Indigenous Land Rights in Israel

Introducing the Negev–Bedouin land issue from the international indigenous land rights perspective, this comparative study suggests options for the recognition of their land. The book demonstrates that the Bedouin land dispossession, like many indigenous peoples', progressed through several phases that included eviction and displacement, legislation, and judicial decisions that support acts of dispossession and deny the Bedouin's traditional land rights.

Examining the *Mawat* legal doctrine on which the State and the Court rely on to deny Bedouin land rights, this volume introduces the relevant international law protecting indigenous land rights and shows how the limitations of this law prevent any meaningful protection of Bedouin land rights. In the second part of the work, the Aborigines' land in Australia is introduced as an example of indigenous peoples' successful struggle for their traditional land rights. The final chapter analyzes the basic elements of judicial recognition of the land and shows that the basic elements needed for Bedouin land recognition exist in the Israeli legal system.

Proposing practical recommendations for the recognition of Bedouin land, this volume is a key resource to scholars and students interested in land rights, international law, comparative studies, and the Middle East.

Morad Elsana is a research scholar and professional teacher at the American University (DC). Prior to this role, he served as a visiting assistant professor of law at the Californian Western School of Law, fellow of the Israel Institute. Elsana is the recipient of several prestigious fellowships such as The Fulbright Outreach fellowship; The NIF Civil Rights Leadership fellowship; and the McGill University "Middle East Program for Civil Society & Peace Building" fellowship. His research focuses on human rights, indigenous peoples' rights, legal pluralism comparative law, racial justice, and the Arab Minority in Israel.

Routledge Studies in Middle Eastern Politics

99 Erdoğan's 'New' Turkey
Attempted Coup d'état and the Acceleration of Political Crisis
Nikos Christofis

100 The Iraqi Kurds and the Cold War
Regional Politics, 1958–1975
Hawraman Ali

101 Islam, Jews and the Temple Mount
The Rock of Our/Their Existence
Yitzhak Reiter and Dvir Dimant

102 Saudi Interventions in Yemen
A Historical Comparison of Ontological Insecurity
Caroline F. Tynan

103 Middle Eastern Monarchies
Ingroup Identity and Foreign Policy Making
Anna Sunik

104 Nationalism and Islamism in the Kurdistan Region of Iraq
The Emergence of the Kurdistan Islamic Union
Mohammad Salih Mustafa

105 Indigenous Land Rights in Israel
A Comparative Study of the Bedouin
Morad Elsana

For a full list of titles in the series:
https://www.routledge.com/middleeaststudies/series/SE0823

Indigenous Land Rights in Israel

A Comparative Study of the Bedouin

Morad Elsana

Routledge
Taylor & Francis Group
LONDON AND NEW YORK

First published 2021
by Routledge
2 Park Square, Milton Park, Abingdon, Oxon OX14 4RN

and by Routledge
52 Vanderbilt Avenue, New York, NY 10017

Routledge is an imprint of the Taylor & Francis Group, an informa business

British Library Cataloguing-in-Publication Data
A catalogue record for this book is available from the British Library

Library of Congress Cataloging-in-Publication Data
A catalog record has been requested for this book

ISBN: 978-0-367-18314-1 (hbk)
ISBN: 978-0-429-06074-8 (ebk)

Typeset in Times New Roman
by codeMantra

To those who have never given up their ancestor's land; to those who have never been deceived by the delusional colonial recognition of their land. To all the Palestinians, especially the Bedouins, to all the indigenous peoples around the globe I dedicate this work.

To my parents (my late father Abdallah Salman Elsana and my mother Sarah Elsana), to the people who supported me after my father, my uncle Nawaf Assanea', my brothers and my sisters.

Last but not least to my wife Abeer and my kids: Amer, Ghaith, Ahmad, and Zakaria, I dedicate this work.

Contents

Acknowledgements

The production of a book is always a team effort. Here, too, a number of individuals and institutions deserve special gratitude for their contributions, which helped this book see the light of day.

Special thanks to my academic advisors Professor David Hunter from the American University -Washington College of law, professor Salman Elbedour (Howard University), to professor Oren Yiftachel from Ben-Gurion University, to Dr. Durgham Saif, to my editors Katty Felder, and Grace McMillan for their reviews and comments throughout the writing and editing of the first and final versions of the multiple chapters of this book. Their efforts, comments, and ideas were invaluable. A special thanks to the lawyers Mr. Ziyad Sana and Mr. Khalil Elsana from Elsana Law Firm in Beer-sheva (Israel), who provided their valuable opinions on several legal issues regarding Bedouins in the Negev/Naqab.

I am grateful to the Fulbright (IIE) and Israel Institute for providing funding for my research and the publication of this book. Their generous grants permitted the writing and editing of this book.

I am also grateful to (1) The *Georgetown Journal* of *Modern Critical Race Perspectives* (MCRP), (2) *The Journal Jurisprudence*, and (3) *California Western International Law Journal* for granting me permissions to reuse materials previously published in their journals in the following article:

1 Morad Elsana, The Recognition of Indigenous People's Land: Application of the Customary Land Rights Model on the Arab-Bedouin Case in Israel, 7 George T. J. Law Mod. Crit. Race Perspect. 45–68, 1 (2015).
2 Morad Elsana, *The Role of the Judiciary in Dispossessing Indigenous Peoples' Land: The Bedouin Case in Israel*, 34 J. Juris. (Fall 2018).
3 Morad Elsana, *Indigenous Peoples' Land: The Case of Bedouin Land in Israel*, 49 Cal. W. Int'l L.J. 61, 1 (2018).

I also appreciate the work of the anonymous reviewer/s who provided me with many valuable ideas that tremendously improved my book. I also would like to express my gratitude to the Routledge, Taylor and Francis Group, especially Ms. Titanilla Panczel, a senior editorial assistant at the

Middle Eastern, Islamic and Jewish Studies for her consistent support along my first publishing journey.

Last but not least, I am grateful to my family, especially my wife, Abeer Alsane-Abu Dayyeh and my beloved son Amer Elsana, who were constantly reading and editing my drafts, showing support and understanding by helping, listening, and sharing my dilemmas, tolerating many absence days, and my long working nights. To all of them, I am most thankful.

1 Introduction

The dispossession of indigenous peoples' land rights remains one of the most common human rights issues around the world.[1] However, despite its disastrous consequences on indigenous peoples and recent indigenous rights' advocacy achievements on both national and international levels, the problem remains.

This study intends to add another stone to the literature in this field. Namely, it will introduce the dispossession of indigenous land in an additional part of the world, the Negev/Naqab region, the southern part of Israel through different circumstances (i.e., timing, location, sociopolitics) while showing the actions, policies, legislations, and ideologies that "collaborate" to dispossess the land of those "weak peoples" permanently. These similarities show that the actions taken against the Bedouin fall into the same category of activity against indigenous peoples in many places around the world, namely, the category of settler–colonialist occupation.

As is well known, the issue of indigenous land dispossession accelerated after Europeans discovered the New World and began conquering, occupying, and colonizing indigenous peoples' land.[2] This was similar to the classical colonization, soon it took the form of settler colonization (settler–colonial occupation). Obviously, the expansion of settler colonization required the dispossession of land for the settlement of the new immigrants in the colonies; thus, Europeans refused to acknowledge most indigenous peoples' rights, denying their sovereignty and freedom to practice their culture. On several occasions, they even denied their basic right to exist.[3]

The issue of indigenous peoples' land rights has been approached from several research frameworks such as settler–colonialism, multiculturalism, indigeneity, apartheid, and many others. Among the many, however, settler–colonialism has been the most prevalent framework used to study this issue, since "It is a framework that highlights commonalities in the history and contemporary situation of indigenous peoples in many parts of the world."[4] According to Rowe and Tuck, settler–colonialism is

> The specific formation of colonialism in which people come to a land inhabited by (Indigenous) people and declare that land to be their new

> home. Settler colonialism is about the pursuit of land, not just labor or resources. Settler colonialism is a persistent societal structure, not just an historical event or origin story for a nation state. Settler colonialism has meant genocide of Indigenous peoples, the reconfiguring of Indigenous land into settler property.[5]

Steinman also notes that settler–colonial framework is the most dominant among indigenous peoples' land issues.[6] This framework imbedded the dominant issues of conflict between indigenous peoples and states.

Patrick Wolfe in his comparative article, "Settler Colonialism and the Elimination of the Native," writes that access to land is the primary motive of settler colonialism and therefore settler–colonialism is an eliminatory process. Wolfe emphasizes that "the primary motive for elimination is not race (or religion, ethnicity, grade of civilization, etc.) but access to territory." And because "Settler colonialism is inherently eliminatory…." Wolfe further states that[7] the "settler–colonial project [relies] on the elimination of native societies."[8] Citing Raphael Lemkin, he states that "[…] settler colonialism […] strives for the dissolution of native societies. […]; it erects a new colonial society on the expropriated land base – as [he] puts it, settler colonizers come to stay: invasion is a structure not an event."[9] Therefore, "Settler colonialism destroys to replace."[10]

Settler colonials justify indigenous peoples' land dispossession by colonial ideology that claims *they could better use of the land.* According to Wolfe, "The ideological justification for the dispossession of Aborigines was that "we" could use the land better than they could."[11]

As Glenn states, "The settler goal of seizing and establishing property rights over land and resources required the removal of indigenes, which was accomplished by various forms of direct and indirect violence, including militarized genocide."[12] Glenn continues, noting that "Settlers sought to control space, resources, and people not only by occupying land but also by establishing an exclusionary private property regime and coercive labor systems, including chattel slavery to work the land, extract resources, and build infrastructure."[13]

Glenn writes that unlike classical colonialism settler colonialism came to stay. Thus, it aimed to acquire the land essential for permanent settlement. To realize this, colonialism had to first eliminate indigenous peoples. Such elimination was done in a variety of ways: genocide, forced removal, or through assimilation. Later, settler–colonialism acquired the indigenous land through imposing property regimes that transformed land ownership from indigenous peoples to settlers. Settlers adopted an ideology that justified elimination of indigenous peoples' land claiming that indigenous peoples are savage, uncivilized peoples who do not efficiently use the land. Thus, indigenous peoples inevitably had to give way to civilized Europeans.[14]

Veracini, in his book *Settler Colonialism: A Theoretical Overview*, notes that "Settler colonialism is a global and transnational phenomenon"[15] that dominated the past but continues to exist in the present. Veracini shows that settler colonialism is a resilient formation that rarely ends.[16] Veracini also notes that "settlers come to stay."[17] They also are founders of political orders…they carry with them a distinct sovereign capacity. Unlike colonialism, "settler colonialism wants Indigenous people to vanish."[18]

Several scholars such as Wolfe, Rodinson,[19] Abu Saad, Yiftachel,[20] Kedar, Amara, Nasasra,[21] and Elsana have conceptualized the Bedouin-Israel relationship through colonialism, mainly settler colonialism.[22] Ismael Abu-Saad and Cosette Creamer describe the Israeli policies that aim to transform the Bedouins from land-based pastoralists into urbanized laborers detached from their land in order to dispossess them of it. They examine the evolution of Israeli policies toward the Bedouin (forced urbanization) and discuss the settler-colonial vision inherent in the implementation of the urban model.[23] Oren Yiftachel "suggests a more comprehensive approach [...] in which the plight of Bedouins in Israel is analyzed through an internal colonial lens."[24]Yiftachel argues that the colonial framework, which includes settler society, indigeneity, and "gray space," is a sound framework within which policy, territory, economics, and politics affecting the Bedouins in Israel can be analyzed and credibly explained.[25]

Nadera Shalhoub-Kevorkian, from the Hebrew University, also views the Bedouin through settler colonial lenses.[26] In *The Biopolitics of Israeli Settler Colonialism: Palestinian Bedouin Children Theorise the Present*, she writes:

> The circumstances of the Bedouin in the unrecognised villages of the Naqab illustrate how Israeli settler colonialism operates across every realm of life, all the while producing new technologies and vocabularies to justify, dismiss, and deny the pain and fear colonised children live.[27]

Along with Shalhoub-Kevorkian, Tatour, whom also views the Bedouin land issue through a settler-colonial lenses.[28] In her recent article "The Culturalisation of Indigeneity: the Palestinian-Bedouin of the Naqab and Indigenous Rights," Tatour approaches the Bedouin rights issue mainly from a settler-colonial perspective.[29] She discusses the case of the Bedouin, who (the Bedouin) have lived in the area for centuries, as they became subject to Zionist control (settler colonialism) during the early formation of Israel. As Israel continued to gain power the Bedouin were marginalized and pushed out of their land. The Bedouins found themselves under new regulations and laws that they did not even have a say in. As is typical for settler colonialism, the Israeli settlers wanted the land and the native Bedouin people were in the way so they created new laws or adopt laws that define Bedouin land as inhabited by body, or deserted land, "Mawat" or dead land. To quote Tatour:

> Israeli courts, on their side, have adopted the 'dead land doctrine,' enshrining in their rulings the colonial view of the Bedouin as nomads and of the Naqab as an empty and awaiting settlement and civilization. The denial of the Bedouin right to their land has been total.[30]

This policy gave Israel a legal and moral greenlight to take Bedouin's land rights and destroy their villages. At the same time, Tatour argues that the recognition of the Bedouin as indigenous has been "premised on the principle of cultural distinctiveness,"[31] which, among other things, has had the "sidelining of settler colonialism as the defining feature of Bedouin indigeneity"[32] effect.

Some scholars define the relationship between the State and the Bedouins of the Negev as an ethnic cleansing framework. According to Ilan Pappe the demolition of mosques and villages, in addition to the proclamations of officials that their dream is to see a million Jews come to the Negev in order to solve the Bedouin problem, are clear signs of ethnic cleansing within the region.[33] This idea is further supported by Gordon and Ram, who noted that settler colonialism in the Negev is either similar to traditional settler colonialism in North America and Australia, or like how it was in Rhodesia before the settlers lost control of the territory; impossible to modernize and normalize due to the factors present from the indigenous other.[34] Pappe further adds that the Israel's policy towards the Bedouins in the Negev is strategic, as the state, press, and Israeli academia largely declares the Bedouins an existential threat to the state.[35]

The denial of land rights has been devastating to many indigenous peoples' communities. It affects all aspects of their existence, including their economy, sovereignty, and ability to practice their traditional way of life. As mentioned above, indigenous land dispossession was carried out in several ways: By conquest and occupation,[36] followed by more sophisticated and even cunning means,[37] such as political and legal means. Such methods have also allowed the colonizing state to legitimize acts of dispossession and block any legal or political options for indigenous peoples to assert their land rights.[38]

Furthermore, many indigenous peoples around the world lost their land "by a complex of different tools employed by successive administrations" used by states.[39] In addition to the well-known examples of the United States, Canada, Australia, and New Zealand, other examples can be found in Bangladesh, Latin America, and many other places around the globe. Rajkumari Chandra Kalindi Roy in his book, *Land Rights of the Indigenous Peoples of the Chittagong Hill Tracts, Bangladesh,* describes how the State of Bangladesh employed many tools under the disguise of "state development plans" to seize indigenous Chittagong Hill Tracts lands.[40] Roy discusses "the different tools employed by successive administrations to exploit indigenous people from their traditional resources and divest them of their ancestral lands and territories."[41] In addition, Roy shows that development programs are not implemented in a culturally appropriate manner with the consent and participation of indigenous peoples.[42] Thus, they serve to push vulnerable indigenous peoples into greater impoverishment and hardship.

It's important to remember that indigenous peoples did not quietly accept the dispossession of their land.[43] Throughout the years of Western conquest, they aggressively and bravely fought to protect their land from colonization.[44] In the beginning, they physically resisted the acquisition and the occupation of their land by engaging in aggressive wars against their foreign invaders. Later, having lost those wars, they had no choice but to struggle through the colonialist system operating under the Western legal system in an attempt to assert their land rights.

Unsurprisingly, the colonial systems supported colonial policies and approved the dispossession of many indigenous groups of their land. In his book, Knafla also presents a comparative study of "the role that courts and legislatures played in the extinguishment and acquisition of Aboriginal title and land."[45] Even when these colonial states recognized and adopted indigenous legal systems, the recognition was to no avail or only very limited. As Povinelli notes in her book the recognition of indigenous peoples' rights was only a "cunning recognition" and meant to continue the colonization in its new mode.[46]

One has to also consider the change of the international legal doctrine on the issue of treaties between governments and Indigenous peoples.[47] Gilbert in his book shows that originally, indigenous treaties with colonial powers were considered valid international treaties and thus part of the Law of Nations.

> It was, after all, the British authors of the Royal Proclamation of 1763 who recognized indigenous groups as 'nations' and acknowledged the duty of the crown to negotiate with them, nation to nation, to determine the nature of Native rights.[48]

However, during the 19th century, as a result of the states parties change of interests, indigenous peoples lost their international entity status; indigenous peoples were thus no long considered international entities. As a result, these treaties became domestic matters. This change deprived indigenous peoples not only of their land but also their sovereignty, as they become "subject of colonial powers," rather than nations.[49]

Later, during the last few decades (since the 1960 until 1990s), as a result of a longtime struggle, indigenous peoples succeeded in bringing their issues to the attention of the international community, making some progress in their movement toward rights recognition.[50] As Knafla explains,

> Since World War II, international law has had an increasing influence in settler-state authority over Aboriginal peoples. Recognition and accommodation of Aboriginal rights to land and self-government in international forums have encouraged Aboriginals, especially in the past decade, to articulate a conception of their unique collective rights and to negotiate them as state to state, people to people.[51]

During that time, several international organizations, such as the International Labor Organization (ILO), raised the issue and called for recognition of indigenous peoples' land rights.[52] Others articulated instruments Universal Human Rights Instruments that recognize and protect indigenous peoples' rights. In 2007, the international community, in a landmark move, recognized indigenous peoples' land rights through the United Nations Universal Declaration for the Rights of Indigenous Peoples.[53]

During the late 20th century, the struggle for land recognition took place in several countries, including but not limited to Canada, Australia, and New Zealand.[54] As a result, several states began to recognize indigenous peoples' land rights.[55] In addition to the fact that the recognition is considered a landmark success it also informs other indigenous peoples as well as other states of the possibility of recognizing indigenous peoples' rights.[56] As Knafla and others show these examples give hope to other indigenous peoples as they continue to struggle to keep their traditional land.

The recognition of indigenous peoples' land came as a result of many factors relating to the nature of each indigenous group, their state's political and legal systems, but also as a result of new developments in international law on indigenous and human rights issues.[57] Different countries have had different reasons for recognizing indigenous peoples' land rights. Some countries have recognized indigenous peoples' land as part of their desire to bring about "historical justice"[58]; others have acknowledged that indigenous people cannot be ignored forever; and still others succumbed to local, regional, and international pressure[59] to recognize indigenous peoples' land rights. In his book *Recognising Aboriginal Title: The Mabo Case and Indigenous Resistance to English-Settler Colonialism*, Peter Russell describes the struggle of indigenous peoples in Australia and the sociopolitical circumstances surrounding the recognition of their land.[60]

Different states have also recognized different types of rights, whether it be full ownership, native title, or the use of traditional lands for cultural activities, such as the recognition by the state of Minnesota of the fishing rights of indigenous peoples on some of the state's lakes. States identify different legal sources for indigenous land rights. Some viewed these rights arising from indigenous legal systems that were in place when the colonists arrived.[61] These rights become enforceable in common law courts through the doctrine of continuity.[62] Others viewed the common law as the source. For example, the British common law acknowledged indigenous peoples' use and control over land at the time the British Crown acquired sovereignty. This gave rise to real property rights leading to recognition of indigenous land rights.[63] Natural law, fundamental principles of justice, and inherent human rights provide a third source for indigenous rights.[64] In the end, some states, like Canada, have relied on common law;[65] others, like Australia, have relied on a combination of common law and international law to define indigenous land.[66] In South Africa, the court recognized indigenous land ownership based on indigenous customary law.[67]

The issue of recognition is at the center of the debate. The need for recognition is indispensable for indigenous peoples. It is important for them to be able to be part of their countries. Indigenous peoples need to feel an equal worth of other groups in their countries. As Taylor states, recognition is capable of forming groups and nations like indigenous peoples.[68] Thus, "...the demand for recognition is now explicit. And it has been made explicit, [...], by the spread of the idea that we are formed by recognition."[69]

Recognition is an essential element for the cohesion of states and societies. Taylor also states that "Multinational societies can break up, in large part because of a lack of (perceived) recognition of the equal worth of one group by another."[70] On the other hand, he notes, "We could say that, thanks to this idea, misrecognition has now graduated to the rank of a harm...."[71] For this reason, "The 'struggle for recognition' is fast becoming the paradigmatic form of political conflict in the late twentieth century."[72]

In his book *The End of History and the Last Man*, Francis Fukuyama places the struggle for recognition as one of the two engines that drive human development. Fukuyama states: "There are two separate motors driving the historical process. *The first* is economic [...] and *'The second motor is what Hegel called the 'struggle for recognition'.*"[73]

According to Fukuyama:

> Human beings desire not just material well-being; they [also] seek recognition of their dignity and status on the part of other human beings, and this demand for recognition is the fundamental passion that underlies politics. The desire for recognition can take many forms, from recognition of one's gods or holy places to recognition of one's national identity within the community of nations. Modern politics is based on the idea, [...], that the only ultimately rational form of recognition is universal recognition of all human beings on the basis of their equal dignity as moral agents.[74]

Another approach of recognition relies on the theory of multiculturism. According to Sarah Song, "The idea of multiculturalism in contemporary political discourse [...] about how to understand and respond to the challenges associated with cultural and religious diversity."[75]

The change in political and cultural perspective by which nation-states are organized, and the adoption of a new political and social perspective on the organization of a nation-state, resulted in nation-states recognizing their multiethnic and multicultural character.[76] And as an essential need to reflect such changes on their rights these states started to accept additional changes in other fields including changes in legislation and judicial fields known as legal pluralism. This legal pluralism brought about the recognition of indigenous peoples' collective-historical rights.

Similarly, Guzman notes that in the 1990s, as a result of changes in the world order and in the world view of the relationship between the nation-state and minority groups, but mainly as a result of the new vision that sees multiculturalism as the optimal way of civil coexistence, many countries started to "reassess" their attitudes towards minorities, including indigenous peoples.[77] As she states, "The multiculturalism that took place in the 19th century [...] led to a change in the state's approach to the law of indigenous peoples, a change that created legal pluralism,"[78] that have led to a more susceptibility to recognize indigenous peoples' rights.[79]

The adoption of the political philosophy of multiculturalism has led to many changes on all levels. One of these changes is "reinvention" of legal pluralism (i.e., recognition of the legal systems of other groups). In recent years, several states have concluded that the recognition of indigenous peoples' law is necessary to build a "modern, multicultural and equal state"[80] to preserve indigenous peoples and their culture, and adopt historical justice concepts (acknowledging and redressing historic wrongs) that would benefit the state and the natives on many levels.[81] Many immigrant countries such as Canada have come to see legal monism as an obstacle to the recognition of indigenous rights and have turned to legal pluralism to understand and embrace the rights of other groups such as indigenous peoples, religious groups (Jews or Muslims) migrant groups. These changes have been translated in several fields; in the legal field, as Guzman points out, they were "translated" by legal pluralism."[82]

Critic to recognition

Despite the importance of recognition, however, many scholars have criticized it on both theorical and practical levels. Some even saw the recognition as a continuation mode of colonialism.[83] One prominent theorist, the late Frantz Fanon, who in his influential book *The Wretched of the Earth,* argued that "the major weapon of the colonizers was the imposition of their image of the colonized on the subjugated people."[84] As Drabisky notes, Fanon strongly rejected the recognition through the colonizer. He rejected the recognition he perceived as humanity created by the colonizer. According to Drabisky, "Fanon is concerned with how a dialectics of recognition might simply mean elevation of the Black person to a sense of humanity created by and modeled on white people."[85] Therefore, "Fanon resists at every turn the desire for recognition if that recognition proceeds from an inevitably colonial sense of standard or measure."[86]

On a practical level, recognition has not always been beneficial to indigenous peoples. As Knafla writes, "Although Aboriginal title doctrine has become part of the common law, legislatures strive to provide for the recognition and protection of that title in ways that are not always beneficial."[87]

As has been shown by many scholars recognition of indigenous peoples' rights has been very limited.[88] Furthermore, recognition is often "empty" of any real value. As Elizabeth A. Bovinelle shows in her groundbreaking book *The Cunning of Recognition* the theory of recognition is in fact an empty one that does not grant a meaningful recognition.

Povinelli's book examines how multicultural forms of recognition reinforce liberal regimes that discriminate against them (IP) rather than open them up to a true cultural democracy.[89] Povinelli also argues that the multicultural legacy of colonialism perpetuates unequal systems of power, by demanding that they identify with an impossible standard of authentic traditional culture.[90] Povinelli explains that "the inequity of multiculturalism arises not from its weak ethical commitment to difference but from its strong [...] vision of a new national cohesion."[91] According to Tatour, Bovinelle's critics have contended that multiculturalism is seen as a continuation of the colonial domination.[92]

In her book *Red Skin, White Masks*[93] Glen Coulthard rejects the colonial politics of recognition as a dominant mode of negotiation and decolonization between the nation-state and indigenous nations.[94] According to Dereher and Mondal, "Coulthard challenges recognition as a method of organizing difference in liberal politics. She questions the assumption that contemporary difference and past histories of colonialism between the state and Indigenous peoples can be reconciled through a process of acknowledgment [recognition]."[95]

Notwithstanding significant achievements, many states refuse to recognize indigenous peoples' land rights and continue to rely on colonial–settler's legal theory, which supports legal doctrines and denies indigenous land rights, such as the Discovery doctrine, the *Terra Nullius* doctrine, and the *Mawat* doctrine.[96] Some of these colonial countries enacted laws that enable indigenous peoples to submit petitions and applications to courts in order to assert their land rights. However, in practice, courts continue to deny indigenous peoples' applications and affirm state acts of dispossession. In effect, "the issue is being domestically contained and not being resolved in any systematic way."[97] The efforts of indigenous peoples on both national and international levels to recognize land rights have often failed, making it one of the most widespread contemporary human rights issues.[98]

The Bedouins in Israel

The Bedouins in Israel have a different history but similar process, land setter colonialism and land dispossession. The State of Israel (from now on referred to as "State") refuses to recognize Bedouin land rights[99] and to recognize Bedouin land rights according to the laws of the Ottoman Empire and the British Mandate.[100] Further, Israel does not recognize the Bedouins as an indigenous group and thus refuses to recognize their land rights under international law.[101]

Land use, possession, and ownership have thus been issues between the Bedouin and the State for over half a century. Recently, these issues have resurfaced because of State attempts to "resolve" the issue and find a permanent solution. In other words, the State wishes to completely dispossess the Bedouin and transfer Bedouin land to the State once and for all.[102]

The State's view on Bedouin land rights is simply that they have none.[103] Here too the state relies on legal doctrines to deny Bedouin land rights; it claims that Bedouin land is *Mawat* land. *Mawat* land is a categorization of land as barren or unclaimed and owned by the state.[104] By designating traditional Bedouin land as *Mawat*, the State has appropriated Bedouin land. Courts in Israel have accepted the State's position and approved the State's acts of dispossession.[105] The State and the courts' interpretations of the *Mawat* doctrine, however, do not comport with traditional notions of *Mawat* land. Such use of old legal doctrines brings to mind the use of the *terra nullius* and the discovery doctrines in Australia and Canada.[106]

Generations of Israeli scholars view the Bedouin as "people of the desert," lacking a sense of land ownership or notions of proper land use.[107] To Western eyes, land use and development potential is the primary means of valuing land.[108]

Bedouin lived on their land for generations and land ownership defines their society in many ways. Their attachment to the land is reflected by their ardent refusal to abandon their traditional lands or their land rights. They have continually rejected all the State's offers of compensation and settlement.[109]

The State of Israel has denied Bedouin indigenous rights in several ways. One is by denying Bedouin customary law. The Ottoman Empire and the British Mandate, who controlled Bedouin territory prior to the establishment of Israel, recognized Bedouin land rights.[110] The Ottomans accepted tribal land ownership without formally recording title in the Land Registry Office (*Tabu*).[111] They recognized Bedouin tribal judicial systems and established the tribal council in Beersheba to deal with Bedouin issues, including issues of land ownership.[112] The fact that the Ottoman Empire tried to regulate land rights in 1858 with the introduction of the Ottoman Land Act and the *Tabu* (Land Registry Office in the Ottoman empire), according to which individuals were permitted to use *Mawat* land only if they had got permission from the state, still did not deny Bedouin tribal land rights.[113]

The British Mandate that followed the Ottoman Empire guaranteed security, protection, and recognition of Bedouin land rights, as long as the Bedouin cooperated with the British government. To accomplish these goals, the Mandate administration enacted the Tribal Court Regulation of 1937 and officially established Tribal Courts for the Bedouin. The Mandate government did not apply restrictive or archaic legal doctrines on the Bedouin, and Bedouin continued to own their land according to their customary laws.

In light of these policies, the Bedouin continued to follow tribal law to govern various matters, including land rights. According to Bedouin tradition, land ownership and land rights are determined by Bedouin law and, when disputes arise, by the Sheikh's decisions. To disregard tribal law and follow State law would be considered an insult to the Bedouin culture and tribal rules.

After a brief introduction of the Bedouin land issue in Chapter 1 and a short introduction of the Bedouin tribal system and their land issue in Israel in Chapter 2, Chapter 3 introduces the dispossession of Bedouin land in two phases. The first occurred during the first years of the establishment of the State, and the second is the current ongoing land dispossession following the 2003 Negev Plan, Goldberg Committee, and Prover Plan. Chapter 3 describes the methods of dispossession by executive, legislative, and judicial means. As part of the discussion, the chapter addresses land tenure in Israel and the policy against Arab land in order to show how the general context of land policy supports Bedouin land dispossession and expropriation. In particular, Chapter 3 introduces how the State has employed administrative means to evict, displace, and concentrate the Bedouin in small villages in order to dispossess their land.

Legislatively, the State has also enacted laws that provide legitimization for the dispossession of Bedouin land. Particularly, the Land Rights Settlement Ordinance of 1969, which established a process of land title settlements to address unsettled land rights throughout Israel. The Ordinance created new rules for land settlement claims, determined the jurisdiction of courts, and outlined the applicable law to be applied during the settlement process. In effect, the settlement process applied archaic land doctrines, entrapped many Bedouins in red tape, and even reversed typical notions of civil procedure and due process.

After that, the Israeli judicial system took action in response to Bedouin counterclaims regarding the land settlement process established by the Land Rights Settlement Ordinance of 1969. Relying on two premises – first, that Bedouin land is *Mawat* land, and second that Bedouin did not revive the land, i.e. make the land productive according to Western notions – the judiciary addressed Bedouin land rights. Culminating with the Alhawashelah decision and the Albeck Committee to investigate Bedouin land rights, the State denied Bedouin land rights. As a result, all State-sponsored avenues to gain recognition of land rights were closed to the Bedouin.

After failing to get their land rights through the national system, Bedouin turned their eyes to international law hoping to get protection for their land rights, only to discover the weakness of international law and its inability to support their land rights. Chapter 4 introduces the protection of indigenous peoples' land rights under international law, which includes regional legal systems and major international actors such as the World Bank. It also introduces the application of international law to the Bedouin in Israel and shows the limitations of international law with regard to the protection of Bedouin land rights in Israel.

Chapter 5 introduces and articulates the process of aboriginal land recognition in Australia. It follows the Aboriginals' struggle for recognition of their land rights from prerecognition to recognition and discusses the legal and nonlegal reasons behind the recognition. It first introduces the major events of their struggle, such as the campaigns for equal rights and campaigns against discrimination, the referenda, and the land movement. Then it introduces the beginning of land legislation, the Woodward Commission, and the judicial recognition in *Mabo (No.2)*. The conclusion of the chapter compares some of the Australian events, policies, and struggles with the Bedouin plight and highlights lessons for the Bedouin case.

Finally, Chapter 6 contains two parts: the first discusses the methods of land recognition, and the second part applies these methods to the Bedouin case. The methods of land recognition discussed in this final chapter originated in Australia, South Africa, and Nicaragua and rely on the approach of "recognition of customary land rights." In addition, it highlights the basic elements of the approach and introduces the requirements for the application of the approach. The second part constructs a vision for Bedouin land recognition. It shows that the Bedouin case in Israel includes the basic requirements needed to apply the customary law approach. Namely, the Israeli legal system includes the basic elements for recognition of customary land rights (i.e., legal principles that recognize customary land rights, the existence of an indigenous group that can be defined as a community with a strong connection to land and a system of law).

The importance of this study cannot be underestimated. Although scholars like Emanuel Marx,[114] Joseph Ben–David,[115] Joseph Ginat,[116] Avinoam Meir,[117] and Tovi Fenster[118] and political geographers like Oren Yiftachel[119] have studied the Bedouin community and the Bedouin issue, these studies often focus on the sedentarization of Bedouins[120] and the significant consequences for Bedouin culture since the establishment the State and the subsequent attempts to settle these seminomads. Only a few of these scholars focus on the Bedouin land rights issue as an indigenous rights issue.[121]

This research fills an essential gap in this field of research by looking at the Bedouin land issue from the perspective of indigenous land rights.[122] This text describes Bedouin land dispossession, their struggle, and the limitations of national and international systems to protect their rights. It also compares the Bedouin land issue to other indigenous land issues to suggest new options for Bedouin land recognition. This study demonstrates how the Bedouin case illustrates methods of land dispossession similar to other indigenous groups' dispossession in the wake of colonial settlement by those with similar goals supported by similar ideologies to the State of Israel.

Notes

1 Erica-Irene Daes, *Prevention of Discrimination and Protection of Indigenous Peoples and Minorities: Indigenous Peoples and Their Relationship to Land* ¶ 124 (U.N. Sub-Commission on the Promotion and Protection of Human Rights, Final Working Paper E/CN.4/Sub.2/2001/21, 2001).

2 S. James Anaya, Indigenous Peoples in International Law 3 (2004).

3 *See* First Nations Summit, Implementation of Jurisprudence Concerning Indigenous Peoples' Rights: Experiences from the Americas – A Canadian Perspective 19–20 (2005), *available at* http://www.fns.bc.ca/pdf/Implementation ofJurisprudence_IP1005.pdf; *see also* Peter H. Russell, Recognising Aboriginal Title: The Mabo Case and Indigenous Resistance to English-settler Colonialism (2006) (discussing how Aboriginal peoples' leaders and state representatives, such as Edward Woodward, head of the Woodward Commission, traveled from Australia to the United States and Canada to learn about the recognition of indigenous peoples land rights); Ephraim Yuchtman-Yaar & Ze'ev Shabat, Magamut Bahevrah Hayesrailit [Trends in Israeli Society]1218 (2003) (discussing former Israeli Prime Minister Golda Meir's denial of the existence of a Palestinian nation).

4 Evelyn Nakano Glenn, *Settler Colonialism as Structure: A Framework for Comparative Studies of U.S. Race and Gender Formation*, 1 Sociology of Race and Ethnicity 52–72, 57 (2015).
5 Aimee Carrillo Rowe & Eve Tuck, *Settler Colonialism and Cultural Studies: Ongoing Settlement, Cultural Production, and Resistance*, 17 Cultural Studies ↔ Critical Methodologies 3–13, 4 (2017).
6 Erich W. Steinman, *Decolonization Not Inclusion: Indigenous Resistance to American Settler Colonialism*, 2 Sociology of Race and Ethnicity 219–236, 221 (2016).
7 Patrick Wolfe, *Settler Colonialism and the Elimination of the Native*, 8 Journal of Genocide Research 387–409, 387 (2006).
8 *Id.* at 391.
9 *Id.* at 388.
10 See *Id.* at 388–389. Wolfe writes that "As Theodor Herzl, founding father of Zionism, observed in his allegorical manifesto/novel, "If I wish to substitute a new building for an old one, I must demolish before I construct." In a kind of Realization[1] that took place half a century later, one-time deputy-mayor of West Jerusalem Meron Benvenisti recalled,

> As a member of a pioneering youth movement, I myself 'made the desert bloom' by uprooting the ancient olive trees of al-Bassa to clear the ground for a banana grove, as required by the 'planned farming' principles of my kibbutz, Rosh Haniqra.
> 9

[...] "The ideological justification for the dispossession of Aborigines was that 'we' could use the land better than they could, ..."
11 *Id.* at 389.
12 Glenn, *supra* note 4 at 52
13 Glenn, *supra* note 4 at 52.
14 *Id.* at 67.
15 L. Veracini, Settler Colonialism: A Theoretical Overview 2 (2010).
16 *Id.* at 100.
17 *Id.* at 97.
18 *Id.* at 14, 25, 82, 145.
19 Maxime Rodinson, Israel: A Colonial-Settler State? 35 (1st ed. 1973) "FN35: Wolfe states that "Israel is also, of course, a partial exception here, though not so substantial an exception as is asserted by those who claim that Israel cannot be a colonial formation because it lacks a single commissioning metropolis. From the outset, the Yishuv co-opted Ottoman, British and US imperialism to its own advantage, a reciprocated opportunism involving what Maxime Rodinson neatly glossed as "the collective mother country."
20 Oren Yiftachel, *Epilogue: Studying Naqab/Negev Bedouins—Toward a Colonial Paradigm?*, 8 HAGAR Studies in Culture, Polity and Identities 83–108.
21 Mansour Nasasra, *The Ongoing Judaisation of the Naqab and the Struggle for Recognising the Indigenous Rights of the Arab Bedouin People*, 2 settler colonial studies 81–107, 82, 83, 89 (2012).
22 Ahmad Amara, Ismael Abu-Saad & Oren Yiftachel, Indigenous (In)Justice: Human Rights Law and Bedouin Arabs in the Naqab/Negev (2013).
23 *Id.* at 8.
24 *Id.* at 11–12.
25 *Id.* at 11–12.; Yiftachel, *supra* note 19.
26 Nadera Shalhoub-Kevorkian, *The Biopolitics of Israeli Settler Colonialism: Palestinian Bedouin Children Theorise the Present*, 15 Journal of Holy Land and Palestine Studies 7–29 (2016).

27 Nadera Shalhoub-Kevorkian, *The Biopolitics of Israeli Settler Colonialism: Palestinian Bedouin Children Theorise the Present*, 15 Journal of Holy Land and Palestine Studies 7–29, 23 (2016).
28 Lana Tatour, *The Culturalisation of Indigeneity: The Palestinian-Bedouin of the Naqab and Indigenous Rights*, 0 The International Journal of Human Rights 1–25, 6 (2019).
29 See generally, Tatour, *supra* note 27.
30 *Id.* at 6.
31 *Id.* at 5.
32 *Id.* at 5.
33 Pappe, Ilan. *The Naqab Bedouin and Colonialism: New Perspectives.* 57.
34 Neve Gordon & Moriel Ram, *Ethnic Cleansing and the Formation of Settler Colonial Geographies*, 53 Political Geography 20–29, 25 (2016).
35 Pappe, Ilan. *The Naqab Bedouin and Colonialism: New Perspectives.* 66.
36 *See generally* Jérémie Gilbert, Indigenous Peoples' Land Rights under International Law: From Victims to Actors (2006) (describing methods of land dispossession).
37 See generally, Elizabeth A. Povinelli, The Cunning of Recognition: Indigenous Alterities and the Making of Australian Multiculturalism (2002).
38 See for example David Kretzmer, The Legal Status of the Arabs in Israel 50 (1990) where he writes "then they locked the land Ownership..." means they legally prevented any options for land restoration.
39 Rajkumari Chandra Kalindi Roy, Land Rights of the Indigenous Peoples of the Chittagong Hill Tracts, Bangladesh 88 (2000).
40 *Id.* at ??
41 *Id.* at 84–88.
42 *Id.* at 114–116.
43 Bill Yenne, Indian Wars: The Campaign for the American West 55–56 (1st ed. 2008) Describing the Yakima War.
44 Louis A. Knafla, Aboriginal Title and Indigenous Peoples: Canada, Australia, and New Zealand 173 (2010).
45 *Id.* at 1.
46 Povinelli, *supra* note 36 at 176 See also 181.
47 Jérémie Gilbert, Indigenous Peoples' Land Rights under International Law 43 (1st ed. 2006).
48 Knafla, *supra* note 43 at 24.
49 ilbert, *supra* note 46 at 43.
50 Knafla, *supra* note 43 at 24.
51 *Id.* at 24.
52 *See generally* Anaya, *supra* note 2.
53 G.A. Res. 61/295, U.N. Doc. A/Res/61/295 (Oct. 2, 2007), *available at* http://www.unhcr.org/refworld/docid/471355a82.html.
54 Knafla, *supra* note 43 at 1–2.
55 *Id.* at 5. See for example, Australia, New Zealand, and Canada.
56 *See* Russell, *supra* note (discussing how Aboriginal peoples' leaders and state representatives, such as Edward Woodward, head of the Woodward Commission, traveled from Australia to the United States and Canada to learn about the recognition of indigenous peoples land rights).
57 See Knafla, *supra* note 43 at 43 (Comparing the different approaches of recognition. See also Peter Russel, describing land recognition in Australia – Mabu Case).
58 President Tsai presides over third meeting of Presidential Office Indigenous Historical Justice and Transitional Justice Committee, https://english.president.gov.tw/News/5222 (last visited Jul. 14, 2019).
59 Australia, for example.

60 Peter H. Russell, Recognising Aboriginal Title: The Mabo Case and Indigenous Resistance to English-settler Colonialism 6–7 (2006).
61 Kent McNeil, *Judicial Treatment of Indigenous Land Rights in the Common Law World* 5 (CLPE Research Paper No. 24/2008, 2008).
62 M. Walters, *The "Golden Thread" of Continuity: Aboriginal Customs at Common Law and under the Constitution Act, 1982* 44 McGill L. J. 711 (1999); Russell Lawrence Barsh, *Indigenous Rights and the Lex Loci in British Imperial Law*, in *Advancing Aboriginal Claims: Visions/Strategies/Directions* 91 (Kerry Wilkins ed., 2004).
63 *See* Kent McNeil, Common Law Aboriginal Title 196–221 (1989).
64 Brian Slattery, *Aboriginal Sovereignty and Imperial Claims*, 29 Osgoode Hall L. J. 681, 690 (1991).
65 Calder v. British Columbia, [1973] S.C.R. 313 (Can.).
66 *Mabo v Queensland (No. 2)* (1992) 175 CLR 1 (Austl.).
67 Yvette Trahan, *Richtersveld Community & Others v. Alexkor Ltd.: Declaration of a Right in Land through a Customary Law Interest Sets Stage for Introduction of Aboriginal Title into South African Legal System*, 12 Tul. J. Int'l & Comp. L. 565 (2004).
68 Charles Taylor, *The Politics of Recognition*, Contemporary Political Theory: A Reader, 64 (1994).
69 *Id.* at 64.
70 *Id.* at 64.
71 *Id.* at 64.
72 Nancy Fraser, *From Redistribution to Recognition? Dilemmas of Justice in a 'Post-Socialist' Age*, 212 New Left Review, 68 (1995), https://newleftreview-org.ezproxy.st-andrews.ac.uk/I/212/nancy-fraser-from-redistribution-to-recognition-dilemmas-of-justice-in-a-post-socialist-age (last visited Aug. 10, 2019).
73 https://web.archive.org/web/20121107234145/http://bev.berkeley.edu:80/fp/readings/Fukuyama.htm.
74 Authors: Francis Fukuyama, (2012), https://web.archive.org/web/20121107234145/http://bev.berkeley.edu:80/fp/readings/Fukuyama.htm (last visited Aug. 20, 2019).
75 Sarah Song, *Multiculturalism* (2010), https://plato.stanford.edu/archives/spr2017/entries/multiculturalism/ (last visited Dec. 23, 2019).
76 From: ESC Rights of Indigenous Peoples Citing Jorge Dandler, "*Hacia un Orden Juridico de Diversidad,*" in *De Amerindia hacia el tercer milenio, Instituto Nacional Indigenista* (UNESCO-INI, 1991), 59. (Jorge Dandler, Towards a Legal Order of Diversity, in De Amerindia towards the third millennium, National Indian Institute).
77 Mireya Maritza Peha Guzman & Sten Schaumburg-Müller, *Legal Pluralism as an Approach to Indigenous and Tribal Peoples' Rights*, in Human Rights in Development Yearbook 2003, 48–50 (2005).
78 Mireya Maritza Peha Guzman and Schaumburg-Müller, *supra* note 57 at 48–50 (The states that recognized indigenous peoples' legal rights).
79 Morad Elsana, *Legal Pluralism and Indigenous Peoples Rights: Challenges in Litigation and Recognition of Indigenous Peoples Rights*, 87 University of Cincinnati Law Review 1043, 18 (2019).
80 Mireya Maritza Peha Guzman and Schaumburg-Müller, *supra* note 76.
81 See the example of the problems surrounding Bedouin's lands because of the State's inability to recognize their customary law and the Bedouins' refusal to give up their rights under the State's law. See also in this context how the state (forbids bigamy) but the Bedouin continue to practice a polygamous lifestyle. This is not the best example, but the best example is the actual control of the Bedouin over their lands in their villages despite the State's law that do not recognize their land rights.

82 Elsana, *supra* note 78 at 26.
83 Tatour, *supra* note 27 at 4.
84 Taylor, *supra* note 67 at 68.
85 John Drabinski, *Frantz Fanon*, *in* The Stanford Encyclopedia of Philosophy (Edward N. Zalta Ed., Spring 2019 ed. 2019), https://plato.stanford.edu/archives/spr2019/entries/frantz-fanon/ (last visited Jul. 17, 2019).
86 *Id.*
87 Knafla, *supra* note 43 at 27.
88 Povinelli, *supra* note 36; Tatour, *supra* note 27; Knafla, *supra* note 43.
89 Povinelli, *supra* note 36 at 6.
90 H. W. Wilson Company, Book review digest 963 (2003); Jon Altman & David Martin, Power, Culture, Economy: Indigenous Australians and Mining 10 (2009).
91 Povinelli, *supra* note 36 at 38.
92 Tatour, *supra* note 27 at 4 Tatour states "However, as critics have contended, multiculturalism is not a move away from liberal racism and colonial domination but rather its continuation."
93 See generally Glen Sean Coulthard, Red Skin, White Masks: Rejecting the Colonial Politics of Recognition (2014).
94 Ragina Johnson & Brian Ward, *"A sense of hope and the possibility of solidarity" | International Socialist Review*, /issue/103/sense-hope-and-possibility-solidarity (last visited Dec. 23, 2019).
95 Tanja Dreher & Anshuman A. Mondal, Ethical Responsiveness and the Politics of Difference 177 (2018).
96 For more about the Mawat Doctrine see Oren Yiftachel, Alexander (Sandy) Kedar & Ahmad Amara, *Re-Examining the 'Dead Negev Doctrine': Property Rights in the Bedouin-Arab Space*, 14, 7–147 Mishpat Umimshal (2012).
97 Charlene Yates, *Conceptualising Indigenous Land Rights in the Commonwealth* (Commonwealth Policy Studies Unit Concept Paper, March 2004), *available at* http://www.docstoc.com/docs/72939815/Indigenous-Land-Rights-and-Resource-Management-in-the-Commonwealth.
98 Daes, *supra* note ("One of the most widespread contemporary problems is the failure of States to recognize the existence of indigenous land use, occupancy and ownership, and the failure to accord appropriate legal status and legal rights to protect that use, occupancy or ownership.").
99 Noa Kram, The Negev Bedouins: Struggles for Land Rights and Cultural Survival in Israel (2011).
100 Thabet Abu-Ras, *Land Disputes in Israel: The Case of the Bedouin of the Naqab*, Adalah's Newsl., April 2006, at 2.
101 Human Rights Watch, Off the Map: Land and Housing Rights Violations in Israel's Unrecognized Bedouin Villages (Mar. 2008), *available at* http://www.hrw.org/reports/2008/03/30/map.
102 Id.
103 Oren Yiftachel et al., *Re-Examining the 'Dead Negev Doctrine': Property Rights in the Bedouin-Arab Space*, 14 Mishpat Umimshal, 7–147, 11 (2012).
104 *See infra* Chapter 2.D.
105 CA 218/74 Salim El-Huashlla v. State of Israel (Alhawashelah) 38(3) PD 141 [1974] (Isr.); CC 3316/04 Esa Farhood Alasibi v. State of Israel PM (unpublished) (2009) (Isr.); CC 7161/06 Suleiman Aluqbi v. State of Israel PM (not yet published) (2012) (Isr.).
106 *See infra* Chapter 4.
107 *See* Havatzelet Yahel et al., *Fabricating Palestinian History: Are the Negev Bedouin an Indigenous People?*, Middle E. Q., Summer 2012, at 3 (denying the indignity of the Bedouin of the Negev).

108 *See* Ahmad Amara, *Okbi judgment and testimony of Prof. Ruth Kark in court [Psak din Aluqbi veedotah shel prof Ruth Kark bbet hameshpat]*, Hagada Hasmalit, http://hagada.org.il (last visited Sept. 6, 2012) (describing how scholars support the State's view despite historical facts).
109 Y. Ben-David, Feud in the Negev: Bedouin, Jews, Land (1996).
110 Yiftachel et al., *supra* note 24, at 31–32.
111 Ghazi Falah, *Israeli State Policy toward Bedouin Sedentarization in the Negev*, 18 J. of Palestine Stud. 71, 76 (1989).
112 Birzeit University, Informal Justice: Rule of Law and Dispute Resolution in Palestine 31 (2006).
113 *See generally* Yiftachel et al., *supra* note 24.
114 *See* Emanuel Marx, Bedouin of the Negev (1967).
115 *See* Joseph Ben-David, Social Change among the Bedouin of the Negev: Transition from Tribal Organization to Urban Community (1988).
116 *See* Joseph Ginat, Bedouin Bishah Justice: Ordeal by Fire (2012).
117 *See* Avinoam Meir, As Nomadism Ends: The Israeli Bedouin of the Negev (1996).
118 Tovi Fenster, Participation in the Settlement Planning Process: The Case of the Bedouin in the Israeli Negev (1991) (unpublished Ph.D. dissertation, London School of Economics and Political Science) (on file with author).
119 *Id.*; J. Ben-David, The Settlement of the Bedouin in the Negev 1967–1992, (1993); Joseph Ginat, Blood Revenge: Family Honor, Meditation and Outcasting (1997).
120 Elia Zureik, The Palestinians in Israel: A Study in Internal Colonialism 2 (1979).
121 *See* Ahmad Amara et al., Indigenous (In)justice: Human Rights Law and Bedouin Arabs in the Naqab/Negev (2013).
122 *See infra* Chapters 2 and 3.

Bibliography

Altman, J., & Martin, D. (2009). *Power, Culture, Economy: Indigenous Australians and Mining.* ANU E Press.

Amara, A., Abu-Saad, I., & Yiftachel, O. (2013). *Indigenous (In)Justice: Human Rights Law and Bedouin Arabs in the Naqab/Negev.* Harvard University Press.

Francis Fukuyama. (2012, November 7). https://web.archive.org/web/20121107234145/http://bev.berkeley.edu:80/fp/readings/Fukuyama.htm

Drabinski, J. (2019). Frantz Fanon. In E. N. Zalta (Ed.), *The Stanford Encyclopedia of Philosophy* (Spring 2019). Metaphysics Research Lab, Stanford University. https://plato.stanford.edu/archives/spr2019/entries/frantz-fanon/

Dreher, T., & Mondal, A. A. (2018). *Ethical Responsiveness and the Politics of Difference.* Springer.

Elsana, M. (2019). Legal Pluralism and Indigenous Peoples Rights: Challenges in Litigation and Recognition of Indigenous Peoples Rights. *University of Cincinnati Law Review, 87*(4), 1043.

Fraser, N. (1995). From Redistribution to Recognition? Dilemmas of Justice in a 'Post-Socialist' Age. *New Left Review, 212.* https://newleftreview-org.ezproxy.st-andrews.ac.uk/I/212/nancy-fraser-from-redistribution-to-recognition-dilemmas-of-justice-in-a-post-socialist-age

Gilbert, J. (2006). *Indigenous Peoples' Land Rights under International Law* (1st ed.). BRILL.

Glenn, E. N. (2015). Settler Colonialism as Structure: A Framework for Comparative Studies of U.S. Race and Gender Formation. *Sociology of Race and Ethnicity*, *1*(1), 52–72. https://doi.org/10.1177/2332649214560440

Gordon, N., & Ram, M. (2016). Ethnic cleansing and the formation of settler colonial geographies. *Political Geography*, *53*, 20–29. https://doi.org/10.1016/j.polgeo.2016.01.010

Johnson, R., & Ward, B. (n.d.). A Sense of Hope and the Possibility of Solidarity. *International Socialist Review*. Retrieved December 23, 2019, from https://isreview.org/issue/103/sense-hope-and-possibility-solidarity

Knafla, L. A. (2010). *Aboriginal Title and Indigenous Peoples: Canada, Australia, and New Zealand*. UBC Press.

Kretzmer, D. (1990). *The Legal Status of the Arabs in Israel*. Westview Press.

Mireya Maritza Peha Guzman, & Schaumburg-Müller, S. (2005). Legal Pluralism as an Approach to Indigenous and Tribal Peoples' Rights. In *Human Rights in Development Yearbook 2003)*. Martinus Nijhoff Publishers.

Nasasra, M. (2012). The Ongoing Judaisation of the Naqab and the Struggle for Recognising the Indigenous Rights of the Arab Bedouin People. *Settler Colonial Studies*, *2*(1), 81–107. https://doi.org/10.7790/scs.v2i1.305

Povinelli, E. A. (2002). *The Cunning of Recognition: Indigenous Alterities and the Making of Australian Multiculturalism*. Duke University Press.

Rowe, A. C., & Tuck, E. (2017). Settler Colonialism and Cultural Studies: Ongoing Settlement, Cultural Production, and Resistance. *Cultural Studies ↔ Critical Methodologies*, *17*(1), 3–13. https://doi.org/10.1177/1532708616653693

Roy, R. C. K. (2000). *Land Rights of the Indigenous Peoples of the Chittagong Hill Tracts, Bangladesh*. IWGIA.

Russell, P. H. (2006). *Recognising Aboriginal Title: The Mabo Case and Indigenous Resistance to English-settler Colonialism*. UNSW Press.

Shalhoub-Kevorkian, N. (2016a). The Biopolitics of Israeli Settler Colonialism: Palestinian Bedouin Children Theorise the Present. *Journal of Holy Land and Palestine Studies*, *15*(1), 7–29. https://doi.org/10.3366/hlps.2016.0127

Shalhoub-Kevorkian, N. (2016b). The Biopolitics of Israeli Settler Colonialism: Palestinian Bedouin Children Theorise the Present. *Journal of Holy Land and Palestine Studies*, *15*(1), 7–29. https://doi.org/10.3366/hlps.2016.0127

Song, S. (2010). *Multiculturalism*. https://plato.stanford.edu/archives/spr2017/entries/multiculturalism/

Steinman, E. W. (2016). Decolonization Not Inclusion: Indigenous Resistance to American Settler Colonialism. *Sociology of Race and Ethnicity*, *2*(2), 219–236. https://doi.org/10.1177/2332649215615889

Tatour, L. (2019). The Culturalisation of Indigeneity: The Palestinian-Bedouin of the Naqab and indigenous rights. *The International Journal of Human Rights*, *23*(10), 1569–1593. https://doi.org/10.1080/13642987.2019.1609454

Taylor, C. (1994). The Politics of Recognition. *Contemporary Political Theory: A Reader*. Sage books.

Veracini, L. (2010). *Settler Colonialism: A Theoretical Overview*. Springer.

Wolfe, P. (2006). Settler Colonialism and the Elimination of the Native. *Journal of Genocide Research*, *8*(4), 387–409. https://doi.org/10.1080/14623520601056240

Yenne, B. (2008). *Indian Wars: The Campaign for the American West* (1st edition). Westholme Publishing.

Yiftachel, O. (n.d.). Epilogue: Studying Naqab/Negev Bedouins—Toward a Colonial Paradigm? *HAGAR Studies in Culture, Polity and Identities*, *8*, 83–108.

Yiftachel, O., Kedar, A. (Sandy), & Amara, A. (2012). Re-Examining the 'Dead Negev Doctrine': Property Rights in the Bedouin-Arab Space. *Mishpat Umimshal*, *14*, 7–147.

2 Background

This chapter outlines three major subjects. The first part provides an overview of the Bedouin in general, their tribal structure, and their tribal law. The focus in this part is on Bedouin Tribal Law (*Alorf*), the Bedouin Tribal Land System, and how it works to define and organize their land rights. The second part introduces the Bedouin in Israel, their land disputes with the State, and the main reasons for the dispute. The goal of this part is to shed more light on the main issue of Bedouin land dispossession as well as to introduce their history and other elements essential to understanding the Bedouin land rights issue in Israel. It describes the Ottoman and British land laws that continue to affect Bedouin land rights, and the use the State continues to make with these laws and land rights doctrines, such as the *Mawat* land doctrine. The third part introduces the *Mawat* land doctrine and other methods and techniques the state has been using to possess the indigenous Bedouin land.

The Bedouin, their tribal structure, and tribal law

The Bedouin community of the Negev remains one of the few traditional nomadic cultures in the Middle East today.[1] Within the Israeli Jewish State, they are an Arab minority who belong to the larger Arab majority in the Middle East. "Bedouin" is derived from the Arabic word *badawi* or *badow*.[2] Emanuel Marx, in his book *The Bedouin of the Negev*, defines the Bedouin and describes their life:

> The Arabic term *badawi*, from which 'Bedouin' is derived, denotes a nomadic inhabitant of the desert (*badioh*) who depends for his livelihood on herds of camels and sheep. The word conjures up pictures of camel-herds moving over the vast expanse of the Arabian desert, of billowing black tents, of fierce bearded Arabs in flowing robes, and of daring raiders on swift horses.[3]

The Bedouin organize themselves into tribes or confederations of tribes. In the Negev there are four major confederations: Taiaha, Dolam, Tarabin, and Azazmah. Each of these confederations includes several major tribes called *Ashira*.

Prior to the 1948 Arab–Israeli War, there were 95 Bedouin tribes in the Negev.[4] Following the war, only 19 tribes remained.[5] The rest were evicted or fled during the war.[6] Each tribe occupies and controls a specific territory. Within that territory, individuals own their land. Tribal laws define ownership, use, and other rights related to land, including the passage of people or goods through the territory. Although their rule over territory has been dramatically reduced in Israel, many Bedouin in Israel, Egypt, and other places continue to control several territories, albeit often unofficially.[7]

The tribal structure of Bedouin shapes their social, political, and cultural system. Bedouin social organizations impact their behavior, their rights, and obligations under their tribal legal system. Bedouin tribes share the same language, traditions, and tribal law. However, tribes may be distinguished by differences in their Arabic accent, some of their secondary traditions, and facial features. Such differences allow Bedouin to recognize a person's tribal identity. The tribal system organizes war alliances, confederations, and marriage relations, and manages resources like land, water, and pastures.[8]

*Bedouin tribal law (*Alorf*)*

The Bedouin system of law is still vibrant and relevant to Bedouin life today. Bedouin law is known for its strong ability to enforce customs and order, even under the harshest conditions that come with living in the desert. Bedouin law constitutes a set of rules that control the followers' way of life and determines and enforces rights and obligations.[9] In some areas, Bedouin law surpasses the law of the state. For example, Bedouin law can enforce orders and traditional obligations in the tribe where state law cannot.[10] With regard to land rights, Bedouin law continues to apply; it organizes, defines, and defends Bedouin land rights, whereas state laws may offer the Bedouin very limited legal protection for their traditional tribal land rights.[11]

In some areas, Bedouin law may challenge State law. In the case of Bedouin land in Israel, for example, where the State does not recognize Bedouin tribal land ownership and therefore does not offer substantial legal protections, Bedouin law continues to recognize Bedouin tribal land and protects it, even in cases where the state has confiscated land and denied ownership rights.[12] Bedouin law considers anyone who purchases Bedouin land from the government as trespassing on the tribe's property rights, even though that land was legally (according to the State's law) sold. In such situations, Bedouin law subjects the buyer and his family members to a tribal legal claim, and they could face punishment accordingly. Such tribal law prevents Bedouins from buying another Bedouin's land from the State and forces the State to negotiate land settlement with Bedouin owners.[13]

In intertribe conflicts, as another example, according to Bedouin law, the offender and his tribe or part of it have to leave their village and move to another place to avoid clashes with members from the victim's tribe. In such cases State law cannot protect the Bedouin, meaning the offenders have to leave their homes.[14] Since the State does not have the means to deal with such cases, it accepts the authority of Bedouin customary law. State officers and authority figures, not only in Israel but in many other states in the Middle East, are aware of the power of the Bedouin law and the limitations of state laws among Bedouin. As Egyptian journalist Abdel Ati Samah in the *Almasri Alyawm* newspaper has written, the power of Bedouin law "exceeds the state law power." Awad Ben Khamis goes on to write, "the power of Bedouin law exceeds the state law power."[15]

Bedouin tribal land system

As part of their legal system, the Bedouin established and developed a land system to manage and organize their land rights. Their land system puts in place rules to organize and protect land matters.[16] Bedouin law includes their traditional land rights system, "which governs the allocation of rights and obligations in relation to 'real' or 'immovable' property."[17] Within the confines of this system, they have been trading, selling, purchasing, and renting land among themselves for centuries. They continue to rely on their system today.[18]

For many years, the Bedouin land system was respected by other states that ruled the Negev, such as the Ottoman Empire and the British Mandate.[19] These states allowed the Bedouin of the Negev to own and possess their land according to their land system and did not interfere or dispossess them of their land rights.[20]

The Bedouin land system contains the necessary elements needed to define a land rights system. It recognizes land ownership, and acknowledges trade and other kinds of land transactions, including mortgages of tribal land, gifting of land (e.g., as part of a dowry), and payment of debts with land. As Hanina Porat explains in his article about Bedouin lands, many Bedouin have traded land both inside and outside the tribe. The Bedouin even sold some of their land to Jewish settlers and Jewish organizations before 1948.[21]

Moreover, the Bedouin land system recognizes different forms of land ownership, such as private and public lands. According to Bedouin law, private land means land that is privately owned by individuals; that land is restricted to that individual's use. Public tribal land is land under tribal control designated for tribal collective use, such as land around water wells and water springs allocated for herds of animals such as cattle. The Bedouin land system also defines the borders of each tribe's public lands, and nobody other than the members of a particular tribe is allowed to use it.

In addition, the Bedouin land system provides boundary delineation and geographical definition in order to define people's rights accurately. Bedouin lands are usually delineated by their neighbors' land borders or by natural signs, such as valleys, trees, hilltops, or watersheds.[22] When such natural borders do not exist, owners mark their land boundaries with artificial borders such as stones, a trench, or any other observable signs.[23] The Bedouin land regime defines the legal rights of owners, possessors, and lessees.

Finally, an additional characteristic of the Bedouin land system is its recognition of a variety of land uses. The Bedouin use their land for personal and public matters, such as traditional seasonal agriculture,[24] pastoral needs, hunting, other sports, and religious observations as well.[25]

The Bedouin land issues in Israel

The Bedouin in Israel are divided into two groups. One is located in the northern part of the State in the Galil and the other is in the southern part of the State in the Negev. In addition, there are a small number of Bedouin who live in the Center Region of the State in cities like Lod and Ramleh.[26]

The Bedouin are part of the Arab–Palestinians citizens of the State of Israel.[27] Their population is estimated to be between 180,000–210,000[28] people, making up three and a half percent of the State population.[29] They represent about 15 percent of Arabs in Israel overall, while their representation of total population of the Negev (Arabs and Jews) is 24 percent.[30]

The Bedouin have lived in the Negev for many centuries, well before the establishment of the State of Israel. Some claim that Bedouin have inhabited the Negev since the fifth century C.E.,[31] while the Bedouin themselves insist they have been living in the Negev from time immemorial and therefore are the native people of the Negev.[32]

Before the establishment of Israel in 1948, the Bedouin in the Negev numbered between 65,000–95,000 people.[33] However, during the 1948 War, the Bedouin population was significantly reduced. Most of the Bedouin population, about 90 percent, was forced to leave or fled the country to neighboring jurisdictions like Jordan, the Gaza Strip, and the West Bank.[34]

After the 1948 War, the remaining Bedouin, about 11,000, were rounded up in closed areas called the *Siyag* ("the fence" in Hebrew) and lived under a military rule in the *Siyag* zone for about 18 years until 1966. During this period, the State put into action a plan that later shaped the policy and laws to dispossess the Bedouin of their traditional land.

Of the current Bedouin population,[35] half live in 16 recognized villages and the other half live in about 36 unrecognized villages.[36] Bedouin who live in the unrecognized villages live under very poor conditions, deprived of very basic rights, such as housing, running water, electricity, basic infrastructure, education, health services, and social services.[37] Furthermore, they are subject to harsh State acts, such as ongoing house demolition, crop destruction, livestock confiscation, and land expropriation, as part of an apparent attempt to dislodge them from their historical villages in order to concentrate them in small villages and dispossess them of their land.[38]

In terms of this research, Bedouin traditional land refers to land that the Bedouin own or once owned according to their tribal law. Such lands are not registered with the State of Israel Land Registry Office. Therefore, Bedouin do not have title deeds or other official documents that prove their land ownership. However, many Bedouin have traditional documents called *Sanadat* (singular: *Sanad)* that define their land rights and define the source of those rights (i.e., by inheritance, purchase, rental, lease, or mortgage). These documents describe the borders of the land, the size, and the owners, just like any other deed.

Land is valuable and important in Bedouin tradition and culture. On the cultural level, the Bedouin consider their land part of their tribal wealth, strength, and sovereignty.[39] Land ownership is a defining characteristic of Bedouin social status and political classification. According to Safa Abu Rabia, "Land constitutes the basis for social stratification in Arab-Bedouin society, representing the primary source of power and prestige."[40] By tradition, only the original Bedouin tribes own land. Tribes that do not own land are not considered to be "original" Bedouin and are called *Falahin*;[41] such tribes were unable to secure their continued existence and thus were placed under the patronage and protection of the original tribes who owned the land.[42] Bedouin have also equated land with honor, making land the most valuable element in their culture – one for which they are ready to fight and die. The Bedouin traditional economy heavily relies on the land resource for maintaining and securing their subsistence.[43]

For a long time prior to the establishment of the State of Israel, Bedouin organized their land rights according to their traditional law and did not register their land in any official land registration system (*Tabu)*.[44] Scholars list several reasons for such lack of registration, including lack of government authority in the Negev and lack of government interest in a poor, deserted area. Some scholars claim that Bedouin economic hardship and their attempts to evade the Ottoman military service and taxes were the reasons for this lack of land registration.[45] Others mention the Ottoman Empire's lack of interest in allocating funds for the enforcement of the land registration law in marginalized locales.

Still other scholars mention culture as the main reason. The Bedouin showed no interest in registering their lands since they had always relied on Bedouin law to protect their rights rather than state law, which was weakly enforced or not at all throughout history. Moreover, many scholars claim that tribes viewed land registration as an indication of weakness, giving the impression that the tribe could not properly defend its land solely through its tribal mechanisms.[46]

Other historical factors played a role in the Bedouin's disinterest with registration, such as the fact that the Bedouin of the Negev enjoyed informal semiindependence in their territory including a fully independent legal system that controlled all their matters including land rights.[47] In addition, the political reality (i.e., the lack of government authority in the Negev) did little to convince the people of the advantages or the consequences of not registering their land rights. Weak Ottoman governments characterized by a lack of state institutions such as police forces and courts contributed to this unwillingness to register land among the Bedouin.[48] Thus, in the historical context of the 19th century and the geographical context[49] of the Negev, all these factors created a *de facto* tribal system that determined the rights and obligations in their region.

After the defeat of the Ottoman Empire in World War I in 1917, the British Empire occupied Palestine and began a new era of rule under the British Mandate. During the British Mandate the government enacted the 1921 *Mawat* Land Ordinance, which provided some opportunity to register land rights within two months. Bedouin, however, did not use this period to register their land.[50] The two-month period was too short to inform the Bedouin about the new law, or allow them to register their land rights accordingly. This was especially true during times where there was no modern means of transportation or communication.[51] Shlomo Swirski and Yael Hasson explained that the Bedouin continued to rely on their traditional system, not understanding the importance of such registration. They added that the Bedouin could not have anticipated that their land rights could one day depend on such registration.[52]

In addition, the hostile political environment during the British Mandate also contributed to the lack of registration. The Arab population, including Bedouin, who knew about the Balfour Declaration of 1917, which established a National Homeland for the Jews on their land, viewed the British Authority as an entity that aimed to transfer their land to the Jewish settlers and therefore could not be trusted. Furthermore, because the Bedouin are an oral culture that does not see a need for documents to prove their rights, they saw no reason to put ownership claims in writing.

Despite the fact that both the Ottoman Empire and the British Mandate authorities recognized the Bedouin legal system and incorporated parts of Bedouin tribal law into their legal codes, Israel refuses to recognize Bedouin tribal law and continues to deny Bedouin rights under its law, especially as they relate to land rights.[53] The State ignores the authority of Bedouin law and its effect on land issues. It ignores the fact that the Bedouin system continues to determine Bedouin land rights even after the State has expropriated tribal lands and registered the land in the name of the State. In some ways, ignoring Bedouin land law limits the State's ownership and use and, more importantly, limits the State's power to freely allocate, sell, or rent Bedouin land to other Bedouin who continue to respect and obey their tribal law.[54]

The existence of two systems and the refusal of each one to recognize the other's authority has been one of the major reasons for the conflict over Bedouin lands. While the Bedouin insist that the refusal of the State to recognize Bedouin tribal law[55] is a main reason for the Bedouin land issue in

Israel,[56] the State insists that the refusal of the Bedouin to acknowledge and accept the State's rule is the main reason for the Bedouin land conflicts. The State's attitude places the Bedouin in a constant conflict between two legal systems, the State system and the Bedouin tribal system. The results of this conflict are devastating, especially in cases where the State allocates Bedouin land to other Bedouin. It is devastating not only for land and property rights, but also for the dissonance that leads to bloody conflicts among Bedouin tribes and threatens the lives of many people.

While Bedouin customary law plays a leading role in land allocation and property rights, other sources of property doctrine affect Bedouin. Bedouin tribal law has remained consistent, but the political landscape in which the Bedouin find themselves has shifted over the centuries. From the Ottoman Empire to the British Mandate to the present-day Israeli government, each ruling power has brought a new set of rules governing property rights that affect Bedouin. In recent decades, the *Mawat* land doctrine has proven to be the most controversial.

The *Mawat* land doctrine

Several Ottoman laws and doctrines determine Bedouin land rights in Israel, but especially the Ottoman Land Law of 1858 and the *Mawat* land doctrine. Such laws and doctrines have gone through several changes and amendments during the British Mandate from 1921 to 1948, and the first years of the establishment of the State of Israel in 1948.

Therefore, to understand the legal status of Bedouin land today it is essential to understand the basic framework of Ottoman Land Law and the concept of *Mawat*. Additionally, it is important to comprehend how the land laws and the definition of the *Mawat* doctrine have changed over time, from the Ottomans, through the British Mandate, and up to the creation of the State of Israel.

The Ottoman Land Code of 1858 divided the lands in the Ottoman Empire into five categories: *Mulk*, *Miri*, *Waqf*, *Matruka*, and *Mawat*.[57] *Mulk* land constitutes land held by private ownership. *Miri* land is held by the state, but usufruct (*Tassaruf*) to an individual holder. *Waqf* land is land devoted to religious purposes. *Matruka* land is land owned by the state and preserved for public use, such as roadbeds or village threshing floors, or land around wells for herd pasturing. Finally, *Mawat* land is barren or unclaimed land owned by the state, such as forests, mountainous areas, deserts, and the like.[58]

The *Mawat* land category, in particular, continues to be relevant to Bedouin land rights because it has determined the recognition (or nonrecognition) of Bedouin land rights for almost a century since the ruling in the Alhawashelah case. The word *Mawat* literally means "dead" in Arabic. The roots of the doctrine of *Mawat* and *Ihya Almawat*, meaning revival of land, date back to the sixth century, in the early days of Islamic *Sharia* law. According to the *Sonnah*, the second source of Islamic *Sharia* Law,[59] several *Hadiths* are relevant to the *Mawat* doctrine and the practice of *Ihya Almawat*.

One *Hadith*[60] states, "He who brings dead land back to life shall himself possess it and he who by force wants to make use of it has no right or title to it at all."[61] Another *Hadith* concerning *Mawat* land states, "Whoso quickens a dead land, it is his; there is no right of expropriation against him."[62]

The doctrine of *Mawat* land has been basic legal doctrine under Islamic law for centuries. The Ottoman Land Code of 1858 codified the doctrine in the modern codex of law and included the concept in the Ottoman Civil Code (*Majallah*).[63] During the Ottoman Empire rule, *Mawat* was defined by the Land Code as

> ...undeveloped or unused land; which was not owned or possessed by anyone; and it was situated in a remote places, at least one and half miles from inhabited areas, at such a distance from towns and villages from which a human voice cannot be heard at the nearest inhabited place.[64]

The *Mawat* doctrine and *Mawat* revival interpretation differs from place to place and from time to time depending on the jurisprudence (*Fiqeh*) and schools of law (*Madhab*) of each state. Thus, the meaning of *Mawat* land has undergone many changes depending on the ruler's identity, the state, the political situation, and the state's interests in the land. Such considerations vastly differ between the Ottoman Period, the British Mandate, and control by Israel.

The Mawat *land doctrine during the Ottoman period*

Ottoman law defined the *Mawat* land category in Articles 6 and 103 of the Land Code of 1858[65] as, "Undeveloped or unused land that was not owned or possessed by anybody and situated in a remote place at least one and one-half miles from inhabited areas."[66] Ottoman policy encouraged the revival[67] of *Mawat* land[68] as part of a policy to encourage agriculture in rural areas to increase tax revenues.[69] As part of that policy, Ottoman legal rules easily recognized land revival, which could then entitle the possessor to a title deed.[70]

In regard to which activities could amount to revival of *Mawat* land, the Ottoman system was less rigid than both the Mandate system and the Israeli system.[71] While the Israeli system requires a continuous cultivation of the land that improves the land in a way that substantially changes its nature,[72] the British Mandate courts took an even stricter approach and demanded almost "the impossible" to recognize revival.[73] As British J. Black interpreted "revival as a total change of land means turn the desert into paradise."[74] On the other hand, in Ottoman law "sowing seed or preparing the land for irrigation" was considered as revival of the land.[75]

The Mawat land doctrine during the British Mandate in Palestine

When Britain occupied Palestine in 1917 it changed many of the land rules including the definition of *Mawat*. During its occupation, Britain had many special commitments it planned to execute in the area,[76] many of which affected the land ownership and the rules of land acquisition in Palestine. These commitments included the Balfour Declaration of 1917 to establish a "National Homeland" for the Jewish people in Palestine and to facilitate Jewish immigration[77] and settlement in Palestine according to the desires of Jewish leadership and the interests of Western States.[78]

During that time, western countries also perceived that establishing a National Homeland for Jews created a solution to the "Jewish problem" in Europe and would enable the transfer of the Jewish-European population out of the continent of Europe.[79] Therefore, as part of their support, in 1920 the principal allied powers and the League of Nations recognized the Balfour Declaration and incorporated it into the mandate on Palestine.[80]

The Mandate Government, acknowledging the importance of land in order to execute the Balfour Declaration and facilitate immigration and settlement of Jews, worked to acquire as much land as possible, mainly land it considered public or state land, as stated in the Mandate Charter.[81] In addition, Forman & Kedar indicated that "Article 6 of the League of Nations' Mandate Charter of 1922 stipulated that the government of Palestine shall facilitate Jewish immigration" and encourage settlement by Jews on the land, including state lands and waste lands not required for important public purposes for the land.[82] Such commitments directed and shaped the land policy of the British Mandate in Palestine.

Because land was vital to the execution of Balfour Declaration, the British government sought ways to own and control land as much as possible in order to settle Jewish immigrants. Changing land laws and creating new laws provided ways to own and control the land. Therefore, in order to secure sufficient land for Jews the Mandate Government started to change land laws and land acquisition rules to ensure the transfer of nonprivate lands to state settlements.[83] As part of the changes, the government revised the *Mawat* land acquisition rules. These rules classified a maximum amount of land as *Mawat* land and blocked the acquisition of *Mawat* land by the indigenous people of Palestine in order to transfer it to the state.[84]

In 1921, the British Mandate Administration enacted the 1921 Mawat Land Ordinance, which effectively prevented Palestinian land acquisition of *Mawat* land by revival.[85] The Ordinance stated that, "Those who had already acquired rights could claim title by registering their interest at the land registry within two months of the publication of the Ordinance."[86] According to many scholars, this short notice was clearly intended to prevent *Mawat* land acquisition.[87] The results were two-fold: it stopped the acquisition of *Mawat* land and dispossessed those who could not register land they had revived within the prescribed time period of two months.

Despite the attempt to codify a maximum amount of land as *Mawat* land, sources indicate that the policy of the British Mandate toward the *Mawat* lands was inconsistent and harsh compared to the Israeli policy. Although the British Mandate *Mawat* Land Ordinance aimed to stop *Mawat* land acquisition and facilitate the transfer of the maximum amount of land to the government, in practice, the Mandate Government did not totally stop *Mawat* land acquisition, and it continued to recognize acquisition of *Mawat* land that had been revived without the authorities' consent and outside the two-month period.[88] According to Hussein Abu Hussein "During the British rule, it was the practice to grant title deeds . . . to those able to show that they had revived land prior to the 1921 Ordinance without consent."[89] Abu Hussein explained that such a policy could be justified under the Mandate obligation to "Safeguard the civil and religious rights of all the inhabitants of Palestine," a dictate mentioned in the Mandate's Charter.[90] Abu Hussein considers this deviation from the law as, "Strong evidence that the British themselves did not intend the 1921 Ordinance to sweep away at a stroke all the acquired rights of the Bedouin."[91]

The Mawat land doctrine in Israel

In Israel, the *Mawat* land doctrine has undergone many changes and adjustments in order to serve the State's policy of land expropriation and land control. The State, through legislation and case law, has changed the rules of acquisition of *Mawat* land in a way that has limited the ability of Arabs (which include the Bedouin) to acquire title to *Mawat* land.

First, courts established rules that distinguish between *Mawat* land and *Miri* land, which resulted in much more land being considered as *Mawat* land.[92] The definition of *Mawat* land was changed and modified in a series of Court decisions such State of Israel v. Salah Badran (Badran Case)[93] and State of Israel v. Abdallah Mousa Rahal (Rahal Case).[94] "The courts then made it impossible for Palestinians [including Bedouin] to establish rights over Mewat land"[95] and transferred much of the *Mawat* land to state land.

In addition, mainly relying on the *Mawat* land doctrine, courts established *theories of interpretations* to reject Palestinian (includes Bedouin) land rights.[96] During the adjudication of land cases, courts strictly applied the Ottoman and British laws in order to deny Arab land rights.[97] The High Court has also insisted on a restrictive interpretation of the meaning of revival of *Mawat* land, holding that it must involve an *improvement of the land* in a way that *totally changes the nature of the land*, and it must involve a *continuous cultivation of the land.*[98] Such conditions proved to be impossible to meet, especially on Bedouin land considering the Bedouin's seminomadic lifestyle.

The *Badran* case exemplifies the High Court's strategy to restrict Bedouin land rights. In this case, the High Court confirmed that according to the court's definition of *Mawat* land, the disputed land was classified as *Mawat* land and therefore rights could not be acquired by prescription. In addition, in applying the *Mawat* Land Ordinance of 1921, Courts ruled that those who revived *Mawat* land prior to 1921 but failed to register their interest within the two months lost their rights. As Abu Hussein states, "Unlike the Mandate authorities, who had, in practice, tended to recognize unregistered rights over *Mawat* even after 1921, the Israeli High Court applied the terms of the 1921 Ordinance strictly and denied Palestinians' [Arab Israeli and Bedouin] land claims."[99] By applying this strict condition, the Court denied many Arab land claims.

After the *Badran* decision established precedent for the *Mawat* land doctrine in Israel, all subsequent land cases followed the Court's approach, including cases involving Bedouin tribal land in the southern part of Israel, starting with the Salim Alhawashelah v. State of Israel[100] (*Alhawashelah* case). At the same time, the Court ignored substantial differences between land in the north (*Badran* case) and the Bedouin land in the south (Alhawashelah) and the Bedouin tribal law.

The *Mawat* Land Ordinance and *Mawat* doctrine have been extensively used to dispossess Arab land in Israel. According to many scholars, Israel has converted many dumans[101] of Arab land to state land through the *Mawat* doctrine.[102] In addition, the *Mawat* Land Ordinance and the *Mawat* Doctrine has a particularly devastating impact on the Bedouin land in the Negev.[103] While the Mandate authorities tended to leniently apply the rules in a way that did not deny claims of land rights where land had been revived without the state's authorization, Israeli courts, in contrast, took the *Mawat* doctrine out of the Ottoman law context and applied it independently to dispossess Bedouin land.[104]

In practice, Israeli courts have been using the British *Mawat* Ordinance as a legal basis to reject Bedouin land rights.[105] Court rulings subsequent to the *Badran* case follow the same definition of *Mawat* land that the court in *Badran* followed. Eventually, Bedouin land rights were definitively determined in the *Alhawashelah* case in 1984. Although there is no major legal distinction between the *Mawat* land of the Negev as a legal doctrine and *Mawat* doctrine elsewhere, many refer to the *Alhawashelah* decision as precedent with regard to Bedouin land rights because it was the first case to squarely address the *Mawat* doctrine regarding Bedouin land in the Negev. In that case, the court accepted the State's argument that during the enactment of the Ottoman Land Law in1858 there were no Bedouin settlements in the Negev and therefore the court held that all Bedouin land is *Mawat* land and thus State land.[106] The effect of the decision was a matter of paramount importance since it determined the fate of all the Bedouin lands in the Negev by classifying Bedouin land as *Mawat* land.

Relying on the *Mawat* Land Ordinance of 1921, the State dispossessed Bedouin of their land, claiming that Bedouin lost their rights by failing to revive and register their land. Thus, the State appealed to the court to deny Bedouin land rights, dismiss Bedouin land claims, and register their land as a State land. In the landmark case of *Alhawashelah*, the High Court confirmed the State's position, and dismissed Bedouin land claims. In this precedent-setting decision, the court stated that the land was *Mawat* land, the Alhawashelah tribe failed to prove they had revived their *Mawat* land, and that the tribe failed to register their rights within the prescribed time. Therefore, they did not acquire any rights to the land.[107]

Conclusion

In summary, the *Mawat* doctrine during the three ages – the Ottomans, British Mandate, and Israeli – reveals that while the Ottomans encouraged land revival and recognized *Mawat* land after revival with few requirements, the British Mandate changed the land laws in Palestine to prevent *Mawat* land acquisition by the Bedouin for colonial and political reasons. Yet, in practice, the Mandate did not intend to unilaterally deny acquired land rights based on the fact that people did not receive consent or did not register their rights. The British Mandate continued to recognize land revival, even when claimants revived the land without the authorities' consent. However, unlike the Ottomans and the British Mandate, Israel redefined the *Mawat* interpretation to fit its goals of creating a land policy aimed at dispossessing the Bedouin of their land. The courts have accepted the view of the State and have applied this redefined interpretation to classify Bedouin land as *Mawat* land; the *Alhawashelah* decision and the Albek Committee Report illustrate this perfectly. The main goal has been to transfer Bedouin land to the State; therefore, policies, laws, and case law continue to support the premise that *Mawat* land is State land and courts continue to establish methods and interpretations to reject *Mawat* land recognition and support this goal.

Notes

1 Salman Elbedour et al., *Bedouins of the Negev: Ethnicity and Ethnic Identity among Bedouin Adolescents in Israel*, 2 Int'l J. of Child Health & Hum. Dev. 177 (2009).
2 *Badow Definition*, Baheth.info, http://www.baheth.info/all.jsp?term=%D8%A8%D8%AF%D9%88 (last visited Feb. 12, 2013).
3 Emanuel Marx, Bedouin of the Negev 3 (1967).
4 Human Rights Watch, *Off the Map: Land and Housing Rights Violations in Israel's Unrecognized Bedouin Villages* 12, http://www.hrw.org/reports/2008/03/30/map (last visited Sept. 6, 2016); Joseph Ben-David, Social Change Among the Bedouin of the Negev: Transition from Tribal Organization to Urban Community (1988); Benny Morris, Israel's Border Wars, 1949–1956: Arab Infiltration, Israeli Retaliation, and the Countdown to the Suez War (1997).
5 See also Marx, *supra* note 124; Ghazi Falah, *Israeli State Policy toward Bedouin Sedentarization in the Negev*, 18 Journal of Palestine Studies 71–91 (1989).
6 Aref Abu Rabia, *Negev Bedouin: Displacement, Forced Settlement, and Conservation*, in Conservation and Mobile Indigenous Peoples: Displacement, Forced Settlement, and Sustainable Development (Dawn Chatty & Marcus Colchester eds., 2002); Donald P. Cole, *Where Have the Bedouin Gone?*, 76 Anthropological Quarterly 235–267, (2003).
7 The control of the land in their villages is part of the control of their territory in the Negev.
8 Frauke Heard-Bey, *The Tribal Society of the UAE and Its Traditional Economy*, in United Arab Emirates: A New Perspective 99–100 (Ibrahim Al Abed & Peter Hellyer eds., 2001).
9 Clinton Bailey, Bedouin Law from Sinai and the Negev: Justice without Government (2009).

10 For example, Bedouin continue to practice traditional customs that raise issues, including honor killings and blood revenge.
11 Thabet Abu Ras, *The Arab Bedouin and their Lands in the Naqab – The Tribal Dimension of Steadfastness*, 93 ADALAH'S NEWSLETTER, 1 (2012).
12 *Id.*
13 *Id.* at 4.
14 BAILEY, *supra* note 132 at 60–67; Abu Rabia, *supra* note 127 at 203, 202–211.
15 Samah Abdel Ati, customary law … Bedouin Law that exceeds the law of the State, [alqadaa alorfi … qanoon albado aladi yatajawaz qanon aldawlah] Oct. 14, 2007, http://www.almasry-alyoum.com/article2.aspx?ArticleID=79244&IssueID=827 [Newspaper article].
16 Katherine Blue Carroll, *Tribal Law and Reconciliation in the New Iraq*, 65 MIDDLE E. J. 11, 12 (2011) (stating that tribal or customary law predates shari'a law).
17 KEVIN GRAY & SUSAN FRANCIS GRAY, ELEMENTS OF LAND LAW 3 (5th ed. 2009).
18 Yiftachel, Kedar, and Amara, *supra* note 95 at 44, 101.
19 *Id.* at 38.
20 Mansour Nasasra, *The Ongoing Judaisation of the Naqab and the Struggle for Recognising the Indigenous Rights of the Arab Bedouin People*, 2 SETTLER COLONIAL STUDIES 81, 95 (2012).
21 See generally Chanina Porat, *Policy of Land Purchase and Settlement in the Negev before the War of Independence*, 62 CATHEDRA 123–154 (1991); BAILEY, *supra* note 132 at 43.
22 Safa Abu Rabia, *Between Memory and Resistance, an Identity Shaped by Space: The Case of the Naqab Arab Bedouin*, 8 HAGAR STUDIES IN CULTURE, POLITY AND IDENTITIES 93–119, 104 (2008) (offering examples of land borders).
23 *Id.*
24 According to some research, they used some land for wheat, barley, and even vine plants. *See, e.g.*, Abu Setteh, *Alaraqib Is All Palestine*, PALESTINE LAND SOCIETY, http://www.plands.org/arabic/articles/055.html (last visited Feb. 4, 2013).
25 Sason Bar Tzvi, *Kevri habedouim banegev: emonot, masorit, vepolhan [Bedouin Graves: Beliefs, Tradition and Ritual]*, SNUNIT, http://www.snunit.k12.il/beduin/arti/2440.html (last visited Feb. 4, 2013).
26 Falah, *supra* note 126 at 78.
27 Salman Elbedour et al., *Bedouins of the Negev: Ethnicity and Ethnic Identity among Bedouin Adolescents in Israel*, 2 INTERNATIONAL JOURNAL OF CHILD HEALTH AND HUMAN DEVELOPMENT 177, (exploring Bedouin identity) (2009).
28 Noreen Sadik, *Israel's Bedouin Population Faces Mass Eviction*, NEW INTERNATIONALIST (2013), https://newint.org/features/web-exclusive/2013/07/23/bedouins-face-mass-eviction (last visited Apr. 1, 2020).
29 *Lexicon of Terms: Minorities in Israel, Bedouin*, THE KNESSET (Jul. 2007), http://www.knesset.gov.il/lexicon/heb/bedouim.htm.
30 Spector Shiri Bass, *Sogiot Breut Wesvivah Bakfarim Habedouim Halu-Mokarim Banegev [Environmental and Health Issues among Bedouin in the Negev Unrecognized Villages]* (2011), http://www.knesset.gov.il/mmm/data/pdf/m02809.pdf.
31 PENNY MADDRELL & YUNIS GRINAWI, THE BEDUIN OF THE NEGEV 4 (1990).
32 Yiftachel et al., *supra* note 24, 134–136.
33 MADDRELL & GRINAWI, *supra* note 76, at 6.
34 *Id.*
35 Spector Shiri Bass, *supra* note 152.
36 Ten of which have been recognized between 2000 and 2010 and they are now in the planning phase.
37 HUMAN RIGHTS WATCH, *supra* note 22, at 57.
38 *Id.*

39 Joseph Ben-David, Feud in the Negev: Bedouin, Jews, Land 13 (1996).
40 Abu Rabia, *supra* note 144 at 95.
41 Yosef Ben-David & Amiram Gonen, Floersheimer Institute for Pol'y Stud., Bedouim vebedouim-falahim betahlikh haaiyor banegev [The Urbanization of the Bedouin and Bedouin- Fallakhin in the Negev] 11–12 (2001).
42 Bailey, *supra* note 132.
43 *See* Soliman Abu Bader & Daniel Gottlieb, *Poverty, Education and Employment in the Arab-Bedouin Society: A Comparative View* 137 (ECINEQ, Society for the Study of Economic Inequality Working Paper, 2009), *available at* http://ideas.repec.org/p/inq/inqwps/ecineq2009-137.html (discussing the importance of land in the Bedouin traditional economy).
44 Some lands are registered, such as Abu Karen land and Altorkmani land, but they are not Bedouin tribal land.
45 George Bisharat, *Land, Law, and Legitimacy in Israel and the Occupied Territories*, 43 American University Law Review, 467 (1994), http://digitalcommons.wcl.american.edu/aulr/vol43/iss2/3; Shlomo Swirski & Yael Hasson, Invisible Citizens: Israel Government Policy Toward the Negev Bedouin 14 (2006); Penny Maddrell, Bedouin of the Negev 4–5 (1st ed., 1989).
46 Ben-David, *supra* note 161.
47 Bailey, *supra* note 132; 7 Oren Yiftachel, Re-Examining the 'Dead Negev Doctrine': Property Rights in the Bedouin-Arab Space, 14 Mishpat Umimshal 101 (2012).
48 The Archaeology of Society in the Holy Land 538 (Thomas E. Levy ed., 1995).
49 The historical context is an element that should be taken into account; the Negev region was located between the Ottoman Empire and Egypt. The Ottoman Empire did not control the Negev while it was controlled by Egypt. From the beginning of the 19th century through the mid-19th century, Egypt invaded and controlled the entire region of Palestine, which includes the Negev. After Mohammad Ali Pasha, the Governor of Egypt, withdrew from Palestine in the mid-19th century the Ottomans did not effectively control the Bedouin region. Ottoman rule continued to be weak in the Negev, like many other places, until the eve of the First World War and the establishment of the first city in the Negev, Beer Shiva, in 1900. While the Ottomans controlled the Negev they were pre-occupied with the increasing power of the British in Egypt and the Suez Canal, rather than the Bedouin issues in the Negev.
50 Swirski and Hasson, *supra* note 167 at 100.
51 *See* HCJ 849/00 Shatz v. Minister of Justice 849(5) PD 571 [2000] (Isr.).
52 Swirski & Hasson, *supra* note 90.
53 It is worth mentioning that this occurs only in land rights, and has not happened regarding other property rights or personal status issues (e.g., marriage, divorce, and blood relationship, and agnation), animal tax registration followed the same idea. Native peoples' land rights were denied in almost every colonial state for the simple reason that the colonizing state needed land for colonial projects. *See* Muhammad Bakhit, The Ottoman Province of Damascus in the Sixteenth Century 62, 152 (1982) (discussing taxes on animals, animals were considered another source of revenue, for example, the owner of two sheep or goats was taxed one akche, and young animals became taxable when they joined the herds).
54 *See infra* Chapter 3.A.3.e.; *see also* Batya Roded, *Habedouim lo ma shehashavta [Bedouin: Not What You Thought]*, Haaretz (Jun. 26, 2011); Abu Ras, *supra* note 57.
55 Bisharat, *supra* note 167.

56 Of course, there are other reasons for the lack of recognition, particularly lack of registration, and the ultimate goal to dispossess Arab land and Bedouin land for Jewish colonial reasons.
57 Ottoman Land Act of 1858.
58 Bisharat, *supra* note 167 at 493–494.
59 Radwa Elsaman, *Factors to be Considered before Arbitrating in the Arab Middle East: Examples of Religious and Legislative Constraints*, 1 ARB.BRIEF 8 (2011).
60 Statements or actions of Prophet Muhammad.
61 SITI MARIAM MALINUMBAY S. SALASAL, *The Concept of Land Ownership: Islamic Perspective*, BULL. GEOINFORMASI 285, 297 (1998), *available at* http://eprints.utm.my/4950/.
62 *Id.*
63 Majallah al-Ahkam al-Adliyyah (the civil code of the Ottoman Empire).
64 *Articles 6 and 103 of the 1858 Ottoman Land Act*, INTERNETARCHIVE.ORG, http://www.archive.org/stream/ottomanlandcode00turkuoft/ottomanlandcode00turkuoft_djvu.txt (last visited Feb. 5, 2013); *see* FREDRIC MAURICE GOADBY & MOSES J. DOUKHAN, THE LAND LAW IN ISRAEL 263 (1935); HUSSEIN ABU HUSSEIN ET AL., ACCESS DENIED: PALESTINIAN LAND RIGHTS IN ISRAEL 121 (2003); *see also* CA 218/74 Salim El-Huashlla v. State of Israel (Alhawashelah) 38(3) PD 141 [1974] (Isr.) (defining *Mawat* land).
65 *Articles 6 and 103 of the 1858 Ottoman Land Act*, INTERNETARCHIVE.ORG, http://www.archive.org/stream/ottomanlandcode00turkuoft/ottomanlandcode00turkuoft_djvu.txt (last visited Feb. 5, 2013).
66 FREDERIC MAURICE GOADBY & MOSES J. DOUKHAN, THE LAND LAW OF PALESTINE 263 (1935); HUSSEIN ABU HUSSEIN & FIONA MCKAY, ACCESS DENIED: PALESTINIAN LAND RIGHTS IN ISRAEL 121 (2003); C.A. 218/74 Salim Alhawashelah v. State of Israel (1974), PD38(3) 141 (defining Mawat land).
67 Revival or reclamation of *Mawat* land is "bringing 'dead' land into production" and "ihya al-*Mawat*" means revival of *Mawat*. GERHARD LICHTENTHÄLER, POLITICAL ECOLOGY AND THE ROLE OF WATER: ENVIRONMENT, SOCIETY AND ECONOMY IN NORTHERN YEMEN 27 (2003). In some cases, ihya' al-*Mawat* reclamation or the revival of dead (*Mawat*) land, creates a right of ownership with the claimant being given a *taboo* (title deed). *Id.*
68 *See* MICHAEL R. FISCHBACH, STATE, SOCIETY, AND LAND IN JORDAN 29–35 (2000) (discussing Ottoman land policy in Transjordan).
69 Oren Yeftchel, *The Historical Roots of the Ottoman Land Act*, KARMEL.CO.IL (Nov. 16, 2009), http://www.karmel.co.il/index.php?option=com_content&task=view&id=9646.
70 ABU HUSSEIN AND MCKAY, *supra* note 188 at 109–110, 121–123.
71 *Id.* at 123.
72 *Id.*
73 GILBERT, *supra* note 50 at 156 (on proving the impossible).
74 J. Black stated, "Turn the desert into paradise." CA 218/74 Salim El-Huashlla v. State of Israel (Alhawashelah) 38(3) PD 141 [1974] (Isr.).
75 ABU HUSSEIN AND MCKAY, *supra* note 188 at 123.
76 Bisharat, *supra* note 167 at 497.
77 ABU HUSSEIN AND MCKAY, *supra* note 188 (discussing population transfer, the "Jewish Question").
78 Geremy Forman & Alexandre Kedar, *Colonialism, Colonization and Land Law in Mandate Palestine: The Zor al-Zarqa and Barrat Qisarya Land Disputes in Historical Perspective*, 4 THEORETICAL INQUIRIES IN LAW (2003), http://www.degruyter.com/view/j/til.2003.4.issue-2/til.2003.4.2.1074/til.2003.4.2.1074.xml?onlyResultQuery=chinese (last visited Feb. 4, 2013).

79 For the legitimacy of the transfer theory in that time see MARK MAZOWER, NATIONS, REFUGEES, AND TERRITORY: THE JEWS AND THE LESSONS OF THE NAZI NEW ORDER, IN NO ENCHANTED PALACE: THE END OF EMPIRE AND THE IDEOLOGICAL ORIGINS OF THE UNITED NATIONS, Chapter 3 (2009).
80 JAMIL HILAL, WHERE NOW FOR PALESTINE?: THE DEMISE OF THE TWO STATE SOLUTION 78 (2007).
81 Forman and Kedar, *supra* note 200 at 496–497.
82 *Id.*
83 *Id.*
84 *Id.*
85 ABU HUSSEIN AND MCKAY, *supra* note 188.
86 *Id.*
87 J. Heishen described the difficulties of following state law and the need to recognize custom law. He stated that the point is that times were tough and hard for transportation and political situation to follow the laws in two months.
88 GOADBY AND DOUKHAN, *supra* note 188.
89 ABU HUSSEIN AND MCKAY, *supra* note 188 at 122.
90 Palestine Order in Council, 1922, 13 Geo. 5, art. 2, 6, & 9 (Eng.), *available at* http://unispal.un.org/UNISPAL.NSF/0/C7AAE196F41AA055052565F50054E656.
91 ABU HUSSEIN AND MCKAY, *supra* note 188; Yiftachel, Kedar, and Amara, *supra* note 95 at (arguing that the British did not intend to sweep away the acquired rights of the Bedouins).
92 ABU HUSSEIN AND MCKAY, *supra* note 188 at 123.
93 State of Israel v. Salah Badran 16 PD 1717 [1961] (Isr.).
94 State of Israel v. Abdallah Mousa Rahal (Rahal) 4 PD 29 [1982] (Isr.).
95 ABU HUSSEIN AND MCKAY, *supra* note 188 at 123.
96 Bisharat, *supra* note 167.
97 ABU HUSSEIN AND MCKAY, *supra* note 188 at 123.
98 *Id.*
99 *Id.*
100 CA 218/74 Salim El-Huashlla v. State of Israel (Alhawashelah) 38(3) PD 141 [1974] (Isr.).
101 Duman is a unit of land area equal to 1,000 square meters or about 1/4 acre.
102 ABU HUSSEIN AND MCKAY, *supra* note 188.
103 GOADBY AND DOUKHAN, *supra* note 188.
104 Yiftachel, Kedar, and Amara, *supra* note 95.
105 GOADBY AND DOUKHAN, *supra* note 188.
106 Alhawashelah *38(3)* PD 141.
107 ABU HUSSEIN AND MCKAY, *supra* note 188.

Bibliography

Abu Hussein, H., & McKay, F. (2003). *Access Denied: Palestinian Land Rights in Israel.* Zed Books.

Abu Rabia, A. (2002). Negev Bedouin: Displacement, Forced Settlement, and Conservation. In D. Chatty & M. Colchester (Eds.), *Conservation and Mobile Indigenous Peoples: Displacement, Forced Settlement, and Sustainable Development.* Berghahn Books, pp. 202–211.

Abu Rabia, S. (2008). Between Memory and Resistance, an Identity Shaped by Space: The Case of the Naqab Arab Bedouin. *HAGAR Studies in Culture, Polity and Identities*, *8*(2), 93–119.

Abu Ras, T. (2012). The Arab Bedouin and Their Lands in the Naqab – The Tribal Dimension of Steadfastness. *Adalah's Newsletter*, *93*(May 2012).

Bailey, C. (2009). *Bedouin Law from Sinai and the Negev: Justice without Government*. Yale University Press.

Ben-David, J. (1988). *Social Change among the Bedouin of the Negev: Transition from Tribal Organization to Urban Community*. Ben-Gurion University of the Negev, the Jacob Blaustein Institute for Desert Research.

Ben-David, J. (1996). *Feud in the Negev: Bedouin, Jews, Land*. The Center for the Research of Arab Society in Israel.

Bisharat, G. (1994). Land, Law, and Legitimacy in Israel and the Occupied Territories. *American University Law Review*, *43*(2), 467–561. http://digitalcommons.wcl.american.edu/aulr/vol43/iss2/3.

C.A. 218/74 Salim Alhawashelah v. State of Israel (1974).

Cole, D. P. (2003). Where Have the Bedouin Gone? *Anthropological Quarterly*, *76*(2), 235–267. JSTOR.

Elbedour, S., Onwuegbuzie, A. J., Jiao, Q. G., Abu-Rabia, A., Morad, M., & Merrick, J. (2009). Bedouins of the Negev: Ethnicity and Ethnic Identity among Bedouin Adolescents in Israel. *International Journal of Child Health and Human Development*, *2*(2), 177.

Falah, G. (1989). Israeli State Policy toward Bedouin Sedentarization in the Negev. *Journal of Palestine Studies*, *18*(2), 71–91. https://doi.org/10.2307/2537634.

Forman, G., & Kedar, A. (2003). Colonialism, Colonization and Land Law in Mandate Palestine: The Zor al-Zarqa and Barrat Qisarya Land Disputes in Historical Perspective. *Theoretical Inquiries in Law*, *4*(2). https://doi.org/10.2202/1565-3404.1074.

Gilbert, J. (2006). *Indigenous Peoples' Land Rights under International Law* (1st ed.). BRILL.

Goadby, F. M., & Doukhan, M. J. (1935). *The Land Law of Palestine*. Gaunt.

Human Rights Watch. (n.d.). *Off the Map: Land and Housing Rights Violations in Israel's Unrecognized Bedouin Villages*. Retrieved September 6, 2016, from http://www.hrw.org/reports/2008/03/30/map.

Maddrell, P. (1989). *Bedouin of the Negev* (1st ed.). Minority Rights Group.

Marx, E. (1967). *Bedouin of the Negev*. Manchester University Press.

Morris, B. (1997). *Israel's Border Wars, 1949–1956: Arab Infiltration, Israeli Retaliation, and the Countdown to the Suez War*. Clarendon Press.

Nasasra, M. (2012). The Ongoing Judaisation of the Naqab and the Struggle for Recognising the Indigenous Rights of the Arab Bedouin People. *Settler Colonial Studies*, *2*(1), 81–107.https://www.tandfonline.com/doi/pdf/10.1080/2201473X.2012.10648827 .

Porat, C. (1991). Policy of Land Purchase and Settlement in the Negev before the War of Independence. *Cathedra*, *62*, 123–154.

Spector Shiri Bass. (2011). *Sogiot Breut Wesvivah Bakfarim Habedouim Halu-Mokarim Banegev [Environmental and Health Issues among Bedouin in the Negev Unrecognized Villages]*. Knesset Research and Information Center. http://www.knesset.gov.il/mmm/data/pdf/m02809.pdf.

Swirski, S., & Hasson, Y. (2006). *Invisible Citizens: Israel Government Policy toward the Negev Bedouin*. Adva Center.

Yiftachel, O. (2012). Re-Examining the 'Dead Negev Doctrine': Property Rights in the Bedouin-Arab Space. *14 Mishpat Umimshal*, *7*.

Yiftachel, O., Kedar, A. (Sandy), & Amara, A. (2012). Re-Examining the 'Dead Negev Doctrine': Property Rights in the Bedouin-Arab Space. *Mishpat Umimshal*, *14*, 7–147.

3 Dispossession of Bedouin land

This part introduces Bedouin land dispossession after the establishment of the State of Israel. It describes land dispossession at administrative, legislature, and judicial levels. Administratively, the State evicted Bedouins from their traditional lands. Then, it concentrated those remaining into small villages in the *Siyag* area (*Siyag* is a Hebrew word meaning "fence") and confiscated their land. At the same time, the State enacted several laws that further enabled the dispossession of Bedouin land through legislative and judicial means. Courts made sure the interpretation of the law maintained the same principles.

In addition, this chapter introduces two major elements that constitute the general framework for such policy. The first one is land tenure in Israel, and the second is the State's land policy toward Arab and Bedouin land. It also introduces the important court precedent of *Alhawashelah* and explains how the law and the judiciary reject any recognition of Bedouin land rights. This final part describes how the law in Israel expropriates Bedouin land rights through the use of legal doctrines like the *Mawat* doctrine and other similar techniques that have been used to deny indigenous peoples' land rights.

Land tenure in Israel

Originally, land tenure in Israel relied on Ottoman law enacted by the State of Israel as part of its adoption of the Mandate legal system.[1] After its establishment Israel adopted Article 46 of the Palestine Order in Council 1922 that had adopted the Ottoman law (the *Majallah*).[2] Over time, Israel amended or canceled many of the Ottoman laws and enacted new laws, changing the Ottoman land regime and establishing new property laws.[3] However, despite the changes, many components of the Ottoman land regime remain and continue to define land rights in Israel, especially land rights established before the creation of the State, such as Bedouin land rights in the Negev.[4]

Centralized land regime

After its founding, Israel instituted a centralized land regime based on the principle of national ownership of land. In consequence, the State took control of almost every piece of land by changing the legal categorization of the land needed to establish ownership. Next, the State "locked" land ownership alienation in order to prevent any land transfer from the State to any non-Jewish entity. Later, the State started to use land policy as a tool to achieve other goals, such as controlling Israeli Arabs and Bedouin.[5] In this way, the State acquired control and ownership of 93 percent of land in Israel.[6]

Ideology based on the Jewish belief that the land in Israel was divinely given to the Jewish people and the biblical term "land redemption" shaped land policy and led to the enactment of many laws to support the regime. On a practical level, the need to establish and protect the State during the first years of its existence also led to a concentration of land in the hands of the State. Zionist leaders such as David Ben–Gurion, Avraham Granott, and Moshe Dayan believed that state control of land was an essential element of the Zionist State's existence.[7] After its independence in 1948, the State sought to stabilize and initiate plans for defense, settlement, and development. These plans strongly focused on demography and population distribution, and particularly on a Jewish presence in most areas of the country, a goal that relies heavily on state control of land for its success.[8]

Transfer of land to the state and limitations on land use

During the 1948 War, the State seized a large swath of land, much of it owned by Arabs who were displaced, evicted, or fled from the State. Therefore, the State started to look for ways to transform the land it controlled into land it legally owned.[9] To accomplish this, the State first enacted land laws transferring land ownership to the State.[10] Then, it centralized ownership by placing all public land under a State management agency called the Israel Land Administration (ILA). The State then defined, by a constitutional act called Basic Law: Israel Lands, all land managed by the ILA as State land. The Basic Law: Israel Lands from 1960 defines State land as land owned by the three bodies: The State of Israel, the Jewish National Fund (JNF), and the Development Authority. These three bodies own and manage 92percent of the land in the State and are distributed as follows:

a State land, comprising 79 percent of all lands in Israel.[11]
b The Jewish National Fund (JNF), comprising about 13 percent.
c The Development Authority is a statutory body established by the Development Authority (Transfer of Property) Law-1950 manage these lands.[12]
  In the 1950s, the State transferred to the Development Authority all the Arab land from the Custodian of Absentee Property, a governmental body that took charge of land owned by Arabs who were expelled from Palestine during the 1948 War.[13]

Also, in 1960, the State enacted the Basic Law: Israel Lands.[14] Article 1 stipulates that "ownership of Israel lands, being the lands in Israel of the

State, the Development Authority or the Jewish National Fund, shall not be transferred either by sale or in any other manner."[15]

In addition to the traditional need for land for settlement and development, land policy in Israel has been considered one of the major tools used to achieve other goals, such as population distribution, Jewish presence, and, most importantly, population control.[16] Since the first years of its establishment, the State specifically utilized land policy to tighten control on the Arab[17] population and to dispossess them of their land[18] by limiting their land use and the State allocation of land for Arab development.

Consequently, the only option available for individuals to obtain land is by leasing land from the ILA. Through this agency, the State controls land allocation. Only the State can offer leases of land to individuals, companies, and other entities. As part of its policy to control population growth, population distribution, and economic development, the State deprives its Arab citizens from land acquisition by routinely discriminating against the Arab population.[19]

Further, a large portion of the State land is unavailable to the Arab population. The JNF, for example, sells land only to Jews, and prohibits the selling or leasing of land to Arab citizens. Additionally, while Arab citizens cannot buy or lease public land that belongs to the JNF, Arabs from Jerusalem (who are residents of the State, but not citizens) are banned from buying or leasing not only JNF lands, but any State land. According to Article 19 of the ILA land lease provision, "Under Israeli law, the ILA cannot lease land to foreign nationals,"[20] which includes Arab-Palestinian residents of Jerusalem who are residents, but not citizens of the State. The fact that foreigners (noncitizens) may be allowed to lease land in Israel if they show that they would qualify as Jews under the Law of Return,[21] while physically present Arab citizens cannot, emphasizes how land policy is used to perpetuate inequality within the State of Israel.

The prohibition on Arabs' ability to buy or lease land in certain areas designated for Jews was recently challenged in the Supreme Court in Ka'adan.[22] The Supreme Court decided that such prohibition was discriminatory and impermissible.[23] Despite that decision, in practice Arabs are banned from acquiring most State land both directly and indirectly.[24] The most common method is through "Selection Committees" in Jewish towns that are authorized by law to reject candidates who do not meet specific selection criteria, which discriminate against Arab citizens.[25]

These policies prevent land allocation to Bedouin in the Negev as well, both on the individual and collective levels. On the collective level, particularly, such policies prevent the recognition of many Bedouin villages under the claim that the land belongs to the JNF and cannot be allocated to a non-Jewish settlement. Therefore, understanding the framework of the Arab land issue and its history generally will allow better understanding of the Bedouin land issue.[26]

Land continues to be one of the most pressing issues between the State of Israel and Arabs, including the Bedouin. For years, the State has worked to dispossess and control Arab land, and for years Arabs have tried to protect their land, with limited success.

The roots of the Arab land issue in Israel goes back to the beginning of Jewish (Zionist Movement) settlements in Palestine in the late 18th century and the desire of the Zionist Movement to possess land to establish settlements in Palestine under Ottoman rule. Before the establishment of the State of Israel, Zionist leaders viewed Jewish settlement and control of the land in Palestine as a major component of their success in their struggle for a Jewish State.[27] Menahem Ussishkin, for example, who headed the JNF during the British Mandate, stated that Jewish control of land in Palestine was essential for the establishment of a Jewish State.[28] Avraham Granott, another leader, stated that Jewish control of the land was literally a "question of life and death for Zionism and the Jewish National Home."[29] According to scholars such as David Kretzmer, land was needed not only as a resource for Jewish settlement, but also to transform the social and economic structure of the Jewish people who had been removed from their work in agriculture before they immigrated to Palestine.[30]

After the establishment of Israel, the new leadership adopted Zionist thinking as the State's official ideology. That ideology continued to steer and shape the State's land policy beyond its first years. Zionist leaders believed the State must possess and control the land for Jewish settlement needs. Some went even further and explicitly stated that the Arab population had to be ejected from the land. Israel's first Prime Minister David Ben–Gurion, for example, wrote to his son "… we must expel the Arabs and take their place."[31]

Under this policy, the State amended existing law to include Zionist ideology and canceled laws that did not support its and its goals.[32] Although the State initially operated under the Ottoman and British Mandate land laws, gradually it enacted new laws designed to increase the State's control of land and the eviction of Arab landholders. The Absentee Law and the Land Acquisition Law, both of which dispossessed many Arabs of their lands, provide the most dramatic examples of this policy.

The Absentee Property Law,[33] passed in 1950, authorizes the State to confiscate all Arab absentee property and lands (including that of the Bedouin in the Negev).[34] The law gave the State the right of possession to all land and property of Palestinians who were absent between 1949 and 1952. The State also used this law to confiscate land for military and other public needs[35] and to transfer ownership of all absentee land to the State.[36] The Land Acquisition Law also retroactively legalized the confiscation of land belonging to nonabsentee Arabs without legal authorization. After the War of 1948 those lands were allocated for military bases or Jewish communities.[37]

The State also used the Prescription Law of 1958[38] for Arab land dispossession. The law extended the ten-year period of land cultivation to gain title for *Miri* land[39] to 15 years for land that had not been settled and 25 years for settled land.[40] In addition, the Prescription Law further stated that the new provisions applied even if the 15- or 25-year periods had elapsed before the Prescription Law came into effect.[41] Thus, as Kretzmer shows, a person who had already acquired title through possession under the Ottoman law could be deprived of that title through retroactive application of the extension of the prescription period.[42] According to Mohsen Sabri,[43] by changing the prescription period, the State expropriated about 205,000 dunams[44] of land from Arabs.[45]

Administrative tools, such as planning and zoning, provide additional methods for transferring Arab land to the State or for Jewish development.[46] Through planning laws and policies the State allocated the majority of the Arab land for Jewish settlement, public development, military needs, or other needs, while preventing or reducing land for Arab use. Planning policy affected all Arab land dispossessions but disproportionately Bedouin land in the Negev.[47]

Further, the judicial system played an additional role in Arab land dispossession. Courts subjugated the legal policy and interpretation of law to further Arab land dispossession. They narrowed the definition of Arabs' legal rights in order to deny them land ownership,[48] thus enabling the State to acquire the majority of the Arab land.[49] As part of this policy, the State has made it difficult for Arabs to win land cases in courts, as the law has made it nearly impossible to recognize Arab land rights.[50] Alexander Kedar explains how Israeli law and the "legal activism" exercised by the courts[51] have eliminated any possibility for Arab claimants to win their land claims through the Israeli court system. Kedar argues that ideological reasoning is behind such policy; the connection between the Zionist ideology and the State's laws dictate and stipulate court decisions. Kedar relies on several cases where courts interpreted the Ottoman laws to restrict and even deny Arab land rights.[52] This "judicial activism" protects Jewish land and State land and discriminates against Arabs in land rights. In regard to Bedouin land in particular, the rules for court procedures established by the State were designed for the purpose of denying Bedouin land rights.[53]

Professor Oren Yiftachel sheds light on the reality that the law has limited power when dominated by strong political forces that shape legal policy and even dictate court decisions. He notes that a number of petitions to the Supreme Court[54] regarding Jewish settlements in the occupied territories show a "legal backup – as well as a broad institutional and political legitimization – to the Israeli-Jewish colonialism, and to a distinct and unequal definition of property rights of Palestinians and Jews… creating *de facto* a regime of apartheid."[55]

Land policy toward Bedouin and the dispossession of their land

The dispossession of Bedouin land took place at several levels. At the first level, the State evicted and displaced the Bedouin from their traditional lands. Then, it concentrated those remaining in small villages to the *Siyag* area and confiscated their land. At the same time, the State enacted several laws that further enabled Bedouin land dispossession by additional administrative and judicial means. The courts followed and made sure that interpretation of the law would accord with the State's goals. The State, at all levels, ignored and disregarded Bedouin traditional land rights.

The dispossession of Bedouin land began well before the establishment of the State of Israel in 1948. The desire to purchase Bedouin land for settlement has its roots in the 1930s as part of an effort by the Zionist movement to establish a Jewish presence in the Negev in order to convince the League of Nations to annex the Negev to the Jewish State in the Partition Plan.[56]

Ironically, similar to other indigenous peoples, the first Bedouin land dispossession was facilitated by the international community. In 1947 the United Nations' Partition Plan of Palestine granted about 11 million dunams[57] (about 2,718,159 acres) in the Negev to the Jewish State despite Bedouin claims that the land belonged to them. Of those 11 million dunams Bedouin continue to claim land ownership of less than 650,000 dunams, less than 6 percent of the original partition.[58]

The executive role

The State employed several administrative and executive means to dispossess Bedouin land, including eviction, displacement, and concentration.[59] First, during the establishment of the State of Israel in 1948, the State evicted the majority of Bedouin from their land, while many other Bedouins fled the war. Evictions continued even after the war.[60] As a result, 90 percent of Bedouin were evicted and became refugees in neighboring countries.[61]

Second, the State displaced the remaining Bedouin through relocation. For example, the Assanea were evicted from Laqia village to Tal Arad; the Tarabin were evicted from their lands in Ajbibat village (near Ofakim today) to A'mra village (near Omer); and the Abu Alkeaan were evicted from Kharbet Zobalah to Atir Um Alheran.[62]

Third, after the war ended, the State refused to allow Bedouin who were evicted or had fled to neighboring countries to return to their original land, despite obligations under international law[63] and the international community's demands to allow refugees to return to their homeland.[64] At the same time, the State made many changes to Bedouin land and villages by establishing new settlements for Jewish immigrants on Bedouin land. In conjunction, the State refused to recognize Bedouin villages in order to prevent any land allocation, disconnect the Bedouin from their land, and facilitate future displacement. The Bedouin continue to live in what are known as unrecognized villages.[65]

After Bedouin were rounded up in the *Siyag* area, the State continued its efforts to concentrate Bedouin into smaller areas. In 1956, the State began discussing a variety of possibilities to deal with Bedouin in the Negev.[66] The policy to concentrate Bedouin in the *Siyag* area originated with the military because at the time the Negev was under military rule.[67] That policy stated explicitly that the purpose of concentrating Bedouin in the *Siyag* was to secure land for settling Jews and setting up military bases.[68]

There were several proposals for dealing with Bedouin issue, and "all of the proposals considered shared a common denominator – reducing to a minimum the area on which Bedouin would be settled in the *Siyag* region."[69] The first proposal, led by Minister of Agriculture, Moshe Dayan, aimed to transform Bedouin into an urban proletariat.[70] Dayan, who believed that the State should "transform the Bedouin into an urban proletariat in industry, services, construction, and agriculture,"[71] suggested settling Bedouin in mixed Jewish-Arab localities in the center of Israel, along the lines of Jaffa and Ramle, where they would become urban laborers. The second proposal, led by Yigal Alon, who in the early 1960s served as Minister of Labor, suggested concentrating Bedouin in two or three townships within the *Siyag* area in the Negev.[72] Eventually, the State adopted Alon's plan to settle Bedouin in two to three townships in the *Siyag* area.[73]

Consequently, the concentration policy affected the legal status of Bedouin land and established the major platform for future acts of land dispossession. That policy disconnected many Bedouin from their territory, their villages, and their lands; weakened their rights; and enabled the State to apply laws to confiscate their lands. Later, the State enacted the Absentee Property Law that expropriated all land that was not possessed by its owners. Thus, the land belonging to the 90 percent of Bedouins who were forcibly evicted or fled became State land.

In addition, the evictions and displacement eliminated options that would enable the Bedouin to defend or restore their land rights. These options included claims for land based on a statute of limitations that may have enabled some Bedouin to possess or own land they had been using or occupying for a long time before they were evicted or displaced.

These acts continue to affect Bedouin land rights to this day. In the recent Goldberg Report, for example, the Committee stated that Bedouin who were not in physical possession of their land were not eligible for land as part of their compensation. Instead, the Committee offered them only monetary compensation. Further, Bedouin who lost possession also lost their ability to effectively bargain for land recognition or land compensation. This element is an important one in light of the fact that Bedouin land rights are not recognized under the State law and therefore the Bedouin have no power to seek relief through the State judicial system.

Not surprisingly, the plan to concentrate Bedouin in the *Siyag* Zone deteriorated Bedouin living conditions. Bedouin lived in impoverished conditions due to limitations on movement, employment, and livestock grazing. Later, the State provided no village planning, home building permits, water, electricity, education, or health services. When Bedouin challenged this policy, the State reacted harshly with house demolition. It destroyed every new

Bedouin house, filed criminal charges, and placed severe punishments on Bedouin who built without a building permit.

While the State prevented Bedouin development, it also diligently worked to establish and develop new settlements for Jewish immigrants in the Negev. For those new settlements, the State allocated land, planned towns, and supplied them with every necessary service. During that period, the State established more than 124 towns for the Jewish immigrant population,[74] while refusing to recognize 35 Bedouin villages.

Implementation and concentration

The concentration plan was implemented gradually through five stages. In the first stage, the State recognized the first two Bedouin villages, Tal-Assaba (Tel Sheva) in 1968 and Rahat in 1972, and required the Bedouin to leave their villages and their lands and relocate to the new townships. The State claimed that the purpose of the act was to "modernize" Bedouin society by putting an end to the Bedouin's nomadic way of life and supplying them with modern services.[75]

Most Bedouin vehemently opposed leaving their lands.[76] The State's efforts to relocate them by physical and legal force failed in several instances. Many Bedouin refused to abandon their land or their way of life, claiming that uprooting them from their land would disrupt their traditional livelihoods. They were concerned that concentrating them into two townships would not modernize their society but destroy their culture and their traditional economy based on a combination of cultivating land and raising livestock. The Bedouin were also concerned that the policy would continue to discriminate against them in planning and land allocation and deprive them of their ability to live traditionally with their extended families.

In the second stage, the State established two additional villages in order to settle the evacuees created by the Negev Land Acquisition Law (Peace Treaty with Egypt) 1980[77] from the Tal Almalah area. Despite unsuccessful attempts to force a sedentary lifestyle on the Bedouin for more than ten years (from 1968 to 1979), the State insisted on following its original plan and proceeded to concentrate Bedouin into small townships in the *Siyag* area. In addition to the original plan, the State continued to use every possible opportunity to evict more Bedouin from their traditional lands and settle them in the new townships designated for Bedouin. One such opportunity appeared during the application of the Israel–Egypt Peace Treaty.[78] In 1979, as part of the Israel–Egypt Peace Treaty, the State decided to move military facilities from the Sinai Peninsula (Egypt) on Bedouin land in the Tal-Almalah area, the site of a large Bedouin community. As part of this move, the State not only confiscated large segments of Bedouin land, but also evicted all the Bedouin living in Tal Almalah and relocated them in two new towns, A'arara and Kseyfeh, created solely for the purpose of settling Tal-Almalah evacuees.[79]

In the third stage, the State established three additional villages to settle the Bedouin in new townships. Despite difficulties and Bedouin resistance to the move, the State proceeded to recognize additional villages in an effort to convince more Bedouin to move. In this phase, the State recognized an additional three villages: Segev Shalom in 1984, Hura in 1989, and Laqiya in 1990. Most of them were planned on tribal lands.

In the fourth stage, the State attempted to settle Bedouin from unrecognized villages, but refused to recognize more villages. After recognizing seven villages for Bedouin in the Negev, the State started to put more effort into a two-part plan. The first part evicted the remaining Bedouin population living in 45 unrecognized villages (about 50 percent of the whole Bedouin population in the Negev) to the seven recognized townships. The second part settled Bedouin land title, which meant dispossessing their traditional land.[80] The State put direct and indirect pressure on Bedouin to fulfill these two goals; it refused to recognize additional Bedouin villages while depriving Bedouin in unrecognized villages of basic services such as education, health, housing, running water, and electricity, and applied a tough housing demolition policy.[81]

In the fifth stage, the State changed its policy and recognized additional Bedouin villages. Between the establishment of the Regional Council for the Unrecognized Villages (RCUV) in 1996 and 2008,[82] after a long struggle against the State's discrimination, oppression, and deprivation policy, the State realized that it was impossible to settle all the remaining Bedouin population from 45 villages into the existing seven townships.[83] As a result, it recognized an additional ten villages gradually in different times between the years 2000–2012, for a total of 17 recognized Bedouin villages.[84]

Unexpected results of the concentration process: Bedouin's control of land allocation

The concentration of Bedouin in townships changed many aspects of Bedouin life, but it also changed the way Bedouin exercised control over their traditional land. That change in control became one of the major ways Bedouin started to defend their land.[85] Originally, the State intended the distribution of building lots to be completely independent of traditional notions of Bedouin land ownership. However, those who did receive building lots were required to follow Bedouin law. For example, the original owners of a piece of land made it difficult for those that bought a building lot from the State to use the land. In essence, although the State approved the sale, because the sale was improper under traditional Bedouin law it would not be recognized by Bedouin.

In other examples, during the establishment of Bedouin townships the State signed settlement agreements with Bedouin tribes in which the tribes agreed to allow the establishment of townships on their traditional land. In exchange, the State agreed to designate the town or part of it to specific tribes. In some agreements, the State restricted other tribes from settling in the new town unless the original tribes agreed.[86]

This kind of settlement gave the tribes some privileges and power to control the allocation of their traditional land. Through settlement agreements, Bedouin restricted who could live on their land or vetoed the allocation of building lots to specific members of other tribes.[87] Such control over their land became one of the reasons the State decided to settle Bedouin land rights and eliminate control over the building lots in the Bedouin towns.

Prevention of Bedouin expansion: planning, urbanization, and demolition

In addition to the concentration plan, the State applied planning and urbanization policies in order to prevent Bedouin expansion outside the designated *Siyag* area. Planning and urbanization subjugated the ultimate goal of land dispossession.[88] The State followed a policy of placing the maximum number of Bedouin on a minimum amount of land and minimum number of Jews on a maximum amount of land.[89] One particular part of the State policy would transform the Bedouin into an urbanized society limited to a few small villages.[90] Moshe Dayan, an Israeli leader and the former Israeli Minister of Agriculture, even wished to eradicate the Bedouin culture altogether by settling them in a permanent village and transforming them into an urban people. In an interview with *Haaretz* he stated:

> We should transform the Bedouin into an urban proletariat in industry, services, construction, and agriculture. Eighty-eight percent of the Israeli populations are not farmers; let the Bedouins be like them. Indeed, this would be a radical move which means that the Bedouin would not live in this land with his herds, but would become an urban person who comes home in the afternoon and put his slippers on . . . the children would go to school with their hair properly combed. This would be a revolution, but it may be fixed within two generations. Without coercion but with government direction... this phenomenon of the Bedouin will disappear.[91]

Planning policy and planning laws have been influential tools to prevent the Bedouin from returning and using their land. The Planning and Building Act of 1965,[92] for example, has been used extensively as a basis to evict many of the Bedouin from their land, relocate them to townships, and strip them of their legal land rights.[93] The Act authorizes the State to use a speedy process of administrative orders to demolish any house or building in areas that are not designated for housing.[94] At the same time, the State refuses to allow planning and development in many Bedouin villages, including housing.

However, despite the recognition of the additional villages and the State's increasing pressure on the Bedouin to relocate, the majority of them refuse to leave their land and move to the new townships. They prefer to continue living on their traditional land in their villages. The State could persuade only about half the Bedouin in the unrecognized villages to move to the newly established townships. Bedouin also opposed the sedentarization plan because it confiscated their lands while doing little to improve their living conditions. They preferred to stay and protect their lands.

In response, the State passed many laws that dispossessed Bedouins' land rights, such as the Negev Land Acquisition Law (Peace Treaty with Egypt) 1980[95] and the Public Land Law (Trespasser Eviction) 1981 (Amendment 2005).[96] The State also made many changes to support its position, such as evicting Bedouins, thereby disconnecting them physically, economically, and emotionally from their land[97]; destroying their traditional economy, which relies on land; undermining their traditional leadership; and literally changing the Bedouin landscape by building towns and projects on their land. These laws and acts demonstrate to both Bedouin and the courts that restoring the land to Bedouin is not an option to be adjudicated in courts.[98] Instead, the only available solution is compensation.[99]

The legislative role and the ordinance regime

Legislation is the second method of land dispossession. Legislation not only dispossesses the Bedouin of their land, but also legitimizes Bedouin land dispossession.[100] From the beginning of its establishment, Israel has achieved land dispossession with the Absentee Law in 1950 and the Land Acquisition Law in 1953. After the War of 1948 it was less acceptable to evict Bedouin from their villages than during the war. Therefore, the State began using other, less aggressive and more "modern" or "civilized" means to evict Bedouin from their lands, relying more on legislation to add legitimacy for land dispossession.

Legislation regarding land dispossession can be divided into two groups. The first group deals generally with legislation that facilitated the dispossession of Arab land, such as the Absentee Property Law (1950) and the Land Acquisition Law (1953).[101] The second group of laws specifically pertains to Bedouin land dispossession, such as the Land Rights Settlement Ordinance (1969)' the Negev Land Acquisition Law (Peace Treaty with Egypt) 1980 (The Peace Law); and the Public Land Law (Trespasser Eviction) 1981 (Amendment 2005).

These laws directly and indirectly enabled and legitimized the dispossession of Bedouin land. They "created the 'alleged' mechanism and framework for the investigation for Bedouin land rights,"[102] which resulted in the dispossession of most of their land.[103] Such laws also helped shape local public opinion and the international community's opinion of the legality and the morality of the State's policy and actions.

Land rights settlement ordinance of 1969

Among the legislations, the Land Rights Settlement Ordinance of 1969 is the most devastating. The Ordinance created a process of land title settlement that ensured the dispossession of Bedouin land. In 1969, the State passed the Land Rights Settlement Ordinance of 1969 as part of its ongoing policy to control land.[104]The Ordinance intended to settle all outstanding land claims in the entire State. It has affected the Bedouin and their land rights more than any other tool because Bedouin lands have long been considered unsettled lands in Israel.

The Ordinance, through sophisticated and extraordinary steps, established new rules for land settlement claims, determined the jurisdiction of courts, and articulated the applicable law for the land settlement process.[105] It requires anyone claiming rights to land to submit a "land title settlement claim" (Memo Claim) to the Land Rights Settlement Officer within the Ministry of Justice.[106] Then, the Land Settlement Officer investigates and assesses the claim. If the Officer approves the claim, he registers the land in the name of the claimant (plaintiff). But, in case of a disputed claim, the Officer must transfer the case to the District Court for further determination. Only the Court is authorized to settle disputes concerning land rights and reject a claim.[107]

Article 17(a) of the Ordinance states: "Upon publishing a settlement notification in a town, every person who claims land rights shall appear . . . and submit his memorandum of claim in the prescribed form."[108] Articles 43 and 44 of the Ordinance determine both the appropriate court jurisdiction and the applicable law in court in case of dispute between claimants.[109] Article 43 provides that only courts shall have jurisdiction over disputes regarding land settlement, and if there are any conflicting claims between two or more claimants, the Land Settlement Officer shall transfer the dispute to court.[110] This eliminates other forms of resolution, such as arbitration. Article 44 outlines the law the courts should apply when evaluating a claim. It provides that:

a A court shall judge by land laws that are in effect during the trial, and take into account the rights of real estate by law and by equity.
b The court shall not be obliged to act according to the Ottoman law rules that prohibit courts to hear the case based on documents that were not registered or under the laws of Ottoman evidence.[111]

The land settlement process: Bedouin land claims and obstacles

During the process of land title settlement, many Bedouin filed land title settlement claims. According to official State numbers, Bedouin filed 3,220 claims for about 991,000 dunams (about 245,000 acres) of land.[112] However, some believe that Bedouin claims exceeded 991,000 dunams for a total of 1,216,000 dunams (about 300,000 acres).[113] Many other Bedouin were excluded from the process altogether. For example, the Alazazimah tribes who own about 225,000 dunams (about 55,500 acres), located in Sahl Albagar (*Har Hanegev* region), were prevented from filing settlement claims due to the fact that the State excluded their land from the settlement process because it had previously been expropriated for military needs.[114]

It is worth mentioning that Bedouin who were excluded from the title settlement process never relinquished their land rights. They continue to claim and demand their land rights and ask the State to recognize their land claims on every possible occasion. During the Goldberg Committee's hearings in 2008, leaders and other tribal members demanded recognition of their land rights despite the fact that they had not submitted land claims pursuant to the Land Rights Settlement Ordinance of 1969.[115]

Finally, relying on the Ordinance rules, the Land Settlement Officer refused to recognize Bedouin traditional land ownership, claiming that the Bedouin do not possess title deeds and categorizing their lands as *Mawat* land, making the land State land. The Officer refused to accept the Bedouin's traditional evidence as sufficient to prove their rights. In addition, Bedouin documents, such as contracts for land purchase (*Sanadat*), could not convince the Land Settlement Officer to accept their claims of ownership. Instead, the Land Settlement Officer and later the courts required a title deed of registration from the Ottoman or British Land Registry Office as the only legitimate evidence of land ownership. Ironically, however, when Bedouin decide to sell their land to the State, the State recognizes Bedouin land rights based on such documents or based on Bedouin law in order to perform the sale.[116]

The Land Settlement Officer forwarded disputed land claims to the District Court.[117] The Court also rejected all Bedouin claims and refused to recognize any of their land rights.[118] When Bedouin appealed to the High Court, the High Court also rejected their land rights and ordered the land registered under the name of the State. In the *Alhawashelah* case, where members of the Alhawashelah tribe appealed the District Court's decision to the High Court, the latter rejected their appeal and decided that Bedouin land in that case was *Mawat* land.[119] Based on the Alhawashelah decision, the Court rejected all subsequent Bedouin land claims.[120] The Court ruled that Bedouin lands were State lands[121] and that the Bedouin had no land rights. To this day, not a single land claim has been ruled in favor of the Bedouin claimants.[122] That collective rejection of land rights means that no Bedouin has land rights within the Negev, a characteristic of indigenous peoples' land problems in many settler states around the world.

As a result, the Bedouin lost trust in the State system and refrained from bringing additional land cases for adjudication. They believe that the courts in Israel are politically motivated and biased and do not attempt to create an equitable outcome. Dr. Amer Alhozail, a Bedouin activist and founder of the Regional Council for the Bedouin Unrecognized Villages, states that there is no benefit for Bedouin to go to court since Bedouin lose every case.[123]

Essentially, in the minds of the Bedouin, courts constitute a "rubber stamp" for the State's land dispossession policy.

The Bedouin's limited understanding of the land settlement process

Land title settlement was an unfamiliar and strange process for Bedouin. Many of them did not understand the process, its goals, or the documents they received from the Land Registrar Officer. Bedouin did not trust the process, and, at the beginning, many refused to participate in the process or submit claims.[124] To overcome these obstacles, the State made an extraordinary effort to convince as many Bedouin as possible to submit claims by calling upon all Bedouin to do so. The State sent officers to tribal leaders to convince them to submit claims on behalf of their tribes, and warned them about the consequences of not of submitting. The State appeared to put forth these efforts, not to recognize or fairly adjudicate land rights as promised, but in order to collect information about Bedouin land and the owners and to entangle them in a legal process that would strip them of their land rights.

While some Bedouin refused to participate, others mistakenly thought that the State was registering their land in the Land Registry and recognizing their land ownership, especially because they were requested to show evidence (either through documents or witnesses) of the land claims and to define the borders and the size of their land. This was understood by many Bedouin as proving their land ownership. In addition, at the end of the process, they received official documents signed by the State Officer of the Land Registration Office, under the Ministry of Justice. Many Bedouin were illiterate, and they could not read the content of the documents they received. In fact, some Bedouin mistakenly thought the copies of the application forms they received from the Land Settlement Officer in the Ministry of Justice were title deeds for their land or an equivalent. Therefore, many Bedouin mistakenly refer to the settlement documents as title deeds or official documents that prove their land ownership.[125]

The ordinance regime: the effect of legislation

The many laws the State passed create a new regime of Bedouin land dispossession.[126] However, the Ordinance is particularly notable. The Ordinance eliminates the previous land regime, introduces a new regime that regulates Bedouin land, and effectively ensures Bedouin land dispossession.

The Ordinance is based on the presumption that the Bedouin do not hold any land rights. Therefore, it requires them to go through a politicized legal process to prove their rights. The Ordinance disregards Bedouin traditional land rights and sets the platform for the State policy of land dispossession in the Negev. The Ordinance does not recognize customary law nor land rights based on customary law.[127]

In addition, the Ordinance establishes a set of rules that ensures the supremacy of the State and inferiority Bedouin legal rights. It supports the State's legal position and undermines the Bedouin position. Article 135 "classifies all *[M]awat* lands as State property, unless formal legal title could be produced."[128] Since the State classifies Bedouin land as *Mawat* land, it essentially classifies Bedouin land as State property.[129] Such articles give a clear privilege to the State over Bedouin claimants and facilitate the expropriation of their land by legal means.

Furthermore, the Ordinance preserves the State's right to object to any Bedouin claim without requiring the State to prove any rights or connection to the Bedouin land. Article 22 of the Ordinance states "The State's rights in land shall be investigated and will be settled whether officially sued or not, all rights in land that have not been proven by other claims shall be registered in the name of the State."[130] In addition, Article 53 grants the State the ultimate right to object to settlement of title claims. The article states "If an objection was filed in one of the matters mentioned in Article 51 and 52, the Settlement Officer shall transfer the matter to the court, and the court may order the registration of the possessor as the owner of the land, if it finds that the mentioned conditions were met."[131]

The Ordinance also replaced the traditional order of Civil Law with a new order, especially for Bedouin land cases. While generally the party who claims rights against the possessor submits his claim, serves as plaintiff, and proves his claims, the new order requires Bedouin, who are the possessors of the land, to submit claims, serve as plaintiff, and carry the burden of proof in order to prove their land rights.

Forcing Bedouin to serve as plaintiffs has several consequences, but mainly it places the burden of proof on them. Generally, in a civil legal process the plaintiff submits the lawsuit, summons the defendant, and carries the burden of proof of his claim. In the case of land possession, the rule places the burden of proof on the plaintiff. That rule indicates that whoever claims rights against the possessor must submit his claim in court and prove it.[132] According to Article 43 of the Ordinance, for either side to be able to own the land, both the Bedouin and the State, must prove his rights.[133] Under Article 45 of the Ordinance, when neither the Bedouin nor the State agree to serve as a plaintiff, the court decides which side should be the plaintiff and bear the burden of proof.[134] In the Bedouin land case, however, the Ordinance changed the traditional order and ordered the Bedouin to submit lawsuits for land settlement,[135] then the State summons the Bedouin to court and forces them to serve as plaintiffs and carry the burden of proof.[136]

The Ordinance also transforms the status of Bedouin from "owners of land" or land possessors to "claimants of land."[137] This transformation has a tremendous effect on Bedouin land adjudication in courts, resulting in a long complicated legal process that denies Bedouin land rights.[138] The process requires Bedouin who appeal for land ownership to prove their rights, while those who agree to accept compensation are not required to do so.

In latter cases, the State recognizes Bedouin rights based on their traditional law. The State's "acceptable paradox" does not find any representation in the legal process. Bedouin are required to prove their land rights exactly like anyone who does not have any traditional connection to the land. Such changes contradict basic rules of due process and evidence and delay adjudication, harming Bedouin ability to bring evidence to prove their claims.

A careful analysis on the macrolevel reveals that the State rather than the Bedouin should be the plaintiff because the State is the party that acts and behaves as a plaintiff. The State is interested in obtaining or acquiring rights through the legal process. It claims rights against the Bedouin who are in possession (or owners) of the land.[139] The State claims a right, summons Bedouin owners to court, and controls the legal process, while Bedouin behave as defendants by trying to defend their rights in court. In the land settlement process the State is also the party who initiates the legal process and forces the Bedouin to file their claims. As mentioned, in the 1970s the State forced the Bedouin to file land title settlement claims and in 2003 the State also filed counterclaims and forced the Bedouin to adjudicate their land settlement claims in court. Therefore, the State should be defined as the plaintiff and carry the burden of proof.

The State's control of the legal process is another factor that should be taken into consideration. The State decides when to start the process and when to freeze it, and against which tribe to submit claims, and it control many other important elements of the process ignoring the basic rules of fair legal process such as the time passed and statute of limitation. Only through colonial "legal magic" does the impossible become possible against indigenous peoples.[140] The timing of such acts has a tremendous effect on the Bedouin claims because it defines and controls the ability of the Bedouin to provide evidence and call witnesses to court. These limitations eventually lead to their inability to prove their cases.

One blatant example of how the State undermines the Bedouin position can be found in the State's ability to delay adjudication of Bedouin land claims. Bedouin claims remained pending for 35 years after the Land Settlement Process began in the early 1970s. That delay severely harmed the Bedouin's ability to bring evidence to court particularly because of the Bedouin oral culture. During the delay, many Bedouin claimants lost their ability to prove their land rights as many claimants and many witnesses passed away, and much of the major evidence was lost with them. This is significantly important and crucial due to the fact that the court requires evidence from 1921, the year of the British *Mawat* Ordinance or before.

Further, the Ordinance places the ultimate power to adjudicate Bedouin land in the hands of the State. The State then abuses that power by managing and manipulating the process in order to weaken the Bedouin's legal position and undermine their ability to prove their land rights.

Negev Land Acquisition (Peace Treaty with Egypt) 1980

Negev Land Acquisition is another legislation the State utilized to dispossess Bedouin land. In 1980, the State signed the Camp David Peace Agreement with Egypt. According to the agreement, Israel agreed to withdraw from the Sinai Peninsula and remove its military bases from Egypt. Among the many available places in the Negev, the State decided to locate military airport and military bases only on Bedouin land in the Tal-Almalah region, a major concentration of Bedouin tribes that owned a large part of the Bedouin lands.[141]

In order to avoid legal intervention by Bedouin or human rights groups the State passed the Negev Land Acquisition Law (Peace Treaty with Egypt) 1980[142] (Hereinafter: The Peace Treaty Law) that imposed Bedouin eviction and land dispossession and set up the compensation process by law. The law allowed the State to evict all Bedouin in the Tal-Almalah area to the designated townships of Arara and Ksyefeh and confiscate their land in exchange for small amounts of compensation fixed by law.

Originally, the Peace Treaty law was designed specifically for the Tal Almalah region, but later it became the law that applies to all Bedouin land settlement matters, especially regarding land compensation. The law defines both the monetary component and land component of compensation.

The Peace Agreement not only physically dispossessed Bedouins of their land, but also forced inadequate and discriminatory compensation upon them. By comparison, in the same year the State evacuated many Jews from settlements that Israel established on Egyptian land. The State paid less than 10 percent to Bedouin of what it paid to Jewish settlers who were relocated from the Egyptian territory of the Sinai Desert in the 1980s.[143] That comparison is similar to the compensation the State paid to the Bedouin and what it paid to the Jewish settlers who were evicted from Gaza Strip in 2004.[144]

Following the Peace Agreement, the State worked to confiscate as much Bedouin land as possible.[145] From these seizures, an expression arose among the Bedouin "Israel got the peace, the settlers got the compensation and the Bedouin paid the price." Yosef Algaze echoed these sentiments: "The Bedouin paid the price for the peace with Egypt."[146]

Public Lands Law (Eviction of Squatters) (see Adalah)

In 2005, the government enacted another piece of legislation as part of its ongoing efforts to confiscate Bedouin land. The legislation, part of an amendment to the Public Land Act, aimed to further dispossess Bedouin land. The law gives local authorities the power to issue orders for the removal of squatters from public land without judicial review, a step that previously had been mandatory. The obvious purpose of the Act is to prevent Bedouin from using their traditional land, which the State defines as public land, and to quickly evict them if they do.[147]

In sum, the State, through the passage of several legislative acts, established a system that dispossesses Bedouin using legislative tools. Israeli legislation has established a mechanism that targets Bedouin land rights on multiple levels. Such laws not only facilitate Bedouin land dispossession but also enable and legitimize land dispossession by the executive and judiciary branches.[148]

The judicial role

Adjudicating Bedouin land claims in courts: the Alhawashelah case

After the Bedouin filed their land claims to the Land Settlement Officer, the State refused to accept their ownership claims. In response, the State filed counterclaims against all Bedouin land settlement claimants.[149] This action marked the beginning of the process of Bedouin land dispossession through the judiciary system.[150] Few cases were adjudicated in the early 1970s, but recently the judicial method has become the main tool for Bedouin land dispossession. Because Bedouin do not possess title deeds, the State bases its argument on two premises. First, the State argues that Bedouin land is *Mawat* land. Second, that Bedouin were required to revive the land and did not do so. Therefore, the State claims that the land in question is State land and Bedouin have no rights to it.

The State's act of filing counterclaims turned Bedouin claims into "disputed claims,"[151] meaning they must be forwarded to the court for adjudication.[152] Therefore, the Land Settlement Officer transferred Bedouin claims to the court for adjudication. In court, Bedouin claimants found themselves in a labyrinthine process in order to prove their land rights. Obstacles include the obligation to follow the State's law and its rules of evidence.[153] Under such rules, Bedouin carry the burden of proof and must introduce sufficient evidence to prove their ownership of the land. This requirement may include providing official documents from the mid- and late-19th century to the beginning of the 20th century. Often Bedouin have been unable to present this evidence in court.

At the same time, courts disregarded and refused to recognize Bedouin customs, laws, and evidence. Unlike the Ottoman and the British Mandate approach, courts in Israel followed a new approach established under the Land Rights Settlement Ordinance and other subsequent laws and court decisions.[154]

Proving land rights in court

In general, to prove land ownership a plaintiff introduces a title deed or other equivalent documents. However, Bedouin do not have title deeds and thus cannot prove their ownership in this way. They must provide evidence that proves their land rights through an alternative method. In fact, in a case of unsettled land like Bedouin land, title deeds do not exist at all. Therefore, the only available option to the Bedouin is litigation, in which they must introduce detailed evidence to prove their land rights, including the source of their right (i.e., by purchase, inheritance, land revival, or long time of possession); the type of land (*Miri*, *Mulk*, *Waqf*, *Matruka*, or *Mawat*); and location, including the exact borders of the land and its neighbors. With *Mawat* land, claimants must prove another two elements: revival of the *Mawat* land, which means continuous land cultivation; and authorization or consent to revive the land, meaning they have to prove that they have received consent from state authorities (Ottoman or British Mandate) to revive that land prior to 1921. Many obstacles such as Hebrew language proficiency, lack of trust, and political hostility make the process very difficult. Further, the fact that the State does not recognize Bedouin oral culture eliminates the possibility to prove their land rights in any other way.[155]

In order to streamline what evidence is needed to prove their rights, Bedouin usually try to prove one of two options, either that they have been legally possessing *Miri* land for the prescription period or prove that they have revived *Mawat* land.[156] Under the first option, which is the preferred option, claimants have to prove that the land is *Miri* land, rather than *Mawat* land, and that they have legally acquired possession without violence or opposition from the previous owner, and they have been in possession of the land since that time. The main obstacle with this option is proving that the land is *Miri* land, especially since the court decided in several cases, including Alhwashleh, Alasad, and Alsibi, that all Bedouin lands are *Mawat* land because at the time the Ottoman Land Code was enacted in 1858 there were no settlements in the Negev.

Alternatively, under the second option, the *Mawat* option, claimants must prove that they have revived[157] *Mawat* land.[158] To prove revival of *Mawat* land claimants must prove three elements: 1) the type of land they are claiming according to the Ottoman law[159]; 2) authorization to revive the land from the Ottomans or the British Mandate prior to 1921; and most importantly, 3) a persistent "use of land" (cultivation) with no interruption. This "use of land" must show a significant change in the land as a result of that use.[160] Each one of these three elements is nearly impossible to prove, let alone all three together.[161] In several cases the court has demanded proof of land use according to non-Bedouin traditions, meaning use of the land according to an agricultural standard rather than a Bedouin-pastoral standard.[162] This requirement is problematic on both the practical and theoretical levels. On the practical level, it deprives the Bedouin of the right to recover land right based on their pastoral culture. It also leads to the denial of Bedouin claims for pastoral land.

On the theoretical level, pastoral lands rights are the core issue of nomadic peoples' land rights problems. The basic theory of land rights relies on "effective occupation" proven by cultivation, an agriculture test.[163] The principle of "effective occupation" of the land has been the basic rule for land use and ownership. Major western theorists such as Locke and Hegel described the "cultivation test" or "agricultural argument" as the basic way to prove occupation of land in order to prove possession and acquire land rights. "The 'agricultural argument' promotes the view that only cultivation of land can be regarded as a 'proper' occupation of land, and only agriculture can be regarded as a basis of a real land tenure system."[164] According to Locke "uncultivated land was not possessed closely enough to constitute property."[165]

Pastoral culture is a problematic element for nomadic indigenous peoples, including Bedouin. "Nomadic peoples are not regarded as legal occupiers of any particular land as they do not to have '*a fixed abode*, and definite territory belonging to the people by whom it is occupied.'"[166] The law discriminates against Bedouin culture and their use of land on the same basis; therefore, the court does not recognize their use of land as a kind of use that grants them land rights.[167]

Unlike Israeli law, international law, despite the theory of possession, protects some land rights of nomadic peoples. Article 27 covers nomadic peoples' right to land to the extent that they can prove a historical cultural attachment to their lands."[168] However, it only protects rights to use, rather than rights to own.

Not surprisingly, the requirements for revival have been almost impossible to meet, since they simply do not fit the Bedouin culture and way of life in the desert.[169] Justice Abraham Halima, who wrote the decision in Alhawashelah, in one of his lectures regarding Bedouin land, showed that it is almost impossible to prove such claims.[170] The abovementioned arguments were tested for the first time in Alhawashelah, which began in the District Court of Beer Sheva, and then in the Court of Appeals in 1984.

The Alhawashelah case

In 1969, as part of the land settlement process, members from the Alhawashelah tribe, who reside in Gaser Asser Village in the southern part of the Negev, filed a land claim with the Land Settlement Officer asking him to approve their land claim and register their land in their name. However, the Land Settlement Officer rejected their application, and therefore they appealed to the District Court of Beer Sheva. In July 1972, the District Court also rejected the Alhawashelah claims.[171] Following the District Court's decision, the Alhawashelah tribe appealed to the High Court. However, before the Court issued its decision, the State appointed a Committee to examine Bedouin land rights in the Negev.

The Albeck Committee, Alhawashelah, and the Mawat Land Doctrine

As mentioned, in 1975, after the District Court of Beer–Shiva issued the Alhawashelah decision,[172] in which the court accepted the State designation of

Bedouin land as *Mawat* land,[173] and while the High Court was adjudicating the Alhawashelah case, the government appointed a special committee from the Ministry of Justice. The Committee, headed by Pleah Albeck, inquired into the legal status of Bedouin land rights and became known as the Albeck Committee.

In October 1975, the Committee issued its report. It stated three points: first, all lands of the Negev (*Siyag* area) are *Mawat* lands because when the Ottoman Lands Code 1858 was published, there was no permanent settlement in the Negev; second, no Bedouin can acquire any rights, even under possession and continuous cultivation; and third, all Bedouin land is State land.[174]

The Committee also stated that it was unacceptable to evacuate Bedouin without compensation after so many years of living in the area simply because there was no rural or urban settlement in 1858. Therefore, the Committee devised an arrangement called *beyond the letter of the law* under which the State would compensate Bedouin in return for relinquishing the lands in their possession or that were in their possession in the past and to which they claim rights.[175]

According to Shlomo Swirski, the report summed up three principles of the policy applicable to Bedouin land to this day: first, nonrecognition of ownership rights of the Bedouin to the lands based on the Ottoman and British land laws; second, compensation is "beyond the letter of the law;" and third, the evacuation principle, which makes compensation conditional upon leaving their land and moving to one of the government-planned townships.[176]

In accordance with the Committee's recommendations, the State did not bring any other Bedouin land cases to be adjudicated. Instead, it began to offer the Bedouin compensation and to convince them to settle their land claims through negotiation outside of the court.[177]

During this phase, the Bedouin continued to demand recognition of their land rights, but the State continued to refuse. It continues to consider only two options when settling their land claims: the legal option, meaning litigation in court, and the land settlement option that could include monetary and land compensation. Neither of these options suggests satisfactory recognition of Bedouin land rights and the Bedouin have rejected both options.

However, unlike the State's expectation, when the State halted adjudication of the counterclaims, only a small number of Bedouin agreed to settle their land claims in exchange for compensation.[178] The Bedouin realized that they had no chance of winning their land claims in court,[179] and welcomed the decision to freeze the adjudication of their land claims. This in turn relieved the pressure to settle their land claims according to the State's unfair offers.

Alhawashelah in the high court of justice

In 1974, a year before the Committee report, three members of the Alhawashelah tribe appealed the District Court's decision to the High Court of

Justice.[180] The Alhawashelah tribe claimed that they owned the land and appealed to register it in their name. However, since their land had never been registered in a Land Registry, they had never possessed a title deed that would prove their ownership.

The State, represented by Pleah Albeck, who served as the head of Albeck Committee, claimed that according to Articles 6 and 103 of the Ottoman Land Code, Bedouin land was *Mawat* land.[181] Articles 6 and 103 define *Mawat* land as remote from an inhabited place, located in a deserted place, and not allocated to anybody or possessed by anybody. Therefore, the State argued that the land should be registered in the name of the State, according to Article 155 of the property law.[182] It also claimed that the appellants had no land ownership because they did not prove they had revived the land. The State argued that the appellants had not cultivated the land and had not registered the land under their name.

In response to the *Mawat* argument, the Alhawashelah members claimed that they had in fact revived the *Mawat* land. They claimed that they had possessed and cultivated the land since time immemorial, long before the British Ordinance of 1921, and that it should be recognized as revival.[183]

As mentioned, a claimant who seeks to prove revival of *Mawat* land has to prove three elements: 1) that he possessed the land; 2) cultivated the land for long time[184], and 3) has received authorization from the relevant authorities according to either the Ottoman Land Code of 1858 or the British Mandate Ordinance of 1921. This 1921 Ordinance was the last chance to get consent to revive *Mawat* land, because the British Mawat Land Ordinance of 1921 put an end to *Mawat* land acquisition through revival. Accordingly, in order to prevail, the Alhawashelah members had to prove that they had possessed the land, revived it, and acquired rights in the period preceding the Ordinance of 1921, or during the Ottoman rule between 1858 and 1915 -- 60 years before their case had reached the court in Israel. In addition, the claimants also had to prove that they had obtained Ottoman or British Mandate authorization.[185] Needless to say, the claimants could not meet this burden.[186]

As a result, the High Court dismissed the appeal, affirmed the State's position, and ordered the Alhawashelah members' land to be registered as State land. Justice Avraham Halima who delivered the decision stated that the claimed land was *Mawat* land, according to the 1858 Ottoman Land Code and the 1921 British Lands Ordinance. The court rejected the Alhawashelah tribe's argument that they had "revived" the land and acquired ownership rights.[187] Through this decision, the court adopted the State's policy as it appeared in the Albeck Report, and it became legal precedent and the governing rule for all Bedouin land cases. The Alhawashelah decision also illustrates how the State report of the Albeck Committee became the court rule and the law regarding Bedouin land rights.

The Alhawashelah decision is considered a landmark decision for Bedouin land rights. It was the first Bedouin land case to reach the High Court producing a detailed decision on the merits. The decision defines Bedouin land as *Mawat* land and creates legal precedent for the dispossession of all Bedouin land in the Negev.[188] It sealed the fate of Bedouin land claims, creating a situation where Bedouin land rights cannot be legally disputed. In practice, the State simply introduces Alhawashelah as precedent in response to Bedouin claims. It argues that Bedouin land is *Mawat* land, and thus claims should be dismissed under the same reasoning as Alhawashelah. The court in turn, relying on Alhawashelah, denies every Bedouin land claim without exception.[189] Not one Bedouin tribe or individual has ever succeeded in winning his land case.[190]

In recent cases, cases from 2004, the process of adjudicating Bedouin land cases introduced the simplicity of dismissing Bedouin land claims.[191] The court, the Bedouin, and the State know in advance the result. Courts have been accepting the argument that Bedouin land is *Mawat* land as a fact, rather than a legal claim requiring proof. Therefore, in recent cases courts have been using the same form for each decision, changing only the technical information, such as names, the size of the land claim, and the date.[192]

By substituting its policy, the State has been ignoring centuries of Bedouin traditional land ownership, its characteristics, and their unique use of land.[193] Courts refuse to acknowledge that Bedouin have a different set of characteristics that require different approaches of investigation to determine ownership.[194]

In several cases, courts ignored elements supporting Bedouin rights. Courts also refused to recognize Bedouin's traditional *Dirah* as a "settlement" for the purpose of land rights recognition. Further, courts denied their traditional use of land for pastoralism to satisfy the use of land requirement for proving *Mawat* land revival. As Tawfiq S. Rangwala stated, "The Israeli courts would not recognize tents as settlements and denied that pastoralism as practiced by the Bedouin constituted 'working' the land."[195] Courts ignored traditional Bedouin land regimes that organize their land rights according to their culture.[196] The courts also ignored the fact that Bedouin land is desert that relies on seasonal rain and seasonal cultivation. Thus, even when the Bedouin revive the land, that revival could not change the land as significantly as the courts demand.

Halt on Bedouin land settlement 1984–2003

After the Albeck Report was issued in 1975, the State froze the process of land settlement. Despite the fact that the law had been decided in favor of the State, it did not bring further Bedouin land claims cases to court adjudication, except in a few circumstances.[197] The few cases that were adjudicated during this period reached court for a specific purpose other than the general process of land title settlement. For example, the State may have wished to put pressure on specific tribes to force them to settle their land or refrain from opposing the development of specific projects on their land.[198]

Bedouin who became aware of the consequences of the legal process refused to bring their land claims to court. They appeared in courts only when they had no choice but to defend their land rights. Mainly, they sought judicial protection of their land against the State, hoping to prevent State acts of dispossession or expropriation only to find out that courts do not recognize any of their rights. In some cases, where Bedouin appealed to the court to protect their land, they were surprised to find that courts not only did not offer any protection but also ruled against them and dispossessed their land rights.[199]

Between 1984 and 2003, the State continued to reject the recognition of Bedouin land rights and continued to expropriate their land when they refused to accept the State's offers for land settlement. Most Bedouin refused to relinquish their lands or to settle. Some Bedouin refused as a matter of principle and some due to inadequate offers of compensation.[200] This situation brought the issue to a deadlock, with no solution that both Bedouin and the State could accept.

The government viewed this deadlock as an obstacle impeding the development of the Negev. This created another reason for the government to continue with aggressive plans and policy to end the Bedouin land issue.

The Negev Plan and the second phase of Bedouin land dispossession

For many years, the State considered the Bedouin land issue as the main obstacle preventing the development of the Negev.[201] State leaders are convinced that the bedouin land claims and the fact they continue to live on their historical land are the main reason behind their refusal to leave their land and move to the new townships. Many political leaders and State officials believe that by solving or eliminating the land settlement issue the State will remove obstacles and clear the way for the development of the Negev.

In 2003, after a long period of stagnation in land settlement, the government decided to confront the Negev issue through the Negev Plan 2003.[202] As part of the plan, the government decided to improve services and infrastructure in the recognized townships and to guard the State's lands in the Negev against Bedouin trespassing or theft of State land.[203]

In practice, the plan aimed to resettle Bedouin from unrecognized villages into designated township and settle Bedouin land claims.[204] Therefore, the government began adjudicating Bedouin land claims that had been frozen since 1975 according to the Albeck Report recommendations.

Bedouin who did not welcome the plan were concerned that their land would be taken from them to serve Jewish development needs and settlement programs in the Negev.[205] They believed that the main goal of the plan was to evict them from their land, concentrate them in small villages, and dispossess them of their lands.[206] Therefore, they rejected the plan, refused to cooperate, and started to advocate against the plan. They called upon all Bedouin to be steadfast, to defend and keep their land, not move to the townships, and not to settle their lands.[207]

Counterclaims

In 2004, as part of the Negev Plan, in a step designed to put additional pressure on Bedouin and coerce them to settle, the State renewed the adjudication of Bedouin land claims and started to submit counterclaims against Bedouin claims. The State vowed to adjudicate all Bedouin land claims and put an end to the Bedouin land problem. To make the plan more effective and assertive, it allocated special budgets and hired a special team of lawyers and experts.[208]

The process of counterclaims forces the Bedouin either to settle their land claims or appear in court and adjudicate their land claims.[209] If claimants do not appear in court to adjudicate their claims, the court dismisses their claims and registers the land under the state's name.[210] The government also raised the compensation offer for a limited time of three years to speed up the process from 20 to 30 percent.[211] At the same time, it warned that refusal to settle land claims would result in loss of land and compensation.

The results were devastating for Bedouin land rights. Shortly after 2004, the State brought more than 130 claims and won 40 rulings relating to about 25,000 dunams that were registered in the name of the State.[212] As of April 2012, Bedouin lost every land case brought and tried in court. Bedouin claimants continue to be summoned to the Land Settlement Office one by one, or tribe by tribe, to settle their land claims.

The compensation option

Compensation includes monetary compensation, land compensation, or a combination of the two.[213] However, the compensation offered by the State is extremely inadequate. As a result, most Bedouin have rejected compensation offers for more than four decades.[214] The land component of the compensation is limited and restricted to a small number of claimants based on the size of the claimant's land (over 400 dunam). In several cases, the State promised to compensate Bedouin with land but the State never delivered.[215] In several other examples, the State agreed to offer agriculture land as part of the compensation, but when they received the land the State refused to give them a title deed and refused to register the land in their names.[216] In other instances, the State offered Bedouin land in deserted places that had a lower value than their original land and that was unsuitable for their needs. In other examples, the State simply claimed that it could not find land to offer to the Bedouin. In one particular example, members of the Alamor and Azabarga tribes agreed to leave their land in Tal-Almalah in 1983. In exchange, the State promised to give them five dunams of agriculture land, but for 18 years the State claimed that it could not find land to fit their needs.

In 2001, they appealed to the Supreme Court, but still did not receive their promised land.[217]

The second component of the compensation is monetary compensation. The Peace Law of 1980 and ILA decisions define the eligibility and the amounts of the compensation.[218] Generally, the State pays Bedouin between 1,100 to 3,000 NIS (approximately $300–800)[219] for each dunam of land.[220] Then, the State later sells the same land for about $80,000–$150,000 for each dunam.[221]

A comparison of Bedouin relocation compensation to Jewish relocation compensation also sharply illustrates the disparity. A Jewish family evicted from the Gush Gatif settlement in Gaza received more than a million Shekels in compensation.[222] By comparison, a Bedouin family evicted from the Bedouin village of Tarabin received approximately 70,000–150,000 Shekels, about 5 to 10 percent of the compensation received by a Jewish family.[223]

The litigation option

The second option is litigation, a legal procedure preserved and designated for claimants who reject the State's offer for land settlement. In such cases, the State forwards Bedouin land claims to the court, where they have two options. They may either appear in court and present their arguments and evidence and adjudicate their land claim, or they may boycott the legal process and not appear in court in protest against the injustice of the legal process in courts. This latter option results in an "absence ruling," a decision that accepts the State's claim in the Bedouin's absence and declares their land as State land.[224] The results are harsh, devastating, and regarded as a "total loss" of the Bedouin land claim. In such cases, the State deprives Bedouin their land and also any compensation they could have received if they would have agreed to settle the land with the State.

The results of both options appear to be the same. Claimants who choose to appear in court lose their land claim and, as a consequence, lose their land rights. On the other hand, claimants who do not to appear in court receive an "absence decision" and lose their land rights too. Therefore, Bedouin are forced to "choose" to settle their land claims to avoid losing absolutely everything. In practice, "the State submits counterclaims and the Bedouin settle their land claims."[225]

In the case of Aluqbi,[226] where serious efforts of research and legal advocacy were applied, the case ended up with yet another decision similar to the *Alhawashelah* decision – the Court denied Bedouin land rights. The decision further proves that courts are so wed to the legal precedent of the *Mawat* doctrine that Bedouin have no chance in local courts.

At the same time, according to the Bedouin activist Mr. Amer Alhuzayel, there are many other Bedouin who continue to resist the State's efforts to dispossess them of their land. They do not attend court, as they prefer to lose "in absence" than to appear before a court they do not trust, believing that appearing in court could give legitimacy to the State's action.[227] In light of this reality, the State decided to appoint a governmental committee to investigate the issue and suggest a new policy in this matter.

The Goldberg Committee

On October 28, 2007, as part of the second phase of Bedouin land dispossession, the government established a committee to examine the issue of the Bedouin settlement in the Negev[228] and suggest guidelines for a policy on the Bedouin settlement in the new townships, including their land claims settlement. The government also asked the Committee to issue recommendations on policies to regulate the Bedouin settlement, including proposals for new legislation.[229]

In January 2008,[230] the Minister of Construction and Housing (MOCH) appointed a committee of eight members, headed by emeritus Supreme Court Justice Eliezer Goldberg. The Committee focused on transferring the Bedouin in the unrecognized villages to the townships and settling land claims. Six of the eight members were Jews who represented the government interests. Only two Bedouin representatives were appointed by the minister. The two Bedouin members were affiliated with the government cause rather than Bedouin rights community. None of the members came from Bedouin NGOs or Bedouin rights groups.

Reasons for establishment of the Committee

Many reasons brought about the establishment of the Committee. Some related to the Bedouin struggle and their living conditions, but some also related to the State's settlement project and policy of land control. The State needed land to move the military and security facilities from the center of the State near Tel-Aviv in order to sell and use the expensive land for other more profitable projects.

In addition, the strengthening Bedouin struggle and the growing appearance of Bedouin issues in national and international media shamed and embarrassed the State.[231] Furthermore, in some cases, the visible struggle succeeded in changing the State's settlement plans, or impeded or hampered their goals. From 1996 to 2007, the Bedouin struggle for their rights was notably strengthened. Several national and international organizations started to work for the Bedouin cause and advocate for their rights. They started to submit petitions to local courts, the Supreme Court, and other tribunals; to file reports to international bodies; and to approach the local and international media to raise awareness of Bedouin issues like living conditions, unrecognized villages, and land dispossession.[232] Human rights organizations started to demand and urge the State to provide basic services to Bedouin in the unrecognized villages, such as health services, education, infrastructure such as roads, and electricity for schools. When the State refused, they submitted petitions to courts and litigated for Bedouin rights, and succeeded in many cases to force the State to establish health clinics, build schools, pave roads, and provide many other rights and services.[233]

On the planning and building level, many NGOs along with community leaders challenged the State planning policy. In several petitions to the Supreme Court, they managed to get decisions that canceled the expansion of the master plans of some Jewish towns that aimed to annex lands that belonged to Bedouin villages.[234] In other petitions they succeeded in freezing parts of the National Master Plan (*tama* 4/14), which ignores the Bedouin villages, and they were able to get a decision that required the National Planning and Building Council to amend the Master Plan in a way that has to take into account the existence of Bedouin villages in their future planning.[235] These achievements, for the first time, forced the State to take the Bedouin villages into consideration when developing the Beer–Sheva Metropolitan Plan.[236]

The Bedouin response

The Goldberg Committee was perhaps the first attempt of the government to handle the Bedouin land issue in a comprehensive way. However, the State's motivation was not to ease Bedouin suffering or to find a just and fair solution for their land issue, rather they were motivated by the State's desire to control land and respond to the right-wing demands to "protect State land" and stop Bedouin "trespassing" and "stealing of the State's land."[237] Therefore, Bedouin did not pin many hopes on the Committee's work.

From the beginning, Bedouin claimed that the Committee was not built to create a fair and just solution for the Bedouin plight but rather to approve the State's policy of evicting Bedouin and expropriating their land.[238] Especially in light of the State's efforts to evict many Bedouin tribes from their villages in a collective manner, such as the Alhawashelah tribe from Khashem Zanneh-Almadbah village, the Annabari tribe from Tal-Arad village, the Abu Alkea'an tribe from Um Alheran village, the Annasarah tribe from Assrreh village, and many others. In addition, Bedouin remained distrustful of the State's plan to remove Bedouin from their land in exchange for a better place and better living conditions after the experience of the 1980 Tal-Almaleh eviction.

The Peace Tent conference and the call to boycott the Committee

The Bedouin response was strong. They called upon the Bedouin to refrain from participating in its deliberations.[239] In a communique from the Peace Tent in Rahat City, Bedouin leaders, who included leaders from the Regional Council of the Unrecognized Villages (RCUV), the High Follow-Up Committee for Arab Citizens of Israel, and many NGOs that advocate for Bedouin rights, called for a boycott of the Committee and asked Bedouin to refrain from appearing before the Committee or from submitting any written positions.

The Goldberg Report

During the yearlong process, the Committee heard from State officials, representatives from local and international organizations, and some Bedouin who did not boycott the Committee. Finally, in November 2008, the Committee issued its report and submitted it to the Prime Minister.[240] The Report drew up general guidelines and recommendations for the government on how to deal with the issue of Bedouin settlement.

Although the report acknowledged, for the first time and in a very limited way, some of the historical injustices that had been inflicted on the Bedouin as a result of the forced eviction to the *Siyag* area, the recommendations, as a whole, did not answer the minimum expectations of the Bedouin community. The report was disappointing with regard to three major issues: 1) land rights, 2) recognition of their villages, and 3) demolition of their homes.[241]

Regarding the issue of land, the Committee failed to recognize Bedouin land rights and did not suggest any just or fair solution. Instead, it suggested similar mechanisms and methods that had failed in the past. The Committee even added new methods and mechanisms that further discriminate against Bedouin and deprive them of some of their compensation rights, namely 20 percent land ownership as part of their compensation.

As for the second substantive issue, the issue of recognition of their villages, the Committee failed to specify unequivocal recommendations regarding the recognition of the Bedouin unrecognized villages on an equal and just basis. Instead, it suggested that only villages with a sufficient population in locations that do not conflict with other plans may be recognized. Ultimately, the Committee's report did not suggest any major change. It did not propose any substantial solution for any of the three issues in conflict: recognition of Bedouin land, recognition of their villages, and demolition of their houses.[242]

To make matters worse, many Bedouin consider the report to be the current source of their woes and troubles. It accelerates the process of Bedouin land confiscation, supports the policy of house demolition, and encourages uprooting their villages. Most importantly, it established the platform for the Praver plan, the plan the State adopted to execute the recommendations of the Goldberg Committee, meaning eviction of Bedouin from their villages and confiscation of their land.

The Praver Plan

In 2009, a short time after the Goldberg Committee issued its report, the government established another committee headed by Ehud Praver (or Prawer), former deputy chairman of the National Security Council. This committee became known as the Praver Committee. The government asked the Committee to prepare a plan for the implementation of the Goldberg Committee's recommendations as they appeared in the Goldberg Report, namely[243]: a) the settlement of Bedouin land claims; b) planning of new towns for Bedouin; and c) enforcement of the law with regard to the Bedouin illegal house construction (i.e., house demolition).[244]

In May 2011, the Committee submitted its recommendations in a report known as the Praver Committee Report.[245] The Report suggested new compensation offers for Bedouin claimants. It suggested the State would compensate Bedouin for claims on possessed land (land designated as agricultural land) and for claims regarding land not possessed by claimants. The Report suggested offering Bedouin claimants parcels of land up to 50 percent of the claimed land.[246] But this applied only to possessed land. During the last 60 years, the State moved the majority of Bedouin from their land and deprived their land possession rights; therefore, the number of land holders (possessors) is very small. For claims regarding land not possessed by claimants, which constitute the majority of Bedouin claimants, the Report suggested offering Bedouin monetary compensation only. The Report recommends depriving this group of any part of their land as compensation.

With respect to the issue of planning arrangements for Bedouin settlements and recognition of Bedouin villages, the Report stated that "solutions for the existing population will be in the existing seven government-planned townships, in the Abu Basma villages (or by expanding the jurisdiction of such villages) and in new settlements."[247] In this regard, the Report suggested beginning a process of planning that would cover the total Bedouin population in the unrecognized villages. The process of the settlement regulation would include planning expansions for the existing towns to absorb the additional Bedouin concentrations[248] and the establishment of new townships, as necessary.

With regard to recognition of new Bedouin villages, the Report set a high bar of requirements for recognition. It stated that "the establishment of new settlements is contingent upon the 'criteria of population density and continuity', as well as 'an examination of size and economic capacity.'"[249] For years, similar criteria prevented the recognition of Bedouin villages. The Report also included several other elements like a strict timetable and strict implementation rules to ensure completion. Additionally, the proposal includes a "plan for the economic development and growth of Bedouin population in the Negev."[250]

Many human rights organizations believe the results of the Praver Plan could be disastrous for Bedouin if implemented because it suggests the eviction of the majority of Bedouin from unrecognized villages. The Report reveals that only one third of the Bedouin of the unrecognized villages will remain in their current places, while two thirds will be uprooted from their villages and resettled in other Bedouin towns. The Report proposes to displace nearly 30,000–40,000 Bedouin from their villages and transfer them to other Bedouin towns such as Rahat, Kseifa, and Hura.[251] Many villages such as Assir, Alssera, and Um Alhran, with populations of 1,500, 1,000, 500, respectively, will be demolished.[252] In addition, the plan suggests a new segregation process in the Negev. It arranges for Bedouin settlements within a clearly demarcated and separate region in the Negev[253] and separates the Bedouin population from the rest of the State's population.

Amidror amendments

After publication of the Report, many right-wing political parties protested against the plan. Ironically, they claimed that the government was giving the Negev to the Bedouin.[254] As a result of their pressure, Prime Minister Benjamin Netanyahu ordered the National Security Advisor, Jacob Amidror, to review the Report. Accordingly, Amidror looked over the plans and made several amendments that affect the plan on the three major issues: the location of the resettlement, land ownership claims, and level of compensation. The amendments further limited the area designated for the Bedouin settlement. He stated that "no land [compensation] will be given to Bedouin and no Bedouin settlement will be planned west of Highway 40."[255]

In addition, Amidror's amendments decrease the amount of land Bedouin were supposed to get as part of the compensation for their land claims. The amendment specifies that the proposed arrangement would only apply to Bedouin who filed a lawsuit prior to October 1979, and whose claims were not rejected by the Land Settlement Officer or the court. Another amendment provides that the proposed arrangement will apply only to land the plaintiff held and cultivated, rather than claims for grazing lands, which constitute the majority of the claimed land. Further, the amendments held that the determination of land area (for purposes of providing compensation) shall be made according to evidence of cultivation of the land or living on the land close to the time of filing the original claim, provided that the land was not held at that time or in the future by the State.[256]

Bedouin representatives, who already objected to the Praver Plan, claimed that Amidror's amendments made the proposal totally unacceptable, mainly because the amendments dramatically reduced the land Bedouin could get as part of the land settlement. The original Praver Plan proposed an area of 183,000 dunams for Bedouin living in the unrecognized villages in exchange for settlement of their land claims, but after the amendments, the area was reduced by almost half.[257]

Finally, the plan outlines implementation of the Goldberg Commission Report to deal with the Bedouin settlement issue in the unrecognized villages, rather than recognizing their villages and ending the systemic violations their rights. The Plan was prepared without any consultation with Bedouin of the unrecognized villages, and it could lead to the uprooting of tens of thousands of Bedouin from their homes.[258]

Denial of Bedouin land rights under their tribal law as a method of land dispossession

Besides executive, legislative, and judicial means, the denial of Bedouin customary law and their indigenous culture is another method of land dispossession. Recognition of Bedouin tribal law, tribal courts, and tribal characteristics can be found in several levels of Israeli law, including State law, official documents, and case law of the Supreme Court of Israel. One of the best examples of such recognition can be found in Article 45 of Palestine Order in Council 1922–1947, which recognizes the tribal court system in the Negev through the Tribal Court Regulation of 1937. It authorizes the State to establish tribal courts in the Negev and authorizes these courts to rule according to Bedouin tribal law.[259] Both the Palestine Order in Council and the Tribal Court Regulation were adopted into the State law. Regardless of the fact that the Tribal Court Regulations were never applied in Israel and tribal courts were never established, they continue to be a valid law since they were never nullified.[260] Theoretically, a Bedouin tribal court can convene in Beer-Sheva City and rule according to the Bedouin tribal law, argues Elyakim Rubinstein, who served for long time as an Attorney General of the State of Israel.[261]

In addition, on several occasions both the State and the judicial system recognized elements of the unique characteristics of Bedouin in the Negev. For example, in the Supreme Court case *Avitan v Israel Land Authority*.[262] In that case, Avitan, a Jewish police officer, petitioned the Supreme Court against the ILA decision that refused to sell him a building lot in the Bedouin town of Segev–Shalom at a subsidized price similar to the price it offered to Bedouin who were willing to move and live in the Bedouin recognized townships. Avitan claimed that the State discriminated against him based on his ethnicity.[263] The State argued against Avitan's request and claimed that it sells such subsidized residential building lots for Bedouin only as part of the efforts to encourage Bedouin to transfer from a nomadic way of life to a settled way life in the designated townships. The State articulated that "Bedouin in Israel constitute an ethnic minority with character and uniqueness. Bedouin have an old culture and heritage derived from Arab tribes since the period before the advent of Islam. Since then until the half of this century, only a few changes have occurred in the habits and customs of their lives."[264]

Further, the State also recognized the "special character" of the Bedouin society in several official documents. In its response in the Avitan case, it stated: "Given its *special character and unique customs of the Bedouin society that were preserved...* to a great extent even during the process of transition to permanent settlement there was a need to study and consider carefully the needs of the Bedouin society."[265] Furthermore, in the same cases, the State recognized the tribal nature of the Bedouin of the Negev. It indicated that "Bedouin towns were designed, in advance, to Bedouin tribes and certain factions, in light of Bedouin sensitivity to tribal, factions and family affiliations."[266]

The unique tribal character of the Bedouin of the Negev was also recognized in the Supreme Court decision in Abu Ghanem, in which Bedouin petitioned to the Supreme Court against the Ministry of Education, claiming that its policy discriminated against the Bedouin in budget allocation for educational drop-out officers.[267] In that case, the Court indicated again the uniqueness of the Bedouin of the Negev. The Court referred to the Bedouin as a unique population with a different character that deserved an affirmative action in that issue.[268]

However, despite the "recognition"[269] of Bedouin tribal courts, tribal law, and tribal characteristics, the executive, legislative, and judicial branches refuse to recognize Bedouin tribal law and their land rights within the framework of Bedouin law. Both the executive and the legislative branches ignored Ottoman and British law, which recognized Bedouin land rights based on their custom and tribal law. They also ignored the fact that both Ottomans and British Mandate specifically separated Bedouin and Bedouin land rights from other communities in Palestine.[270] The State ignored the Ottoman and British attitude that preserved the Bedouin's historical land rights according to their customs.[271]

The courts also ignored Bedouin customs regarding land.[272] They dismissed the fact that the Bedouin had different interpretations of the elements that would prove land rights. Ideas such as "revival," "settlement," and "use of the land" are defined differently by the Bedouin.[273] The courts did not consider the land's features when interpreting revival of land, mainly the fact that their lands are desert that by its nature does not "change totally by seasonal cultivation" as the courts demanded.

Finally, the courts denied Bedouin pastoralism as a legitimate land use for the sake of *Mawat* land revival.[274] Moreover, the courts refused to recognize Bedouin traditional settlements as settlements for the purpose of land recognition and land revival. The State refused to "recognize tents as settlements and denied that pastoralism as practiced by the Bedouin constituted 'working' the land."[275]

Conclusion

The story of the Bedouin is similar to colonized indigenous peoples'struggles for recognition of their land rights. Colonial states often employ a number of policies affecting indigenous peoples, including physical removal from their land, confinement (i.e., reservations), denial of land rights, and suppression of culture and traditional economy. Like so many indigenous groups, the Bedouin have been stripped of their land rights with little recourse. They have endured occupation and resettlement and the process has destroyed their traditional economy and threatens the survival of their culture. The State of Israel has expelled Bedouin from their land, concentrated them in the *Siyag* area, and refused to recognize their villages. Moreover, the State has disenfranchised the Bedouin and refused to include them in population statistics. As a result, the Bedouin have been left a poor people unable to implement their traditional land-based economy, leaving them dependent on the settler–state economy.

The State of Israel has employed a number of methods to dispossess the indigenous population (i.e., the Bedouin) of their land. These efforts include administrative, judicial, and legislative methods, which have effectively foreclosed any option for Bedouin to legally repossess and hold title to their traditional land. Many colonizing states rely on the notion of *terra nullius* and the Doctrine of Discovery to dispossess indigenous peoples of their land. Likewise, Israel has adopted the *Mawat* land doctrine to declare land traditionally used by Bedouin as state-owned land.

Most importantly, these methods actively disregard traditional Bedouin customs of property ownership and transfer. By refusing to recognize Bedouin customary law, including aspects of Bedouin oral culture and pastoral economy, the Israeli judicial system fails to properly recognize Bedouin traditional land rights. Recognition of Bedouin as an indigenous group with viable indigenous law can pave the way to recognition of Bedouin land rights.

The next chapter introduces the protection of indigenous land under international law and examines the applicability of such law to the Bedouin case in the Negev.

Notes

1 Haya Noach, hakfarim shiyeshnam ve-Aenam [The Existent and the Non-Existent Villages] 31 (2009); Hussein Abu Hussein & Fiona McKay, Access Denied: Palestinian Land Rights in Israel 105 (2003).

2 Palestine Order in Council, 1922, 13 Geo. 5, art. 46 (Eng.), *available at* http://unispal.un.org/UNISPAL.NSF/0/C7AAE196F41AA055052565F50054E656.

3 Meir Delbri, Nehul Nadlan [Land Law in Real Estate Management] 57–59 (1997).

4 Oren Yiftachel, Land, Planning and Inequality: The Division of Space between Arabs and Jews in Israel (2000), [קרקעות, תכנון ואי-שוויון: חלוקת המרחב בין יהודים וערבים בישראל] http://simania.co.il/bookdetails.php?item_id=467581 (last visited Jan 1, 2016).

5 Ian Lustick, Arabs in the Jewish State: Israel's Control of a National Minority (1980).

6 *General Information: Israel Land Administration*, Israel Land Admin., http://www.mmi.gov.il/Envelope/indexeng.asp?page=/static/eng/f_general.html (last updated Mar. 11, 2007).

7 Yehushoa Porat & Yakov Shavit, The History of Eretz Yesrael: The British Mandate and the Jewish National Home 102 (1998)

8 Lustick, *supra* note 234 at 3; Rassem Khamaisi, *Territorial Dispossession and Population Control of the Palestinians, in* Surveillance and Control in Israel/Palestine: Population, Territory and Power (Elia Zureik ed., 2011).

9 Center on Housing Rights and Evictions, Ruling Palestine: A History of the Legally Sanctioned Jewish-Israeli Seizure of Land and Housing in Palestine 37 (2005).

10 Israel Lands – Privatization or National Ownership?, https://www.jewishvirtuallibrary.org/israel-lands-privatization-or-national-ownership (last visited Mar. 25, 2020).

11 *Id.*; ABU HUSSEIN AND MCKAY, *supra* note 188 at 144.
12 5710-1950, 4 LSI 151 (1948–1987) (Isr.).
13 Khamaisi, *supra* note 237 at 310.
14 5720-1960 SH No. 312 p. 56 (Isr.).
15 *Id.*
16 See generally LUSTICK, *supra* note 234 at (discussing how land regimes were used to control Arabs in Israel).
17 The term Arab for the purposes of this paper includes the Bedouin, unless otherwise stated.
18 Khamaisi, *supra* note 237 at 335.
19 Sandy Kedar & Oren Yiftachel, *Land Regime and Social Relations in Israel*, in 1 SWISS HUMAN RIGHT BOOK: REALIZING PROPERTY RIGHTS (Hernando de Soto & Francis Cheneval eds., 2006).
20 Nir Hasson, *Most Arabs Can't Buy Most Homes in West Jerusalem*, HAARETZ (Jul. 21, 2009), http://www.haaretz.com/print-edition/news/most-arabs-can-t-buy-most-homes-in-west-jerusalem-1.280392.
21 *Id.*
22 HCJ 6698/95 Kaadan v. Minhal Mekarke'ey Yisrael, Katzir Cooperative and Others 54(1) PD 258 [2000] (Isr.) (rejecting an Arab family's application to lease a land for housing in a Jewish town. They appealed to the Supreme Court claiming discrimination based on racial identity).
23 *Id.*; *see generally* Sandy Kedar, *A First Step in a Difficult and Sensitive Road* 16 BULL. OF ISRAEL STUD. 3, 3–11 (2000).
24 Moshavim are an example of acceptance committees in the Jewish towns and cooperative agricultural communities. S*ee* CA 7831/08 Navatim: Labor Moshav for Agriculture Settlement, Ltd. v. Zakai Wazman __(_) PD ___ [___] (Isr.).
25 Jonathan Lis & Jack Khoury, *Knesset Panel Approves Controversial Bill Allowing Towns to Reject Residents*, HAARETZ (Oct. 27, 2010), http://www.haaretz.com/news/national/knesset-panel-approves-controversial-bill-allowing-towns-to-reject-residents-1.321433.
26 *See generally* ADALAH, THE LEGAL CENTER FOR ARAB MINORITY RIGHTS IN ISRAEL, NOMADS AGAINST THEIR WILL-THE ATTEMPTED EXPULSION OF THE ARAB BEDOUIN IN THE NAQAB: THE EXAMPLE OF ATIR–UMM AL-HIERAN 18 (2011), *available at* http://www.adalah.org/eng/publications/Nomads%20Against%20their%20Will%20English%20pdf%20final.pdf.
27 KRETZMER, *supra* note 37 at 49.
28 *Id.*
29 DAVID KRETZMER, THE LEGAL STATUS OF THE ARABS IN ISRAEL (1990); ABRAHAM GRANOTT, THE LAND ISSUE IN PALESTINE 12 (1936).
30 KRETZMER, *supra* note 37 at 49.
31 Benny Morris, *Refabricating 1948 Fabricating Israeli History: The "New Historians" Efraim Karsh*, 27 J. OF PALESTINE STUD. 81, 84 (1998).
32 Sabri Jiryis, *Domination by the Law*, 11 JOURNAL OF PALESTINE STUDIES 67–92, 75 (1981).
33 The Absentees' Property Law was meant to serve as the legal basis to transfer the property of Palestinian refugees into the possession of the State of Israel. The law says that the land and property of Palestinian residents and nationals of Arab countries who were in one of the Arab countries or in any part of the Land of Israel that is outside of the area of Israel from November 29, 1947 until a declaration that the State of emergency declared in 1948 ended, which has not yet happened, would revert to the possession of the Custodian of Absentee Property, i.e. the possession of the State. 5710- 1950, SH No. 37, 86 (Isr.).
34 *See id.* at art. 4, 30.
35 Jiryis, *supra* note 261 at 84.

36 M. Cherif Bassiouni & Shlomo Ben Ami, A Guide to Documents on the Arab-Palestinian/Israeli Conflict: 1897–2008 198 (2009).
37 David A. Wesley & E. Marx, State Practices and Zionist Images: Shaping Economic Development in Arab Towns in Israel 113–114 (2008); Yifat Holzman-Gazit, Land Expropriation in Israel: Law, Culture and Society 111–112 (2007).
38 The Prescription Law, 5718-1958, SH No. 251, pp. 112, 251.
39 *Miri* land is the private land according to the Ottoman Land Code of 1858.
40 According to the Ottoman Land Code, a person who cultivated miri land for a period of ten years was entitled to ownership. See Kretzmer, *supra* note 37 at 52.
41 5718-1958, SH No. 251, p. 112, § 29(b).
42 Kretzmer, *supra* note 37 at 53.
43 Mohsen Sabri is a scholar who wrote about the Prescription Law and land transfers from Arabs to the State of Israel. *See* Mohsen Sabri, *maamadam Hamishpati shel Arvee Yisrael [The Legal Status of Israel's Arabs]*, 2 Iyunei Mishpat 568 (1972).
44 A dunam equals 1,000 square meters. See Granott, *supra* note 258 at xii (one acre equals 4,046.8 square meters which equals about 4 dunams, the dunam is 1,000 square meters [10,764 sq ft], or 1 decare).
45 Mohsen Sabri, *maamadam Hamishpati shel Arvee Yisrael [The Legal Status of Israel's Arabs]*, 2 Iyunei Mishpat 568, 569 (1972).
46 Issachar Rosen-Zvi, Taking Space Seriously: Law, Space, and Society in Contemporary Israel 43 (2004).
47 Yiftachel, *supra* note 233.
48 Kretzmer, *supra* note 258 at 52–53; Bisharat, *supra* note 167 at 521.
49 Kretzmer, *supra* note 258 at 52.
50 Jamil Dakwar, *The Supreme Court and the Confiscation of Palestinian Lands: On the Politics of Legal Formalism*, 2 Adalah's Rev. 14 (2000), at 14–15.
51 The legal activism regarding this subject began with case law originating in the 1950s and 1960s and concluded with the 1996 decision in *Shibli* where the court restricted further interpretation of land cases, foreclosing Arab land recognition.
52 Alexandre (Sandy) Kedar, *Minority Time, Majority Time: Land, Nation, and the Law of Adverse Possession in Israel*, 21 Tel Aviv U. L. Rev. 665–746, 665 (1998).
53 Ronen Shamir, *Suspended in Space: Bedouins under the Law of Israel*, 30 L. & Soc'y Rev. 231 (1996).
54 HCJ 114/78 Burkan v. Minister of Finance 32(2) PD 800 [1978] (Isr.) (Palestinian resident of Jerusalem appealing the ban on Arab purchases of housing in the Jewish Quarter); HCJ 390/79 Duikat v. Government of Israel Ld(1) PD 1 [1979] (Isr.) (known as the "Elon Moreh case" in which Palestinians appealed against establishing a settlement on their private lands); HCJ 2056/04 Beit Sourik Village Council v. Government of Israel ___ PD __ [2004] (Isr.) (addressing a petition by Palestinians against the damage that was caused by the Separation Wall to Palestinian residents).
55 Oren Yiftachel, *A Geographer in Legal Space: Teaching Legal Geography as a Journey in an Academic Frontier*, 2 Din U'Dvarim 211, 217 (2005).
56 Chanina Porat, *Policy of Land Purchase and Settlement in the Negev before the War of Independence*, 62 Cathedra 123 (1991) (describing the Zionist movement and establishment of 35 Jewish settlements in the Negev, illustrating the Jewish existence in the Negev).
57 One duman equals 0.247 acres. See Granott, *supra* note 258.
58 Noa Kram, *The Negev Bedouins: Struggles for Land Rights and Cultural Survival in Israel*. 10 (2011).
59 Kedar, *supra* note 281 at 727.

60 Baruch S. Kimmerling & Joel Samuel Migdal, The Palestinian People: A History 172 (2003).
61 Penny Maddrell, Bedouin of the Negev 6 (1989).
62 *Motions to Cancel Ex Parte Demolition Orders Against 33 Homes in the Unrecognized Arab Bedouin Village of Umm el-Hieran in the Naqab*, Adalah, http://adalah.org/eng/Articles/553/Motions-to-Cancel-Ex-Parte-Demolition-Orders-33-in (last visited Feb. 6, 2013).
63 United Nations General Assembly Resolution 194, G.A. Res. 194 (III), U.N. Doc. A/RES/194 (III) (Dec. 10, 1948), recognized the right for the first time. On the other hand, since it is only a General Assembly resolution, it is not binding under international law, as opposed to Security Council resolutions.
64 Article 13 of the Universal Declaration of Human Rights (UDHR) states that "[e]veryone has the right to freedom of movement and residence within the borders of each State. Everyone has the right to leave any country, including his own, and to return to his country." Universal Declaration of Human Rights, G.A. Res. 217 (III) A, U.N. Doc A/RES/ 217(III), art. 13 (Dec. 10, 1948); *see also* International Covenant on Civil and Political Rights, Dec. 16, 1966, 999 U.N.T.S. 171.
65 Shlomo Swirski & Yael Hasson, Invisible Citizens: Israel Government Policy toward the Negev Bedouin 68–83 (2006).
66 *Id.* at 15.
67 Chanina Porat, *Israel's Policy on the Bedouin Issue and Left-Wing Alternatives 1953–1960*, 10 Iyyunim BiTekumat Israel 420, 454 (2000).
68 *Id.* at 454.
69 Swirski and Hasson, *supra* note 167 at 15.
70 *Id.* at 16.
71 Moshe Dayan, *On Land Policy and the Bedouin Problem*, Haaretz, Jul. 31, 1963, *cited in* Issachar Rosen-Zvi, Taking Space Seriously: Law, Space, and Society in Contemporary Israel 60 (2004).
72 Yair Bauml, Yahaso shel hamimsad hayesraili laaravim bayesrael: Mdeniot, Ekronot peolah, haasor hashini 1958–1968 [The Attitude of the Israeli Establishment to the Arabs in Israel: Policy, Principles and Action. The Second Decade, 1958–1968] 310–315 (Ph.D. dissertation, University of Haifa, 2002); Sabri Jiryis, *Domination by the Law*, 11 J. of Palestine Stud. 67, 84 (1981).
73 Oren Yiftachel & H. Yacobi, *Control, Resistance and Informality: Urban Ethnocracy in Beer Sheva, Israel*, in Urban Informality 228 (A. Roy & N. Alsayyad eds., 2003).
74 Central Bureau of Statistics Statistical Abstract of Israel, 104, 106 (2012), *available at* http://www.cbs.gov.il/shnaton63/st02_07x.pdf.
75 Ismael Abu Saad, *Socio-Political Upheaval and Current Conditions of the Neqab Bedouin Arabs*, in Indigenous (In)Justice: Human Rights Law and Bedouin Arabs in the Naqab/Negev 28 (Yiftachel et al. eds., 2013).
76 Human Rights Watch, *supra* note 125 at 22.
77 The Negev Land Acquisition (Peace Treaty with Egypt) Law, 5740-1980 34 LSI 190 (170–182) (Isr.).
78 Rosen-Zvi, *supra* note 275 at 64.
79 *Id.*
80 Land title settlement is a legal process of investigating traditional land rights that are not registered. The process aims to register any rights in the Land Registry Office and issue official title for each land owner.
81 See generally Human Rights Watch, *supra* note 125.
82 Abu Basmah Regional Council, *Moladah [Information about the Village]*, Abubasma.org, *available* at http://abubasma.org.il/index.php?m=text&t=10750&lib=759&la= (last visited Feb. 5, 2013) (in 2008 Moladah Village was recognized).

83 Many reasons could explain the decision, including the court's desire to criticize State policy. In addition, the High Court of Justice issued several decisions ordering the State to build schools, clinics, and streets for Bedouin in unrecognized villages. On the other hand, the seven recognized villages remained poor and many people could not secure building lots to live in the recognized parts if the villages. There were recognized parts of the village and others that remained unrecognized.
84 The number is not fixed. It is expected to increase each time as the State recognizes additional Bedouin villages.
85 *See* Abu Ras, *supra* note 57.
86 For example, the town of Tarabin was designated for the Tarabin tribe and even named after it.
87 *See generally* Abu Ras, *supra* note 57.
88 *See* HCJ 528/88 Eliezer Avitan v. Israel Land Administration Meg (4) PD 297 [1988] (Isr.) (indicating that the main purpose for settling the Bedouin is to protect the State land).
89 Swirski & Hasson, *supra* note 218, at 18 ("maximum number of Arabs on the minimum amount of land"); Sawsan Zaher, *The Right of Arab Bedouin Women to Adequate Housing and Accommodation*, 23 Adalah's Newsl., Mar. 2006, at 1; Amer El Huzeil et al., A plan for the treatment of the Bedouin problem, Center for Legal and Economic Research in the Middle East 9 (1999), *available at* http://www.macro.org.il/lib/2179925.pdf.
90 Falah, *supra* note 34, at 72.
91 Dayan, *supra* note 224.
92 Planning and Building Law, 5725-1965 SH No. 467 p. 307 (Isr.).
93 Human Rights Watch, *supra* note 22, at 71.
94 Planning and Building Law, 5725-1965 SH No. 467 p. 307, art. 238 (Isr.).
95 5740-1980 34 LSI 190 (170-182) (Isr.).
96 Many laws expropriate Arab land. See Holzman-Gazit, *supra* note 190; Kretzmer, *supra* note 180, at Chapter 3; Bisharat, *supra* note 201; Noach, *supra* note 152, at 33–40.
97 *See* Dayan, *supra* note 224.
98 *See Mabo v. Queensland (No. 2)* (1992) 175 CLR 1 (Austl.); *Wik Peoples v Queensland* (1996) 187 CLR 1 (Austl.) (addressing the difficulties of recognizing Aboriginal rights due to the new realities surrounding their land).
99 In Aluqbi finding no connection to land after the State evicted Bedouin from their land in the 1950s and refusing to interfere in the State's project to build a Jewish town on Bedouin land). AdminC (BS) 257/04 Association for Support and Protection of Bedouin Rights in Israel v. The National Planning and Construction, PM 2004(2) 7038 (2004) (Isr.).
100 Amer El Huzeil et al., *supra* note 243, at 23.
101 5740-1980 34 LSI 190 (170-182) (Isr.).
102 They created a "complex web of legal mechanisms that imposed insurmountable procedural and evidentiary obstacles that preventing the indigenous Bedouin from effectively protecting their land." Rozen-Zvi, *supra* note 199, at 46.
103 Ahmad Amara, *The Battle for the Land and Housing Rights of the Negev Bedouin*, Housing & ESC Rts. L. Q., Mar. 2008, at 1, *available at* http://www.academia.edu/235048/The_Battle_for_the_Land_and_Housing_Rights_of_the_Negev_Bedouin.
104 According to Porat, Bedouin submitted land claims as early as the 1950s. They based their land claims on documents proving that they had paid taxes. However, the State claimed that no land titles settlement occurred in the Negev; therefore, Bedouin did not possess any proof of land ownership. In addition, the State claimed that tax documents were lost from the State archives. Porat, *supra* note 209, at 457.

105 It started by describing the process, defining the settlement areas, and drafting the orders and notices for the towns.
106 Land Rights Settlement Ordinance [Revised], 5729-1969, 13 OSI 293, art. 17 (293) (Isr.), *available at* http://www.mapi.gov.il/UsefulInfo/MapiRegulations andGuidelines/nevo_pkudat_hahesder.pdf.
107 *Id.* at art. 43("The court only is authorized to hear and adjudicate any dispute about land in a settlement area, and if there were conflicting claims between two or more plaintiffs, the settlement officer shall transfer the dispute to court.").
108 *Id.*
109 *Id.* at art. 43, 44.
110 *Id.*
111 *Id.*
112 Swirski and Hasson, *supra* note 167 at 19.
113 Ronen Shamir, *Suspended in Space: Bedouin under the Law of Israel*, 30 L. & Soc'y Rev. 231, 250 (1996).
114 Yiftachel, *supra* note 91 at 50.
115 Eliezer Goldberg, et al., Din Ve-Heshbon Ha-Vaada Le-Hatzaat Mediniut Le-Hasdarat Hityashvut Ha-Beduim Ba-Negev [Report of the Goldberg Committee for the Arrangement of Bedouin Settlement in the Negev] (2008).
116 Chris McGeal, *Bedouin Feel the Squeeze as Israel Resettles the Negev Desert*, The Guardian, Feb. 26, 2003, http://www.guardian.co.uk/world/2003/feb/27/ israel.
117 C.A. 218/74 Salim Alhawashelah v. State of Israel 38(3) PD 141 [1974] (Isr.).
118 *Id.*
119 *Id.* at 147.
120 Ron Kelley, *Israel's Bedouin: The End of Poetry*, Sept.–Oct. 1998 Americans For Middle East Understanding (AMEU), 1 ("To date, no Bedouin has ever won a land claim. This includes some 3,000 lawsuits by the Bedouin over the past two decades.").
121 HCJ 84/83 El-Wakili v. State of Israel 37(4) PD 173 [1983] (Isr.).
122 *Palestinian Bedouin IDPs, Ongoing Displacement and Land Rights: Israel Poisons Bedouin Land in Abda Unrecognized Villages*, Al Majdal, Mar. 2003, at 37 (reporting that no Bedouin has ever won a land claim to any of the more than 3,000 lawsuits filed over 50 years, and this places the burden of proof regarding Bedouin land claims on Bedouin).
123 Swirski and Hasson, *supra* note 167 at 13.
124 *See id.* at 5 (discussing Bedouin suspicions and attitudes toward state authorities).
125 This is the author's observation during his work as lawyer for the Bedouin community in the Negev from 1997–2009.
126 Kretzmer, *supra* note 37 at 3; Rosen-Zvi, *supra* note 275 at 43.
127 Land Rights Settlement Ordinance [Revised], 5729- 1969, 13 OSI 293, art. 17 (293) (Isr.), *available at* http://www.mapi.gov.il/UsefulInfo/MapiRegulationsand Guidelines/nevo_pkudat_hahesder.pdf.
128 Tawfiq S. Rangwala, *Inadequate Housing, Israel, and the Bedouin of the Negev*, 42 Osgoode Hall L.J. 415, 440–441 (2004).
129 Plia Albeck, Doah mesakem shel tzevet hamomhim leanyan hesder mekarkien ezor hasyag hangev htsfoni [Report of the Team of Experts on the Issue of Land Settlement in the Siyag Area and the Northern Negev], Israel Ministry of Justice (Oct. 20, 1975).
130 Land Rights Settlement Ordinance [Revised], 5729-1969, 13 OSI 293, art. 17.
131 *Id.*

132 This rule is based on two assumptions: first, physical possession of an object by one of the parties, and second such possession provides evidence that the object belongs to its possessor, i.e., if someone holds an object we assume he obtained legally and according to that assumption therefore a person owns what he possess.

133 Land Rights Settlement Ordinance [Revised], 5729-1969, 13 OSI 293, art. 43.

134 *Id.* at art. 45.

135 The Bedouin must defend their land in court. If they do not appear in court they automatically lose their claims and their land.

136 Many Bedouins were surprised to find that when they came to defend their land they were summoned to court as plaintiffs rather than defendants. Some Bedouins did not know about the claims their parents had submitted filed in the land registry long time before legal action had been taken by the State.

137 Land Rights Settlement Ordinance [Revised], 5729- 1969, 13 OSI 293, art. 17(a).

138 *See generally* Joseph William Singer, *Nine-Tenths of the Law: Title, Possession & Sacred Obligations*, 38 CONN. L. REV. 605 (2006).

139 *See generally* Kent McNeil, *The Onus of Proof of Aboriginal Title*, 37 OSGOODE HALL L.J. 775 (1999).

140 Cf. GILBERT, *supra* note 46 at 278.

141 ROSEN-ZVI, *supra* note 275 at 64–65.

142 The Negev Land Acquisition (Peace Treaty with Egypt) Law, 5740-1980 34 LSI 190 (170–182) (Isr.).

143 ELEZER GOLDBERG, HAVADA LEHATSAAT MDINIOT LEHASDARAT HITYASHVUT HABEDOUIM BANEGEV [PROTOCOL OF GOLDBERG COMMITTEE], MINISTRY OF CONSTRUCTION & HOUSING 75 (May 6, 2008).

144 Ezra Hezikia, *Evacuees Act Passed Third Reading*, ARUTZ SHEVA, Aug. 4, 2011, http://www.inn.co.il/News/News.aspx/ 223902.

145 ROSEN-ZVI, *supra* note 275 at 43.

146 Gadi Algazi, *Meshelet yesrael neged ezrahi mdenat yesrael:perek bemelhemt hhatashah neged habedouim [The Israeli government against the citizens of Israel: An Episode of the Attrition War against Bedouin*], HAOKETZ, Jul. 27, 2010, http://www.haokets.org

The new development plans for the Negev are programs for dispossession. Bedouin Arabs passed (were subject to) a huge wave of dispossession during the early fifties, later they again paid the price of peace treaties with Egypt and were pushed away from the little that remained to them....

147 Adalah, *Discriminatory and Anti-Democratic Laws*, ADALAH'S NEWSL., (Feb. 2008), at 1, *available at* http://www.adalah.org/newsletter/heb/feb08/2.php.

148 Forman and Kedar, *supra* note 200 at 494–495.

149 HUMAN RIGHTS WATCH, *supra* note 125 at 18; THE NEGEV COEXISTENCE FORUM FOR CIVIL EQUALITY, *The Arab-Bedouins of the Naqab- Negev Desert in Israel (Shadow Report 2006)* 11–12.

150 See CA 218/74 Salim El-Huashlla v. State of Israel 38(3) PD 141, 151 [1974] (Isr.)

151 Land Rights Settlement Ordinance [Revised], 5729- 1969, 13 OSI 293, art. 43 (293) (Isr.), *available at* http://www.mapi.gov.il/UsefulInfo/MapiRegulationsand Guidelines/nevo_pkudat_hahesder.pdf.

152 *Id.*

153 *Cf.* The Canadian recognition of land rights where the court system modified the rules of evidence and accepted evidence under specific rules according to Aboriginal needs and traditions.

154 *See supra* Chapter 2 (discussing Bedouin tribal law under the Ottomans and the British Mandate).

155 Kent McNeil & Lori Roness, *Legalizing Oral History: Proving Aboriginal Claims in Canadian Courts*, Journal of the West. 39(3), 66–74 (2000), https://digitalcommons.osgoode.yorku.ca/scholarly_works/835 (discussing oral history generally); Abu Rabia, *supra* note 144 at 100 (discussing oral history among Bedouin of the Negev).
156 Abraham Halima, *Negev lands from the Legal Perspective*, Institute for Land Policy and Land Use- dept. of land policy, 33 (1985).
157 *See* CA 218/74 Salim El-Huashlla v. State of Israel 38(3) PD 141, 151 [1974] (Isr.) (defining the concept "revival of *Mawat* land" according to article 1051 of the Ottoman Code where revival is improvement, i.e. preparing the land for agriculture).
158 Kretzmer, *supra* note 258 at 52.
159 See Bisharat, *supra* note 167 (defining Miri, Mulk, Matruka, Waqf, and Mawat).
160 Halima, *supra* note 385.
161 *Id.*
162 Tawfiq S. Rangwala, *Inadequate Housing, Israel, and the Bedouin of the Negev*, 42 Osgoode Hall L.J. 415, 450 (2004).
163 Jérémie Gilbert, *Nomadic Territories: A Human Rights Approach to Nomadic Peoples' Land Rights*, 7 Hum. Rts. L. Rev. 681, 685 (2007).
164 *Id.*
165 *Id.*
166 *Id.*
167 *See generally* Ronen Shamir, *Suspended in Space: Bedouins under the Law of Israel*, 30 L. & Soc'y Rev. 231 (1996).
168 Jérémie Gilbert, *Nomadic Territories: A Human Rights Approach to Nomadic Peoples' Land Rights*, 7 Human Rights Law Review 681–716, 699 (2007).
169 *Id.*
170 Halima, *supra* note 385 at 15.
171 C.A. 218/74 Salim Alhawashelah v. State of Israel 38(3) PD 141, 143 [1974] (Isr.); Swirski & Hasson, *supra* note 218, at 26.
172 Rosen-Zvi, *supra* note 275 at 46–47 (discussing the Alhawashelah decision in the district court).
173 C.A. 218/74 Salim Alhawashelah v. State of Israel 38(3) PD 141, 143 [1974] (Isr.).
174 Swirski and Hasson, *supra* note 167 at 20–21 (quoting the Albeck Report of 1975).
175 *Id.*
176 *Id.* at 21.
177 *See id.* at 9–10.
178 *Id.* at 24.
179 Kelley, *supra* note 349.
180 Rosen-Zvi, *supra* note 275 at 46.
181 Rangwala, *supra* note 391 at 440–441; The Land Rights Settlement Ordinance (1969)135 classified all Mawat lands as State property, unless formal legal title could be produced.
182 5729 -1969, SH No. 575 pp. 259–283 (Isr.).
183 C.A. 218/74 Salim Alhawashelah v. State of Israel 38(3) PD 141 [1974] (Isr.).
184 For 15 years in settled land, and 25 in unsettled land. *See* Kretzmer, *supra* note 180, at 53 (describing the legal status of the Arabs in Israel).
185 Kedar, *supra* note 205, at 686.
186 Halima, *supra* note 309, at 15.
187 CA 218/74 Salim Alhawashelah v. State of Israel 38(3) PD 141 [1974] (Isr.).
188 Kretzmer, *supra* note 180, at 49–50, 60.
189 Havatzelet Yahel, *Land Disputes between the Negev Bedouin and Israel*, 11 Israel Stud. 1–22, 13 (2006).

190 Kelley, *supra* note 349.
191 CC (BS) 3347/04 Jadoa' Alasad v. State of Israel, PM (2004) (Isr.). [Civil Case (BS) 3347/04 Jadoa' Alasad v. State of Israel, (decision delivered Oct. 19, 2009). Tak-Mehozi 2009(4), 1232]
192 *See e.g., id.*; CC 3316/04 Esa Farhood Alasibi v. State of Israel PM (unpublished) (2009) (Isr.).
193 Ignoring traditional law land characteristics and unique land use considerations was inconsistent with State policy and court attitudes which on some occasions acknowledged these unique characteristics of Bedouin culture, including their tribal law). *See e.g.*, Tribal Court Regulation of 5715, 1937, KT 483, 123 (Isr.).
194 C.A. (BS) 7161/06 Suleiman Al-Uqbi et. al. v. State of Israel, (2012).
195 *Id.* at 440–441.; Bisharat, *supra* note 167 at 482.
196 Rangwala, *supra* note 391 at 450–451.
197 Abu Ras, *supra* note 133 at 5–6.
198 *See* CC (BS) 1470/05 State of Israel v. Mohamad Abu Zayed PM (2008) (63) Dinim Shalom 1280 (addressing the issues of preventing State encroachment on Bedouin land and discussing Bedouin land ownership and designating Bedouin land as State land).
199 *Id.*
200 Yahel, *supra* note 418 at 12 ("from 1978 until 2003 agreed settlements of claims were achieved with regard to over 140,000 dumans, most of them in the area of airfields").
201 Adalah, *Nomads against Their Will*, https://www.adalah.org/uploads/oldfiles/eng/publications/Nomads%20Against%20their%20Will%20English%20pdf%20final.pdf (last visited Sept. 24, 2016).
202 Swirski and Hasson, *supra* note 167 at 12.
203 Israeli Government Resolution No. 216 (ARB/I) (Apr. 14, 2003).
204 Noam Sharvit, *When the State Sues Bedouin Compromise*, Globes, http://www.globes.co.il/news/article.aspx?fbdid=1000174638 (last visited Feb. 8, 2013); Swirski and Hasson, *supra* note 89 at 29.
205 Lustick, *supra* note 234 (describing the State policy of control of the Arab minority through land control).
206 *See* Interview by Mohanad Mostafa with Oren Yiftachel, Prof. at Ben Gorion University, at Ben Gorion Univeristy (2011), *available at* http://www.dirasat-aclp.org/arabic/files/Oren_Yiftahel_Kitab_Dirasat_2011.pdf (discussing the Bedouin boycott of the Goldberg Committee).
207 *Qiadat alawasat alarabi tarfud attaanul ma' lajnat Goldberg letasweah alaradi [Arab sector leadership refuses to deal with the Goldberg Committee to resolve the issue of land]*, Arabs48 (Jan. 20, 2008), *available at* http://www.pls48.net/?mod=print&ID=25973 (reporting on the final statement of the Peace Tent Conference for land and housing protection).
208 Adalah, *supra* note 430 at 10.
209 See generally Yahel, *supra* note 418.
210 The Negev Coexistence Forum for Civil Equality, *supra* note 378 at 4, 11, 12.
211 Decisions of the Council at Its Meeting on Mar. 4, 2004, Israel Lands Administration, http://www.mmi.gov.il/hodaotmmiint/show_h.asp?key=525&CodeMaarecet=1 (last visited Feb. 5, 2013) (outlining compensation land prices and construction fields regarding the Negev Bedouin).
212 Yahel, *supra* note 418 at 13.
213 *Id.* at 11–12.
214 Swirski and Hasson, *supra* note 167 at 44–45; Human Rights Watch, *supra* note 125 at 66; The Negev Coexistence Forum for Civil Equality, *supra* note 378 at 25 (comparing Bedouin compensation with compensation paid to Jewish settlers in Sinai and Gaza).

215 S.C. 3341/01 Suliman Hasan Alamor et.al v. Implementation Admin., (2001) HCJ. 4441/01 (Isr.) *dismissed* Feb. 6, 2002. (unpublished) (copy on file with author).
216 For example the Tal Almaleh people and Nassasrah and Alamour tribes.
217 S.C. 3341/01 Suliman Hasan Alamor et.al v. Implementation Admin., (2001) (Isr.).
218 *See* Israel Land Administration Council Decision 858 of May 3, 1999, *available at* http://www.mmi.gov.il/MoatzaWeb/InterHachById.aspx?hachid=858; Israel Land Administration Council Decision 1028 of May 2, 2005, *available at* http://www.mmi.gov.il/MoatzaWeb/interHAchResults.aspx?all=true.
219 As of Feb. 2013, one New Israeli Shekel (NIS) equals approximately US $0.246.
220 Human Rights Watch, *supra* note 125 at 13.
221 For example, Tarabin land near Omer.
222 This comparison should be taken in light of its context. The main difference between the situations arises from the international law perspective: while settlers in Gaza Strip violated international law, traditional Bedouin land rights are protected by international law.
223 Human Rights Watch, *supra* note 125 at 13.
224 Swirski and Hasson, *supra* note 167 at 30.
225 Noam Sharvit, *Hamdenah tovaat habedouim metpashrim [The State Sues Bedouin Compromise]*, Globes, http://www.globes.co.il/news/article.aspx?fbdid=1000174638 (last visited Jan. 8, 2018).
226 File No. 12-21-306 Civil Appeals, Suleiman Aluqbi v. State of Israel (Mar. 15, 2012), Pador Legal Database (by subscription) (Isr.).
227 Swirski and Hasson, *supra* note 167 at 13.
228 *Hovalat tzevet yessum doah vaadat Goldberg lehasdarat hityashvut habedouim banegev [Leading the Implementation Team of Goldberg Commission Report for Bedouin Settlement in the Negev]* Prime Minister's Office, http://www.pm.gov.il/PMO/PM+Office/Departments/policyplanning/goldberg.htm (last visited Feb. 5, 2013).
229 *Establishment of a Committee to Draft Policy for Regulating Bedouin Settlement*, Prime Minister's Office, http://www.pmo.gov.il/Secretary/GovDecisions/2007/Pages/des2491.aspx (last visited Feb. 5, 2013).
230 Shahar Ilan & Yanir Yagna, *Committee: Gov't should Formally Recognize Bedouin Villages in Negev*, Haaretz, Dec. 11, 2008, http://www.haaretz.com/news/committee-gov-t-should-formally-recognize-bedouin-villages-in-negev-1.259322.
231 *See* Concluding Observations of the Committee on Economic, Social and Cultural Rights: Israel, May15–16, 23, 2003, U.N. Doc. E/C.12/1/Add.90 (May 23, 2003), *available at* http://www.unhchr.ch/tbs/doc.nsf/0/b313a3503107f1e6c1256d33002cea38?Opendocument.
232 *See e.g., id.*
233 *See e.g.*, HC 786/04, Ahlam el-Sana v. Ministry of Health (unpublished) [2004] (Isr.) (petition for family health clinics in Lagiyya and Hura in the Naqab).
234 HCJ 6672/00, Jazi Abu Kaf v. Minister of the Interior PD [2000] (Isr.) Pador 02-2-790 (page 2) Takdim Elion 2002(3), 2935 (dismissing a petition to prevent the expansion of the jurisdiction of the Omer Municipality that would encompass the land of Bedouin villages of Tarabin and Mkemen).
235 HCJ 1991/00 Abu-Hamad vs. the National Planning Council PD [2007] (Isr.) Takdim Elion 2007(3), 2542.
236 *See id.*
237 *See* Public Land Regulations (Eviction of Squatters- Eviction Order), 2005, KT 6422, 966 (Isr.).
238 Ismael Abu Saad, *Socio-Political Upheaval and Current Conditions of the Neqab Bedouin Arabs*, in Indigenous (In)Justice: Human Rights Law and Bedouin Arabs in the Naqab/Negev, 49 (2013).

239 Salman Abu-Obaid, *Arab Leadership Refuses to Cooperate with Goldberg Committee for Land Settlement*, SAWT-ALHAQ WALHORIYA (2008).

240 MINISTRY OF CONSTRUCTION & HOUSING, GOLDBERG REPORT (2009), *available at* http://www.moch.gov.il/odot/rashut_beduim/Pages/goldberg.aspx

241 REGIONAL COUNCIL FOR THE UNRECOGNIZED VILLAGES IN THE NEGEV, A RESPONSE TO GOLDBERG COMMISSION REPORT (Dec. 28, 2008) (copy on file with author).

242 REGIONAL COUNCIL FOR THE UNRECOGNIZED VILLAGES IN THE NEGEV, PRINCIPLES PAPER SUBMITTED TO THE COMMITTEE FOR BEDOUIN SETTLEMENT IN THE NEGEV (GOLDBERG COMMITTEE) (Feb. 7, 2008) (copy on file with author).

243 Thabet Abu-Ras, *The Arab Bedouin in the Unrecognized Villages in the Naqab (Negev): Between the Hammer of Prawer and the Anvil of Goldberg*, ADALAH'S NEWSL., Apr. 2011, at 1.

244 Anat Raskin, *Shel me hadamah hazu? Baekvot doah praver lehasdarat hahityashvout habedouit banegev [Whose land? Following the Praver Report on the Regulation of Bedouin Settlement in the Negev]*, 31 MEZRAH, http://www.goarad.co.il/?pid=15&t=mFinal&L1=41&L2=144&item=1847.

245 Prime Minister's Office, *Leading the implementation team of Goldberg Commission Report for Bedouin settlement in the Negev*, http://www.pmo.gov.il/policyplanning/hevra/Documents/goldberg1012.pdf.

246 *Inter-Ministerial Team to Implement Report Recommendations for Regulating Bedouin Settlement- Further Discussion and Transfer of Activities from One Office Space*, PRIME MINISTER'S OFFICE, http://www.pmo.gov.il/Secretary/GovDecisions/2011/Pages/des3707.aspx (last visited Feb. 5, 2013).

247 Praver Report, p. 26, Article 2.5.2:

A report of the Inter-ministerial team for the implementation of the recommendations to regulate Bedouin settlement in the Negev (Prawer Report) [doah hatzevet habenmesradi layisum hamlatzoot havaadah lehasdarat hityashvut habedium banegev] Available at: http://moch.gov.il/Gov_Decisions/Pages/GovDecision.aspx?ListID=f33e0a4b-aa35-4b12-912e-d271a6476a11&WebId=fe384cf7-21cd-49eb-8bbb-71ed64f47de0&ItemID=289 (visited Mar. 11, 2013).

248 Concentrations are the unrecognized Bedouin villages, as the State prefer to call them.

249 Praver Report, p. 24, Article 2.2.1

250 *Id.*

251 Rinat Zafrir, *Israel approves plan to relocate 30,000 Bedouin from unrecognized villages*, HAARETZ.COM, 2011, http://www.haaretz.com/news/national/israel-approves-plan-to-relocate-30-000-bedouin-from-unrecognized-villages-1.383772 (last visited Dec. 31, 2012).

252 ADALAH, THE LEGAL CENTER FOR ARAB MINORITY RIGHTS IN ISRAEL, THE PRAWER PLAN AND ANALYSIS (2011), *available at* http://www.adalah.org/upfiles/2011/Overview%20and%20Analysis%20of%20the%20Prawer%20Committee%20Report%20Recommendations%20Final.pdf (last visited Feb. 5, 2013).

253 *Id.*

254 Ronen Medzini, *Baderekh laeshur: Ketzutz gadol bakarkaot labedoum [On the Way to Approval: Large Cut in Lands for Bedouin]*, YNET, Sept. 1, 2012, http://www.ynet.co.il/articles/0,7340,L-4116414,00.html.

255 *Id.*

256 Zafrir, *supra* note 479.

257 Bedouin representatives define the program "a declaration of war on the Bedouin." *Id.*

258 *ACRI: Discriminatory Prawer Plan Approved*, NEW ISRAEL FUND AUSTRALIA, http://www.nif.org.au/acri_discriminatory_prawer_plan_approved (last visited Feb. 5, 2013).

259 Eliakim Rubinstein, *From the Ancient East to the Middle East: legal dimensions of belonging and distinction between Israel and the neighboring countries*, http://

www.lifshiz.macam.ac.il/m/pages/m0581/m0581194a.html (last visited Oct. 16, 2012).
260 *Id.*
261 *Id.*
262 HCJ 528/88 Eliezer Avitan v. Israel Land Admin. 43(4) PD 297 [1988] (Isr.).
263 *Id.*
264 *Id.*
265 *Id.*
266 *Id.* at 302.
267 *See* HCJ 6671/03 Abu Ghanem v. Ministry of Ed. Nt (5) PD 577 [2003] (Isr.).
268 *Id.*
269 The existence of the Tribal Court Regulation of 5715, 1937, KT 483, 123 (Isr.).
270 The British distinguished the Bedouins, politically and legally, on many occasions. Therefore, it is reasonable to recognize tribal law. See GRANOTT, *supra* note 258 at 89.
271 See ORLY ALMI, NO MAN'S LAND: HEALTH IN THE UNRECOGNIZED VILLAGES IN THE NEGEV 11 (Jul. 2003), *available at* http://www.phr.org.il/uploaded/articlefile_1163421247181.pdf.
272 CA (BS) 7161/06 Suleiman Aluqbi v. State of Israel (unpublished) [2012] (Isr.).
273 See Professional Opinion submitted to District Court regarding CC 7161/06 Suleiman Aluqbi v. State of Israel (arguing that Bedouins acquire a sort of land ownership); see also GRANOTT, *supra* note 258; Bisharat, *supra* note 167 (refusing to recognize the Bedouin settlement as a settlement); Rangwala, *supra* note 391 (refusing to recognize the Bedouin settlement as a village).
274 Ham. (BS) El-Riati v. Batcha, PM 1983(1) 329, 332 (1993).
275 Rangwala, *supra* note 391 at 440–441; Bisharat, *supra* note 167 at 482 see also Professional Opinion submitted by Ruth Kark to District Court regarding CC 7161/06 Suleiman Aluqbi v. State of Israel.

Bibliography

Abu Hussein, H., & McKay, F. (2003). *Access Denied: Palestinian Land Rights in Israel.* Zed Books.

Abu Rabia, S. (2008). Between Memory and Resistance, an Identity Shaped by Space: The Case of the Naqab Arab Bedouin. *HAGAR Studies in Culture, Polity and Identities*, *8*(2), 93–119.

Abu Ras, T. (2012). The Arab Bedouin and Their Lands in the Naqab – The Tribal Dimension of Steadfastness. *Adalah's Newsletter*, *93*(May 2012).

Abu Saad, I. (2013). Socio-Political Upheaval and Current Conditions of the Neqab Bedouin Arabs. In A. Amara, O. Yiftachel, & I. Abu Saad (Eds.), *Indigenous (In)Justice: Human Rights Law and Bedouin Arabs in the Naqab/Negev.* Human Rights Program, Harvard Law School.

Adalah. (n.d.). *Nomads against Their Will.* Adalah. Retrieved September 24, 2016, from https://www.adalah.org/uploads/oldfiles/eng/publications/Nomads%20Against%20their%20Will%20English%20pdf%20final.pdf.

Bisharat, G. (1994). Land, Law, and Legitimacy in Israel and the Occupied Territories. *American University Law Review*, *43*(2), 467–561. http://digitalcommons.wcl.american.edu/aulr/vol43/iss2/3.

C.A. (BS) 7161/06 Suleiman Al-Uqbi et. Al. V. State of Israel, 15 (2012).

Forman, G., & Kedar, A. (2003). Colonialism, Colonization and Land Law in Mandate Palestine: The Zor al-Zarqa and Barrat Qisarya Land Disputes in Historical Perspective. *Theoretical Inquiries in Law*, *4*(2). https://doi.org/10.2202/1565-3404.1074.

Gilbert, J. (2006). *Indigenous Peoples' Land Rights under International Law* (1st ed.). BRILL.

Gilbert, J. (2007). Nomadic Territories: A Human Rights Approach to Nomadic Peoples' Land Rights. *Human Rights Law Review*, *7*(4), 681–716. https://doi.org/10.1093/hrlr/ngm030.

Granott, A. (1936). *The Land Issue in Palestine*. Keren Kayemeth Leisrael.

Halima, A. (1985). *Negev Lands from the Legal Perspective*. Institute for Land Policy and Land Use – Department of Land Policy.

Human Rights Watch. (n.d.). *Off the Map: Land and Housing Rights Violations in Israel's Unrecognized Bedouin Villages*. Retrieved September 6, 2016, from http://www.hrw.org/reports/2008/03/30/map.

Israel Lands – Privatization or National Ownership? (n.d.). Retrieved March 25, 2020, from https://www.jewishvirtuallibrary.org/israel-lands-privatization-or-national-ownership

Jiryis, S. (1981). Domination by the Law. *Journal of Palestine Studies*, *11*(1), 67–92.

Kedar, A. (Sandy). (1998). Minority Time, Majority Time: Land, Nation, and the Law of Adverse Possession in Israel. *Tel Aviv U. L. Rev.*, *21*, 665–746.

Kelley, R. (n.d.). Israel's Bedouin: The End of Poetry. *Americans for Middle East Understanding (AMEU), Sept.–Oct. 1998.*

Khamaisi, R. (2011). Territorial Dispossession and Population Control of the Palestinians. In E. Zureik (Ed.), *Surveillance and Control in Israel/Palestine: Population, Territory and Power*. Taylor & Francis.

Kram, N. (2011). *The Negev Bedouins: Struggles for Land Rights and Cultural Survival in Israel*. The Robert H. Arnow Center for Bedouin Studies and Development.

Kretzmer, D. (1990). *The Legal Status of the Arabs in Israel*. Westview Press.

Lustick, I. (1980). *Arabs in the Jewish State: Israel's Control of a National Minority*. University of Texas Press.

McNeil, K., & Roness, L. (2000). Legalizing Oral History: Proving Aboriginal Claims in Canadian Courts. *Journal of the West*, *39*(3), 66–74. https://digitalcommons.osgoode.yorku.ca/scholarly_works/835.

Prime Minister's Office. (n.d.). *Leading the Implementation Team of Goldberg Commission Report for Bedouin Settlement in the Negev*. http://www.pmo.gov.il/policyplanning/hevra/Documents/goldberg1012.pdf.

Rangwala, T. S. (2004). Inadequate Housing, Israel, and the Bedouin of the Negev. *Osgoode Hall Law Journal*, *42*, 415.

Rosen-Zvi, I. (2004). *Taking Space Seriously: Law, Space, and Society in Contemporary Israel*. Ashgate Publishing Ltd.

Rubinstein, E. (n.d.). *From the Ancient East to the Middle East: Legal Dimensions of Belonging and Distinction between Israel and the Neighboring Countries*. Retrieved October 16, 2012, from http://www.lifshiz.macam.ac.il/m/pages/m0581/m0581194a.html.

Sharvit, N. (n.d.-a). Hamdenah tovaat habedouim metpashrim [The State Sues Bedouin Compromise]. *Globes*. Retrieved January 8, 2018, from http://www.globes.co.il/news/article.aspx?fbdid=1000174638.

Sharvit, N. (n.d.-b). *When the State Sues Bedouin Compromise*. Globes. Retrieved February 8, 2013, from http://www.globes.co.il/news/article.aspx?fbdid=1000174638.

Swirski, S., & Hasson, Y. (2006). *Invisible Citizens: Israel Government Policy toward the Negev Bedouin*. Adva Center.

The Negev Coexistence Forum for Civil Equality. (n.d.). *The Arab-Bedouins of the Naqab- Negev Desert in Israel (Shadow Report 2006).*

Yahel, H. (2006). Land Disputes between the Negev Bedouin and Israel. *Israel Studies, 11*(2), 1–22.

Yiftachel, O. (2000). *Land, Planning and Inequality: The Division of Space between Arabs and Jews in Israel (קרקעות, תכנון ואי-שוויון: חלוקת המרחב בין יהודים וערבים בישראל).* Adva Center. http://simania.co.il/bookdetails.php?item_id=467581.

Yiftachel, O. (2012). Re-Examining the 'Dead Negev Doctrine': Property Rights in the Bedouin-Arab Space. *14 Mishpat Umimshal, 7.*

Zafrir, R. (2011). Israel Approves Plan to Relocate 30,000 Bedouin from Unrecognized Villages. *Haaretz.Com.* http://www.haaretz.com/news/national/israel-approves-plan-to-relocate-30-000-bedouin-from-unrecognized-villages-1.383772.

4 Protection of indigenous peoples' land rights under international and regional systems

The international human rights system, which includes regional systems, is increasingly concerned about indigenous peoples' land rights.[1] The instruments and the documents of the international system provide substantive and procedural tools for addressing land rights, which also influences the work of other human rights institutions and other international bodies such as the World Bank.[2] This body of law increasingly affects domestic policy, legislation, and the judiciary. Australia, for example, adopted the International Convention on the Elimination of All Forms of Racial Discrimination as part of its national law, which led to the recognition of the Aborigines land rights.[3]

However, despite these developments, international law continues to have limited protection of the rights of indigenous peoples. It lacks comprehensive instruments that can prosecute and defend indigenous land rights.[4] The existing instruments are limited by state sovereignty, internal policy, and a state's willingness to accept the jurisdiction of international bodies. The ability of any international system to provide practical protection for indigenous rights depends on a number of elements that includes recognition of such rights and the ability to execute them through judicial and enforcement systems. Therefore, it is often not enough to have protection in the system's documents; there is also a need for a judicial system to execute these rights and enforce them.

This chapter introduces the protection of indigenous peoples' land rights under international law and the limitations of such protection in the Bedouin land case in Israel. It discusses major instruments in international systems and introduces some of the major ones in two regional systems, the Inter-American system and the European system of human rights.

International system and instruments for land rights protection

Although indigenous peoples were not mentioned in the first UN human rights documents, the protection of their rights has been developed and supported through general instruments dedicated to the general protection of human rights. Therefore, for a long time, indigenous peoples had no choice other than to employ general human rights instruments to protect their rights, mainly the UN human rights system.[5]

There are many instruments, documents, and bodies, such as the Declaration on the Rights of Indigenous Peoples, the International Covenant on Civil and Political Rights (ICCPR), the International Covenant on Economic, Social and Cultural Rights (ICESCR), the International Convention on the Elimination of all Forms of Racial Discrimination, the Convention on Biological Diversity, the Rio Declaration of Environment and Development and Agenda 21, the Convention on the Rights of the Child, and many others that protect indigenous peoples' rights.[6] Among these many instruments, the ILO 169, the ICCPR, and protection under environmental instruments are the most relevant to indigenous land protection. The World Bank has also been dealing with several indigenous land issues as part of the development projects it supports. It has issued several documents that recognize and support indigenous land rights.

Indigenous peoples' land rights protection under the ILO

The International Labor Organization (ILO) was one of the first international organizations to devote special attention to indigenous peoples' issues. Since 1930 it has adopted several conventions such as the Convention on Forced Labor (1930) and Convention No. 65 (1936) on penal sanctions on indigenous workers. The Organization has included several measures related to the rights of indigenous workers.[7] Additionally, in 1953 the Organization published a study about the living and working condition of indigenous peoples, which is considered the beginning of important work on indigenous peoples' rights.[8]

Acting under the name of the UN system, in 1957, the ILO adopted Convention No. 107 on indigenous and tribal populations. For 30 years the ILO 107 was the only instrument specifically devoted to indigenous peoples.[9] However, despite its positive aspects, the Convention included elements that negatively affected the rights of indigenous peoples; its assimilation approach in particular was very controversial. During the 1980s many indigenous organizations and the UN Special Reportour Martinez-Cobo called for a revision of Convention No. 107 and its assimilation approach.[10] As a result, in 1986, experts from the ILO recommended a revision to the Convention. The experts concluded that the "integrationist language" of Convention was outdated and even destructive in the modern world.[11]

In another development, in 1989, the ILO adopted Convention No. 169 on Indigenous and Tribal Peoples in the Independent Countries (ILO 169), the most important convention in this regard. Despite the limited number of ratifying states, only 22 countries so far,[12] the Convention underlines the need for new standards, and took the lead in using the term "peoples" instead of "populations."[13]

The Convention promotes the basic theme of the right of indigenous peoples to live and develop their culture according to their own view as distinct communities. It "includes provisions advancing indigenous cultural integrity, land and resource rights, and nondiscrimination in social welfare spheres; and it generally enjoins states to respect indigenous peoples' aspirations in all decisions affecting them."[14]

The Convention is not without shortcomings. It has clarified that use of the term "peoples" is not linked to the question of self-determination.[15] In addition, it set a low level of constraint regarding indigenous peoples' relocation and land dispossession, since it requires only consultation with indigenous peoples rather than consent, as compared to the Declaration on the Rights of Indigenous Peoples (DRIP), which demands consent of indigenous peoples in cases of relocation and land dispossession.

The Convention includes a general supervisory system, which consists of states' reports and a petition system. Ratifying states must periodically send reports to the Organization on the implementation of the Convention indicating whether national laws are in conformity with the Convention. In addition, they have to inform the Organization regarding the progress on the application of the Convention.[16] Indigenous workers' organizations, in turn, can comment on the state's reports that are examined by the ILO Committee of Experts on the Application of Conventions and Recommendations. The Committee can address a "direct request" concerning a state with regard to issues that states should undertake to solve problems.[17]

In addition, the Convention includes a petition system that consists of two procedures. The first allows any state-party, any delegate to the International Labor Conference, or the ILO governing body to file "complaints" against a state that ratified the Convention for any violation of the convention.[18] The second procedure consists of a "representation"; according to this procedure any workers' or employers' organization may file a complaint for a violation of any of the Convention's articles.[19] Filling such a "representation" leads to the appointment of a Committee that examines the case.[20]

The Convention does not include individual petitions, but labor unions or the ILO Government Body could do so on their behalf. As Anaya put it:

> Even though indigenous peoples themselves cannot directly file complaints to the ILO, others could do so on their behalf. There is no requirement that a party initiating a complaint under article 24 or 26 of the ILO Constitution, or the party's constituency, be directly affected by the alleged infraction. Labor unions are especially likely surrogates for indigenous peoples, given the demographic overlap and political alliances between indigenous and labor sectors. Additionally, the ILO Government Body itself is authorized to initiate (according to Article 26) complaints and could do so upon information provided by indigenous groups or by nongovernmental organizations concerned with indigenous peoples' rights.[21]

The covenant on civil and political rights: the Human Rights Committee

The International Covenant on Civil and Political Rights (ICCPR) includes several important provisions that protect, indirectly, the land rights of indigenous peoples. Namely, articles 17, 23, and 27 of the Covenant have proven to protect land right in several cases.[22]

The Human Rights Committee (HRC) under the ICCPR is consistently one of the most developed bodies that protects indigenous peoples' right to use (rather than own) their lands as part of the protection of their cultural way of life.[23] Unlike other human rights bodies, the Committee's jurisprudence has been progressive regarding indigenous peoples' right to enjoy their own cultural way of life. In several cases, "The Committee established a link between culture and traditional forms of livelihood"[24] in order to protect indigenous peoples' land rights. This approach enabled the Committee to protect land rights under several other rights such as the right to culture, the right to economic and social activities, and the right to private and family life.

Protection of land rights under the right to culture in Article 27

The protection of the right to culture under Article 27 of ICCPR is an effective procedure thanks to the UN mechanism of individual petitions, which is one of the important instruments available for victims to access international protection.[25] Article 27 states:

> In those States in which ethnic, religious or linguistic minorities exists, persons belonging to such minorities shall not be denied the right, in community with the other members of their group, to enjoy their own culture, to profess and practice their own religion, or to use their own language.[26]

Additionally, the Convention offers protection under other articles protecting cultural rights, such as Articles 17 and 23. These articles have been successfully used in national and international tribunals to protect indigenous peoples' land rights. Although Article 27 does not mention "indigenous" peoples or communities, General Comment No. 23 on Article 27 confirmed the practice of using Article 27 to protect indigenous rights. General Comment No. 23 states:

> With regard to the exercise of the cultural rights protected under article 27, the Committee observes that culture manifests itself in many forms, including a particular way of life associated with the use of land resources, especially in the case of indigenous peoples. That right may include such traditional activities as fishing or hunting and the right to live in reserves protected by law. The enjoyment of those rights may

> require positive legal measures of protection and measures to ensure the effective participation of members of minority communities in decisions which affect them.[27]

The cultural integrity norm has been the basis of many decisions favorable to indigenous peoples in the UN's HRC.[28] In addition, it has been the basis for several positive decisions in regional human rights systems and national courts; examples can be found in the Inter-American System, the European System of Human Rights,[29] Japanese and Australian courts.

In several cases courts relied on Article 27 to protect indigenous peoples' land use as part of their cultural survival needs.[30] Martin Scheinin describes how the interdependency of the rights of indigenous peoples protects their culture and their very survival.[31] Human rights bodies have held that the cultural integrity norm covers all aspects of indigenous survival needs as a distinct culture. In addition, human rights courts interpret culture to include economic, political institutions, and land use, as well as language and religious practices.[32]

In several cases, the HRC decided to protect indigenous peoples' land rights as part of their culture or as a vital element for the survival of their culture. The principle of "land as a vital element of culture" was also recognized and developed in other regional systems like the Inter-American Commission on Human Rights. In several cases, such as the *Miskito* case and the *Yanomami* case, the Commission demonstrated such protection using this justification.[33] In many of these cases the court found that the protection of indigenous peoples' land rights was essential for the protection of their culture.

In *Sandra Lovelace v. Canada*,[34] an Indian woman lived on a reservation with her parents until she married a non-Indian man and moved off the reservation. After her marriage ended, she returned to the reservation to live with her parents; however, she was deprived of her Indian rights and privileges. The Council deprived her of her right to purchase a home on the reservation. According to the Canadian Indian Act, a woman who marries a non-Indian man loses her Indian status and benefits, such as the right to own a home or live on a reservation. In an effort to reinstate her Indian status, Ms. Lovelace submitted her petition to the Human Rights Committee claiming that Canada's actions violated her rights under Articles 2(1), 3, 23(1) and (4), 26, and 27 of the ICCPR because the Act only strips Indian women who marry non-Indians of their Indian status.[35] In 1981, the Committee accepted the application and decided that the prevention of the petitioner to live on the reservation because of her marriage with a non-Indian man, according to the law over Indians, constituted a deprivation of her cultural identity and a violation of Article 27 of the ICCPR.[36]

Despite the fact that the case is not a land rights case, but more "gender oriented." Before this cases the Canadian law deprived only women of their rights if they married a non-Indian man,[37] the fact that the applicant received her rights to live on the reservation is considered an indirect protection of the right to her land and her traditional territory because the case dealt with gender equality rather than land rights.[38]

The *Kitok v. Sweden* case, decided in 1988, is another case that demonstrates the protection of indigenous peoples' culture under Article 27. In this case, Ivan Kitok, a Swedish citizen from a Sami origin, claimed that the Reindeer Husbandry Act 1971 that deprived him of the right to graze his herd violated his rights under articles 1 and 27 of the Covenant. The Reindeer Husbandry Act divided the Sami people into two groups, reindeer-herding (*sameby*) and nonreindeer herding, and offered traditional rights of herding only for the reindeer-herding group. The government claimed that the Act was restricting the number of reindeer breeders for economic and ecological reasons and to protect the wellbeing of the Sami community.[39]

The Committee did not find a violation of Article 27. It stated that: "After a careful review of all the elements involved in this case, the Committee is of the view that there is no violation of Article 27 by the State party."[40] The Committee agreed that Kitok should not be reintegrated into the Sami community because he did not work within the community for a specified period of time. The Committee found that such restrictions were necessary for the continued viability and welfare of the minority group as a whole and therefore were not a violation of Article 27.[41] In this case, the Committee viewed the Sami lifestyle as part of their cultural right. The Committee decided that the Sami lifestyle was linked to reindeer culture and that Sweden ought to respect this part of the Sami culture.[42]

The third case, *Lubicon Lake Band (Ominayak) v. Canada,*[43] addressed the right of indigenous people to exploit their natural resources. In 1984, the Lubicon Lake Band claimed that the Canadian government that had expropriated their land and granted it to a gas and oil company had violated their right to self-determination and their right to determine their political status and pursue economic, social, and cultural development.[44]

The Committee accepted the application and decided that Canada had violated Lubicon Lake Band rights by allowing the government of Alberta to grant leases for oil, gas, and timber in a territory used by indigenous peoples.[45] In addition, the Committee found that the natural resource development activity compounded historical inequities to "threaten the way of life and culture of the Lubicon Lake Band, and constituted a violation of Article 27 so long as they continue."[46]

These cases show that the Human Rights Committee has successfully protected indigenous peoples' land rights as a cultural right under Article 27.[47] However, this protection is not without limitations, since it only protects rights of land use and does not include protection nor recognition of land ownership rights. In addition, it is limited to member states' that have accepted and signed the First Protocol of the ICCPR. This aspect will be discussed below.[48]

Land as necessary for economic and social activities

In the *Lubicon Lake Band* case, the Committee also recognized that the right of indigenous peoples to engage in economic and social activities is part of their right to enjoy their culture. The Committee stated that: "The right protected by Article 27 includes the right of persons, in community with others, to engage in economic and social activities which are part of the culture of the community to which they belong."[49] According to Benedict Kingsbury, such a decision implies that states violate Article 27 when they do not allocate sufficient land and resources necessary for indigenous peoples to pursue economic activities of central importance to their culture.[50]

In *Lubicon Lake Band*, the Committee even went further and set up a test to solve land conflicts between indigenous peoples and states. The test is based on the state's communication with the indigenous group and economic sustainability.[51] Under this test, the Committee would first examine whether a proper consultation with the concerned indigenous communities had taken place, and second, it would evaluate the effect on the group's economic sustainability (i.e., if the act affects the economic sustainability of "an activity forming an essential element of the indigenous peoples' culture"). If there is no consultation and the state's actions compromise the economic sustainability of the indigenous group, then it would be a violation of their right to culture.[52]

In considering whether the state's actions interfere with the economic activities of an indigenous group in such a way that they threaten the group's way of life and culture, the Committee can take into account historical inequities. Such consideration could indicate a continuous violation of indigenous land rights that would support the group's claim of a violation. In *Lubicon Lake Band*, the HRC took this advanced approach and showed that past wrongs could be used as proof of a continuous violation of indigenous peoples' land rights.[53] In that case, the Committee stated that "historical inequities.... and certain more recent developments threaten the way of life and culture of the Lubicon Lake Band, and constitute a violation of Art. 27 as long as they continue."[54] According to Scheinin, the decision allows the Committee to review new legislation or state action that has any relationship to previous indigenous peoples' land dispossession.[55]

The protection of indigenous peoples' land rights under the right to enjoy their culture is one of the evolving niches for the protection of indigenous peoples' land rights.[56] The beginning of another development of this subject occurred in the HRC during the 1990s when Sami people brought three cases to the HRC under Article 27 against Finland's development projects that were affecting their traditional land and environment. During the deliberation of the three Sami cases the Committee established a new approach to land protection under the protected right of the culture.[57]

In the first case, *Sara et al. v. Finland*,[58] a group of Sami people filed a petition claiming that the Finnish adoption of a new law, called the Wilderness

Act, that authorizes logging activities in their area jeopardized the future of reindeer herding and husbandry. The Committee decided that the petition was inadmissible because the applicants failed to exhaust the available national remedies, and therefore rejected it.

In the second case, *Lansman et al. v. Finland (1992) (Lansman No. 1)*,[59] members of the Sami Herdsmen's Committee filed a petition to the HRC against Finland. They claimed that rights granted to companies for stone extraction from their sacred land disrupt their reindeer husbandry and thus violate their right to culture under Article 27 of the Covenant. The Committee denied the Sami petition. It stated that the amount of the stone extraction had a limited impact on reindeer herding activity in the area and therefore did not violate Article 27.[60] However, the Committee stated that "if mining activities in the area were to be approved on a large scale and significantly expanded by these companies… then this may constitute a violation of the authors' right under article 27."[61] During the deliberation of this case, the Committee confirmed that the Convention protects indigenous peoples' rights not only by traditional means, but it also protects traditional cultures even when they have adopted methods with the help of modern technology.[62] As Gilbert states, during the decision, the Committee adopted a "dynamic approach to what activity constitute 'essential elements' to cultural rights."[63] It viewed the provision of Article 27 as support for an indigenous modern way of life with historical links to traditional life, even though such way of life may have changed over time. Gilbert noticed that such an approach does not develop in a vacuum but reflects a domestic jurisprudence that has started to support such an approach.[64]

As Nesti describes, in the third case, *Jouni E. Lansman et al. v. Finland (Lansman No 2)* (1995),[65] members of the Sami people complained that Finland approved logging activities and construction of roads on their traditional herding lands. Also, in this case the Committee found no violation of Article 27 due to the small amount of logging that did not reach a level that would harm Sami herding activity. However, it stated that allowing large-scale logging may harm the Sami peoples' right to enjoy their culture and therefore may constitute a violation of Article 27.[66]

Protection of indigenous land rights und the right to private life and family life

According to Gilbert, the Committee has also succeeded in protecting indigenous peoples' land rights under other rights such as the right to private life and the right to family life under articles 17 and 23 of the ICCPR.[67] In several cases the Committee acting under the jurisdiction of articles 17 and 23 issued decisions that protected indigenous peoples' land. In the *Hopu et al. v. France* case (1997) two indigenous Polynesians filed a petition to the HRC against France because it had decided to build a hotel in an area that contained an ancestral cemetery. The applicants claimed that building a hotel on their ancestral cemetery violated their private and family rights under various articles of the Covenant, particularly articles 17.1, 23.1, and 27.[68] The fact that France had made a reservation on the application of Article 27 eliminated the applicants' ability to rely on the rights to culture under Article 27 and therefore the applicants relied on the rights to private and the rights to family life under articles 17 and 23 and the ICCPR.[69]

Article 17.1 states: "No one shall be subjected to arbitrary or unlawful interference with his privacy, family, home or correspondence…." Article 23.1 states that: "The family is the natural and fundamental group unit of society and is entitled to protection by society and the State."[70] The Committee accepted the petition and stated that the applicants' relations to their ancestors was an essential part of their identity and their family life. Therefore, the state violated the indigenous right to culture.[71] According to Nesti, in the *Hupo* case the Committee gave a broad interpretation to "the right to privacy and the family right" in order to protect the rights to privacy and the right to family life under Article 17. Nesti also noticed that the Committee in this case followed the European Court of Human Rights approach where in certain cases, such as *Lopez-Ostra*,[72] the court widened the meaning of the right to privacy and family life, home, and correspondence[73] in order to protect other rights such as the right to environment in that case.[74]

The *Hopu* decision[75] represents an important approach for indigenous peoples' land protection under family and privacy rights and constitutes part of the culture protected under the ICCPR. In this regard, as Gilbert indicates, "the HRC has also explored the correlation between cultural heritage protection and indigenous peoples' land rights,"[76] because the Committee recognized that the applicants' relation to their ancestors as part of their culture. As Gilbert put it, "the Committee pointed out that… the applicants' relationship to their ancestors was an essential element of their identity and significant in their family lives, as the burial grounds play an important role in the author's history, culture and life."[77] The decision also demonstrates the interdependence of rights when linked to the notion of indigenous peoples' right to culture.[78] It indicates that "the right to enjoy one's culture should not be restricted as a right based only on Article 27," but expanded to include other rights vital to practice one's right to culture such as the right to use their traditional land.[79]

The development of the protection of the right to culture under international law (mainly under Article 27) gradually influences legislatures and judiciary systems on the national level.[80] It increasingly offers protection to land rights even when states do not recognize indigenous peoples' land rights or when states are not parties to the ICCPR. In a case involving Brazil, the Inter-American Court considered the right to culture under Article 27 as a customary law that protects indigenous rights even in states that are not parties to the ICCPR. As Gilbert describes, "At the national level, the legal recognition of the interrelations between indigenous peoples' right to their lands and the protection of their cultural heritage is increasingly a matter of legislation and adjudication."[81]

In Japan, in *Kayano et al. v. Hokkaido Expropriation Committee*,[82] an indigenous community succeeded in taking control over its traditional territory using legislation designated for cultural heritage.[83] In 1997 the Japanese government enacted the Ainu Culture and Promotion Act, which recognized the existence of the Ainu people. The Act stated that communal property must be returned to its Ainu owners. Based on this Act, the Ainu people filed a claim in a local district court for unfair restitution. In addition to the local legislation, they also based their case on Article 27 of the ICCPR, arguing that the compensation was not fair and therefore violated their minority rights.[84] The Court found a deprivation of important Ainu religious, cultural, and archaeological sites, and thus decided that the expropriation of Ainu from their land was illegal.[85]

Although the Ainu people continue to struggle for recognition of their land ownership,[86] the cultural protection approach provided the community with an indirect legal way to protect and gain control over their traditional territories.[87] The Ainu case illustrates the potential relationship between protection of cultural heritage and land rights for indigenous peoples even where states do not recognize indigenous peoples' land rights. At the same time, it introduces the weakness of the approach, and its inability to recognize indigenous peoples' land ownership.

Another illustration of the interaction between cultural heritage concerns and indigenous land rights on the national level can be found in Australia, where this approach is more advanced due to an increasing awareness of the importance of indigenous cultural heritage and the existence of several laws that protect Aboriginal cultural heritage.[88] These laws include the Aboriginal and Torres Strait Islander Heritage Protection Act of 1984[89] and the Aboriginal Cultural Heritage Act of 2003 of Queensland.[90] In several cases, Aboriginal communities claimed that their land rights are inherently linked to their culture. Courts explored these Aboriginal land claims through references to cultural heritage laws, such as the case of *Noonkanbah Pastoral Co Pty Ltd. v. Amax Iron Corporation*, in the Supreme Court of Western Australia.[91]

In another article, "Nomadic Territories: A Human Rights Approach to Nomadic Peoples' Land Rights," Gilbert explains how the evolution of the new body of human rights law gradually also offers protection to nomadic societies and could provide nomadic peoples with rights to use their lands. Gilbert shows that in addition to the widely accepted fact that the ICCPR provides protection for indigenous land rights, it is also "a significant instrument for nomadic peoples' quest toward territorial rights."[92] In that article he argues that under international human rights law, nomadic peoples are gaining the right to live on their land in their traditional ways through the gradual establishment of a specific body of law dedicated to the rights of nomads.[93]

In conclusion, it is clear how the HRC approaches the protection of indigenous peoples' land rights, mainly under the right to culture under Article 27 of the ICCPR; articles 17 and 23 of the Covenant, the right to privacy and the right to family, were also used and proved to be effective in several cases. Further, such articles protect indigenous land rights not only on the international level but also on national levels as national legislatures and court systems are gradually informed by international decisions developing the interdependence of cultural rights and land use rights.

Other UN treaties and specialized agencies

As Nesti describes, in addition to the above protection under the ICCPR, there are also many UN treaties and specialized agencies that protect or have the potential to protect indigenous rights. Under treaties the Universal Declaration of Human Rights, International Covenant on Economic, Social and Cultural Rights (ICESCR), the Convention on the Elimination of All Forms of Racial Discrimination (CERD), and the Convention on the Rights of the Child (CRC), or the Convention on the Prevention and Punishment of the Crime of Genocide, should be mentioned.[94] The International Covenant on Economic, Social and Cultural Rights (ICESCR) that contains a list of rights, such as the right to adequate standard of living (Article 11) that protects indigenous peoples' right to land, and it could be used against acts of forced relocation.[95]

The CERD also includes provisions that protect indigenous social, economic, and cultural rights.[96] The Convention may consider individual complaints concerning state parties who recognize the competence of the Committee on the Elimination of Racial Discrimination under Article 14 of the Convention,[97] making it an effective and practical method for rights recognition. Further, the fact that racial discrimination is one of the main causes of marginalization and rights' deprivation of indigenous communities makes the Convention very relevant to their struggle.

Additionally, the Convention on the Rights of the Child is one of the rare international conventions that mention indigenous peoples in particular. Many articles refer to indigenous peoples' rights such as articles 5, 17, 20, 29, and 30. Article 30 protects indigenous children right to enjoy their culture and thus protects indigenous land as shown previously.

In her article, *International Protection of the Rights of Indigenous Children*, Cynthia Price Cohen explains the international law of indigenous child's rights by surveying the relevant standards of the convention on the rights of the child.[98] She states that "The Convention on the Rights of the Child protects the indigenous child's rights in three ways: 1) through general principles; 2) through articles protecting the specific rights of indigenous child; and 3) through rights applicable to all children."[99]

In addition to HRC instruments, the ILO, and the World Bank, other UN specialized agencies have provisions that offer additional protection to indigenous peoples' land rights, such as the United Nations Educational, Scientific and Cultural Organization (UNESCO), the Convention against Discrimination in Education (1960), and the Declaration on Race and Racial Prejudice (1978).

The UNESCO has developed several instruments for the protection and promotion of the right to education, cultural heritage, scientific progress, and cultural identity.[100] Also the Convention against Discrimination in Education (1960) contains articles related to indigenous peoples.[101] Article 3 of the Convention states that "States Parties... undertake... [t]o... discontinue any... practices which involve discrimination in education." Article 5 states that "[i]t is essential to recognize the right of members of national minorities to carry on their own educational activities, including the maintenance of schools and... the use or the teaching of their own language..."[102]

Finally, the Declaration on Race and Racial Prejudice (1978) contains provisions that support cultural rights of indigenous peoples. It affirms that all individuals and groups have the right to be different and the right to maintain cultural identity. The Declaration represents another step toward collective cultural rights rather than individual freedoms.[103]

Protection of indigenous land under the environment

Indigenous peoples have also used instruments for environmental protection to protect their land rights. The protection of indigenous peoples' land rights under instruments designated for environmental protection is a developing and promising avenue. The fact that environmental issues are increasingly receiving wider national and international attention increases the potential for protection of indigenous peoples under the same instruments.[104]

International concern for the environment focuses on the loss of biological and cultural diversity. As a result, states and international organizations for environment and development frame their policies and programs as conserving biodiversity.[105] Such policies and programs have important implications for the rights of indigenous populations.[106]

One key factor for this method is the aboriginal perspective about land, which can be quite different among various indigenous and nonindigenous groups. According to Ronald Hill:

> Aborigines view rights to land as originating with the design of the world rather than with alienable legal title. As one Aborigine asserted, "[Europeans] look upon land as 'my land, I own that land,' whereas Aborigines look at something as a part of the whole, a part of themselves, and they are part of that-the land. The land and they are one." Thus, land is seen as part of their "extended selves," something to be preserved and maintained.[107]

Later Hill added:

> ... Aboriginal people have seen it quite differently. They've seen their culture being linked with it, which hasn't been materialistic necessarily.

> They've seen the need for environmental considerations to be preserved in this country, which again isn't necessarily a materialistic priority.[108]

Therefore, thanks to cultures that consider land and the environment part of their spirituality rather than a means of wealth, indigenous peoples can coexist with the environment and live without damaging it. Indigenous land use includes culture and land use as elements necessary to protect the environment.[109]

Thus, the fact that indigenous peoples' land rights are part of the wider debate about environmental protection and human rights allows them to benefit from international obligations to protect the environment and the continued use of their lands and their resources.[110] On a practical level, this kind of protection helps to prevent projects that destroy the environment, prevent the exploitation of resources, and keep companies and other intrusions out of traditional indigenous territory.[111] According to Gilbert, this approach protects indigenous peoples' land in several areas like protected areas in South Africa.[112]

The protection of indigenous peoples' environmental rights is based on two models, the cultural integrity model and the self-determination model.[113] The cultural model, the more pervasive model, recognizes indigenous peoples' environmental rights as part of the protection and preservation of indigenous culture. The self-determination model recognizes indigenous peoples' environmental rights as part of the recognition of their "inherent degree of autonomy and control over their own development."[114]

Recognition of the importance of indigenous peoples' culture as a method to preserve biodiversity and the environment can be incorporated into the emerging international law that takes indigenous peoples' interests into account.[115] In fact, such recognition can be found in several international documents such as the Convention on Biological Diversity, which recognizes the special rights of indigenous peoples in connection with their lands and the environment,[116] and the Desertification Convention, which conceptualizes indigenous practices and ecological knowledge as part of their intellectual property.[117]

The Biodiversity Convention is only one example of an international convention that shows the increasing support for indigenous peoples' rights as part of international environmental law. The Convention also provides support for indigenous peoples' rights of participation, consultation, and compensation. For example, under Article 8(j) states must obtain the "approval and involvement of the holders of [indigenous] knowledge, innovations and practices that encourages" conservation and sustainable use of biodiversity.[118] Further, the Convention on Biological Diversity protects indigenous land, territory, and culture. The Convention is also the only binding document related to the protection of indigenous peoples' environment, and it includes a supervision mechanism.[119]

Agenda 21 is one of the most relevant documents for the protection of indigenous peoples' rights resulting from the Conference on Environment and Development. It is a comprehensive plan for environmental protection.[120] Chapter 26 of Agenda 21 references ILO 169 and the UN Draft Declaration on the Rights of Indigenous Peoples and stresses the relevancy of indigenous peoples to land. Agenda 21 articulates measures the international community ought to undertake to provide environmental protection.[121] It states that "recognition of indigenous peoples' rights is at the base of environment protection and sustainable development."[122]

The environmental discussion after the Conference on Environment and Development of 1992 continued to include the issue of indigenous peoples' rights. In 1994, in her Final Report to the Special Rapporteur on Human Rights and the Environment, Fatma Ksentini stated that "[i]ndigenous [p]eoples have the right to control their lands, territories and natural resources and to maintain their traditional way of life, which includes the right to security in the enjoyment of their means of subsistence."[123]

In 2002, the World Summit on Sustainable Development acknowledged the potential of indigenous peoples as "stewards" of national and global natural resources and biodiversity and reaffirmed the important role of indigenous peoples in sustainable development.[124] Environmental norms provided the basis for several cases protecting indigenous peoples' land.[125] By elaborating the connection between indigenous peoples' cultural survival and their physical connection with their land, the cultural model established a human rights approach to environmental law.[126] In several cases, such as the Yanomami people of Brazil, the Huaorani people in Ecuador, and the Lubicon Lake Band cases, indigenous people succeeded in protecting their environment by relying on the special connection of their cultural survival to their traditional lands. In the recent case of *Awas Tingni,* in particular, the court found that the failure to address indigenous land claims before granting concessions to companies violated Mayagna rights to their traditional property. Metcalf indicates that "the [c]ourt explicitly recognized the intimate connection between indigenous land rights and their cultural survival."[127]

Finally, despite its advantages, protection under environmental instruments has a negative side both practically and theoretically. On the practical level, many indigenous people do not receive protection, especially those who live in states not bound by such conventions. In addition, the protection offered is for "use rights" of land while many indigenous peoples demand ownership of their land. Further, such protection assumes that indigenous people will continue to consume their resources in a way that minimizes damage to the environment. If a group changes their attitude to maximize consumption of their recourses to boost development, they may lose protection under environmental instruments. Moreover, on a theoretical level, the protection assumes that indigenous peoples' rights are an incidental matter to the environmental issue and therefore is not strong enough to answer demands of indigenous groups.

The World Bank

The World Bank has also been an important player in shaping the international law that affects the rights of indigenous peoples. It is a strong player in promoting international policy that supports states' obligations to the development of indigenous peoples.[128] The Bank took the lead among many international bodies to support the indigenous peoples' right of consultation according to the ILO 169. In its Operational Directive 4.20 the World Bank includes "informed participation" and "direct consultation" with indigenous peoples as among the "central activities" to be undertaken in connection with any of the Bank-funded projects that may affect the interests of these peoples.[129]

As Nesti describes, the World Bank funds and participates in many development projects that affect indigenous peoples' land, environment, and survival.[130] Indigenous peoples' complaints against the Bank increased the Bank's awareness about the negative effect on indigenous peoples. As a result, during the 1980s, the Bank started to pay attention to the issue and revise its policy accordingly. Consequently, in 1982 the World Bank issued an Operational Manual Statement (OMS 2.34) titled "Tribal People in Bank Financed Projects," which reflected much of the ILO Convention No. 107 approach toward indigenous peoples.[131] In the OMS, the Bank made clear that it was concerned about the direct and indirect impacts of its projects on tribal peoples.[132] In addition, in its guiding principles the World Bank ordered special programs to mitigate negative effects on indigenous peoples.[133] In 1989 the World Bank issued another Operational Directive on Environmental Assessment (OD 4.00) to guide environmental impact assessment of World Bank's financed projects. In this OD, the Bank made reference to indigenous peoples' practices and did so again in its 1993 New Forestry Policy (OP 4.36). Later, that OD became the Bank's policy in this regard.[134]

The Bank continued to follow up and develop its position on the issue of indigenous peoples. In 1991 it issued a revised Operational Directive (OD 4.20) on Indigenous Peoples, in which the Bank showed additional development on its possession toward the issue. This OD showed that the Bank had improved its approach since the first OD. As Nesti put it,

> The evolution from the first directive is already clear in the title. Indigenous peoples (or other equivalent terms such as indigenous ethnic minorities, tribal groups and scheduled tribes) refer to social groups with a social and cultural identity distinct from the dominant society that makes them vulnerable to being disadvantaged in the development process.[135]

The OD states that the Bank's objectives are both to protect indigenous peoples against potential harm and other negative effects caused by the Bank's development projects, as well as to provide them with new opportunities to benefit from the development process on the basis of informed participation and recognition of the preferences of indigenous peoples.[136]

The World Bank's supervising mechanism and the Inspection Panel

In 1994 the World Bank established an "Inspection Panel" to investigate complaints filed by groups affected by the projects of the International Bank for Reconstruction and Development and the International Development Association.[137] This Inspection Panel offers complainants the opportunity to request an investigation to verify agency compliance with World Bank policies and ODs. In addition, the Bank recognizes that the identities and cultures of indigenous peoples are inextricably linked to the lands on which they live and the natural resources on which they depend.[138]

Despite indigenous peoples' longtime struggle, and the many developments of the Bank, some scholars still believe that the Bank's policies do not answer the demands of indigenous peoples. According to Anaya, in practice, the Bank's actions have not always been faithful to the principles of participation and direct consultation. In a study performed by the World Bank in 1992, more than a third of the Bank's projects affecting indigenous people had not taken into account the principle of consultation with affected communities.[139] Tom Griffiths found that indigenous peoples' experiences participating in World Bank policy processes are often not favorable. He claims that

> World Bank policy processes have failed to address demands that indigenous peoples have made for the last 15 years, e.g., in relation to human rights and free prior and informed consent [...] Meaningful indigenous participation remains absent or superficial ....[140]

The application of international human rights law in Israel and its limitations

The status of international human rights law in Israel and the application of international human rights law are complicated and contain both positive and negative aspects. On one hand, Israel claims to be a democratic state that follows a liberal western regime that respects international human rights and freedoms and is committed to international human rights law.[141] Chief Justice (Emeritus) of the Supreme Court, Aharon Barak, stated that "Israel is part of the international community, and as such, it will conform to that community's norms."[142] Israel has also amended several laws and canceled administrative procedures to follow international law and to follow its obligations under several conventions, such as the Convention against Torture (CAT)[143] and cases such as *Alon Moreh*. In the *Alon Moreh* case, the Supreme Court canceled the government's decision that allowed a group of Jewish settlers to establish a settlement on a Palestinian private land. The court decided that the government's decision contradicted international law, specifically Article 52 of the Geneva Convention, and therefore was illegal.[144]

With regard to international human rights, Israel has signed several human rights conventions that contain protection of major human rights, including indigenous rights and indigenous land rights.[145] It has signed and ratified human rights conventions that contain provisions relevant to indigenous peoples' rights[146] including the following:

1 International Covenant on Civil and Political Rights (ICCPR)[147]
2 International Covenant on Economic, Social and Cultural Rights (ICESCR)[148]
3 Convention on the Elimination of All Forms of Discrimination against Women (CEDAW)[149]
4 International Convention on the Elimination of All Forms of Racial Discrimination (CERD)[150]
5 Convention on the Rights of the Child (CRC).[151]

In addition, while Israel has not opposed the Declaration on the Rights of Indigenous Peoples (DRIP), many reports show that Israel has been constantly violating human rights law, especially regarding the Arab minority in Israel and Arab Palestinians in the Occupied Palestinian Territories.[152] Recently the international community condemned Israel several times for violating international law. As of January 24, 2008, Israel had been condemned 15 times in less than two years.[153] The International Court of Justice Advisory Opinion on the Wall in the Occupied Palestinian Territory and the recent Report of the United Nations Fact-Finding Mission on the Gaza Conflict, also known as the Goldstone Report, accused Israel of no less than war crimes during the 2008–2009 war on Gaza.[154] With regard to the Arab citizens in Israel, the State constantly discriminates against them and violates their human rights in several fields such as employment, education, health services, and planning and land allocation.[155] Further the State constantly violates many Arab and Bedouin rights such as housing by forcibly displacing them from their lands.[156]

One of the major obstacles to the application of international human right law is the limitation the State places on the application of human rights law domestically. Generally, the implementation of international law is accomplished through two major mechanisms, monitoring procedures and complaint procedures. While Israel routinely employs monitoring procedures such as review of development by UN Working Group on Indigenous Population (WGIP); monitoring by the Human Rights Council, its Sub-Commission, and its Special Rapporteur; and monitoring and reporting procedures of the Human Rights Committee and CERD, individual complaints procedures are not available. They are not available either because Israel is not party to the relevant convention, such as the ILO Convention, or because it has restricted the use of such procedures by making reservations to certain provisions, such as Israel's reservation from the First Optional Protocol of the ICCPR, or by abstaining from making the Special Declaration recognizing the competence of CERD.

1 Human Rights Committee and the Committee on Elimination of Racial Discrimination

Both the Human Rights Committee (HRC) and the Committee on Elimination of Racial Discrimination (CERD) can receive complaints from victims of human right abuses. The First Optional Protocol to the ICCPR authorizes the HRC to receive complaints from individuals in countries that are party to the ICCPR that have signed the First Optional Protocol.[157] Article 14 of ICERD authorizes CERD to receive complaints from victims of violations of the rights under the Convention.[158]

Both committees have additional provisions that states must fulfill in order to enable victims to submit complaints and accept jurisdiction for each of the committees. The HRC may consider complaints only if the state is a party to the Covenant and has signed the First Optional Protocol of the ICCPR. The CERD may consider petitions under Article 14, only "if the state is a party to the Convention and has declared that it recognizes the competence of CERD to receive such complaints."[159]

Both procedures are not available for human rights victims in Israel. First, Israel has not signed the First Optional Protocol of the ICCPR and has thus effectively blocked the individual complaint mechanism to the HRC.[160] Second, Israel has not agreed to the optional declaration provided for in Article 14 of CERD[161] and thus Israel has not recognized the competence of CERD to receive complaints from individuals, creating a lack of international human rights protection in several areas. Human rights advocates state that "Israeli citizens… have no international legal remedy, as Israel has not signed the ICCPR's Optional Protocol I."[162]

2 Complaint Procedures connected to the ILO Convention

ILO Conventions also offer two complaint mechanisms. The first is the complaint procedure under Article 24, and the second is the complaint procedure under Article 26 of the ILO Constitution. Although these complaint procedures focus on labor issues, and thus they cannot be invoked directly by indigenous peoples, they nevertheless could be available to address indigenous peoples' rights if the state party signed the relevant convention due to the focus of ILO conventions on indigenous peoples.[163] However, Israel has not signed the relevant ILO Convention No. 169[164]; therefore Bedouin cannot invoke complaint procedures under the ILO either.

3 Declaration on the Rights of Indigenous Peoples

The DRIP does not offer any complaint or monitoring procedures. Unlike customary international law and other binding conventions, the DRIP is only a declarative document and is not legally binding.[165] Israel did not oppose the DRIP during the UN vote to adopt the declaration because it was absent that day. According to officials, the State would not have voted in favor of adoption of the Declaration if it were present. Israel has many reservations to the Declaration and does not intend to follow the Declaration's principles. Adi Sheinman from the State Foreign Ministry stated, "Israel shares the restriction of the states who opposed to the Declaration and therefore it will not apply the principles of the Declaration."[166]

Conclusion

In conclusion, individual communication under the Optional Protocol of the ICCPR and major treaty-based procedures such as the complaint procedures connected to the ICCPR Convention are not relevant to human rights victims in Israel since it is not a signatory of the Optional Protocol of the ICCPR. In addition, Israel has not recognized the competence of CERD to receive complaints from individuals because it has not made the optional declaration provided for in Article 14 of the CERD. Furthermore, Israel is not party to the ILO Convention No. 169 on Indigenous and Tribal Peoples,[167] which limits complaint procedures under the ILO.

At the same time, as the next part of this chapter will illustrate, Israel is not a member of any regional human rights system. As a result, regional procedures such as those found within the Inter-American System are not relevant to Bedouin land rights in Israel. Therefore, in practice, international protection of Bedouin rights is extremely limited, and protection of Bedouin land rights does not exist at all.

Regional systems and instruments for land protection

Although no regional system is relevant to the Bedouin case in Israel, regional systems are introduced here as important part of the comparative law that interacts with international and national law to inform and change norms, legislation, and adjudication on national and international levels.[168] Land rights of indigenous peoples have been promoted through regional systems of human rights law, such as the Inter-American System, the European, and African System, in a way that cannot be ignored. Further, in some cases, regional systems have even adopted more advanced approaches than international systems and have taken the lead in defending indigenous peoples' rights.

1 The protection of indigenous land in the Inter-American System

The Inter-American System is one of the most advanced regional human rights systems in terms of protection of indigenous peoples' rights in general and land rights in specific. The interest of North and South American states in indigenous peoples started even before the creation of the

Organization of American States (OAS) in 1948.[169] However, significant interest in indigenous peoples' issues started in the 1970s, 1980s, and 1990s when the Inter-American Commission of Human Rights (IACHR) addressed violations of indigenous peoples' human rights on several occasions, particularly in response to reports about several states in South America such as Paraguay, Nicaragua, Colombia, Guatemala, Bolivia, and Suriname that raised many of human rights issues. The Commission addressed the violations of indigenous peoples' human rights despite the fact that neither the Inter-American Declaration on the Rights and the Duties of Man (1948) nor the American Convention on Human Rights (1968) contains specific articles about indigenous peoples.[170]

During the 1980s and 1990s the Commission published several reports about indigenous peoples, such as the Report on the Miskito Indians in Nicaragua and the Report about the "Communities of Peoples in Resistance in Guatemala" regarding the Maya Quiche people. Such reports further established the need to address the issue of indigenous peoples' rights in the Inter-American System.[171] In addition, in several cases like *Aloeboetoe*[172] the Commission addressed specific issues of indigenous communities and recognized indigenous peoples' customary law. An attitude that was later reflected in the decisions of the Inter-American Court of Human Rights who, in turn, explicitly took into account indigenous customary law.[173]

The Commission continued to deal with and discuss subjects relevant to indigenous peoples, such as the extinction of indigenous peoples' communities and oil exploration in the Amazon, in order to raise awareness of indigenous peoples' suffering and human rights violations as a result of environment destruction. In some cases it shed a light on the damage oil exploration projects caused to indigenous peoples during the 1970s; in some cases, the damage even led to the extermination of the entire group, like the *Tetetes* and the *Huaorani* communities.[174]

In the *Huaorani* case, for example, oil spills damaged the entire environment by polluting the rivers, making fishing, bathing, and drinking impossible for indigenous communities living in the Amazonian rainforests of Ecuador. In their petition to the IACHR under Article 29 of the American Convention against Ecuadorian government, they claimed that the government violated their right to a healthy environment according to the American Convention. During their petition, they invoked Article 27 of the ICCPR, (Ecuador is a state-party to ICCPR). They relied on the *Lubicon Lake Band* case under the UN Human Rights Committee, and the *Yanonami* case under the IACHR to argue their case.[175] Although the IACHR did not accept the petition of the Huaorani people, in its decision it made important statements about the oil pollution linking it with a violation of the right to life.[176]

Such a case raised awareness about indigenous peoples' human rights violations and the suffering of indigenous communities in the Americas and globally. As Adriana Fabra stated, "The Huaorani action raises awareness both at the OAS level and among the general public about the suffering of indigenous peoples as a result of environmental destruction."[177]

Article 27 in the Inter-American

Regarding land rights protection of the indigenous peoples, the Inter-American Commission took an advanced approach, especially when land use is related to the protection of their culture. In several cases, it held that whenever land is needed for the protection of a cultural right the court will defend that right to land as part of the cultural right.

In the Miskito Indians of Nicaragua case, the Inter-American Commission on Human Rights extended the "special legal protections" of cultural identity under Article 27 to include indigenous ancestral and communal lands. The Commission considered that the issue of ancestral and communal lands as part of "the aspects linked to productive organization" was essential for the protection of their culture.[178]

In another case, the case of the Yanomami of Brazil (1985), the Commission supported the protection of the Yanomami ancestral land under Article 27 despite the fact that Brazil did not sign the Covenant. The Commission considered Article 27 international customary law, and therefore it bound Brazil even though it did not sign the Covenant.[179]

The Awas Tingini *case*[180]

The Inter-American system issued many important decisions that support indigenous peoples' land rights. However, the recent case of *Mayagna (Sumo) Awas Tingni Community v. Nicaragua (Awas Tingni)* is one of the most important ones. In that case, the court recognized for the first time the rights of indigenous peoples to use their land as part of their right to preserve and protect their culture.[181]

The case was initiated in 1996, after Nicaragua granted a Korean corporation logging rights on the lands of the Awas Tingni indigenous community of thc Mayagna. Thc logging liccnsc was issucd without prior consultation with the tribe.[182] In 1998 the Inter-American Commission on Human Rights filed a petition to the Inter-American Court on Human Rights charging Nicaragua with failure to take steps necessary to secure the land rights of the *Awas Tingni* community in the Atlantic Coast region of Nicaragua.

In the decision, the Court stated two important core elements of indigenous peoples' struggle for rights: first, the protection of customary land and resource tenure, according to international human rights law, which includes the basic human right to enjoy the benefits of property; and second, the recognition and protection of indigenous peoples' customary tenure. The court accepted the petition and held that "the international human right to enjoy the benefits of property, particularly as affirmed in the American Convention on Human Rights, includes the right of indigenous peoples to the protection of their customary land and resource tenure." In addition, it held that:

> [T]he State of Nicaragua violated the property rights of the Awas Tingni Community by granting to a foreign company a concession to log within the Community's traditional lands and by failing to otherwise provide adequate recognition and protection of the Community's customary tenure . . . The Court admonished that Nicaragua must secure the effective enjoyment of those rights, which it had not done for Awas Tingni nor for the vast majority of indigenous communities of the Atlantic Coast region of Nicaragua.[183]

Many human rights organizations and experts highlighted the importance of the *Awas Tingni* decision. Claudio Grossman stated that:

> This is a landmark case in the Inter-American System for the Promotion and Protection of Human Rights. It is the first case brought before the Inter-American Court concerning the rights of an indigenous population... It is appropriate that the first such case should examine the property rights of an Indian group because the very culture and existence of the Indian community depends upon the land on which they reside.[184]

The *Awas Tingni* decision established the right of indigenous communities to their land as a basic human right. The Court found that the right to property, as affirmed in the Inter-American Convention on Human Rights, protects traditional land tenure of indigenous peoples, according to their customary law.[185]

2 *Protection of the indigenous peoples' land under the European system*

Two comments are essential at the beginning of this section, the first one about the relationship of Israel to the European Union, and the second one is related to the limited sources of the section, which is a reflection of the limited literature on the subject.

Although Israel is not a member of the European Union and is not a party to the European Convention on Human Rights or the European Court of Human Rights, the development in Europe has a serious effect on it, and therefore serious effects on the human rights of the Arab minority, including Bedouin. First, on the informative level, European legislation and rulings on these matters guide the legislature and the judiciary in Israel. Secondly, these developments indirectly bind Israel through its relationship with the European Union (EU). The EU operates as regional system that works to protect human rights. It does this inside the Union, but also with its partners outside of the European geographical territory through its economic and political relations. Israel has a very complex and far-reaching relation with the Union. Its relations and interests with the EU are key to maintaining human rights[186] and the EU uses these relations to encourage and even enforce human rights, even in states that are not members. Section 2 of the trade agreement between Israel and the EU presents the Union's relations with Israel in maintaining human rights as part of their commercial relation with EU.[187]

Due to the limited resources on the protection of indigenous peoples' right under the European system, this section relies mainly on Patric Thornberry's book, *Indigenous Peoples and Human Rights*. Such scarcity of research on the subject has been noticed by other scholars such as Timo Koivurova who states:

> Probably because there have been no landmark cases decided by the European Court of Human Rights... in favour of indigenous peoples, there has correspondingly been scant interest in studying the problems and possibilities of using the Court as an avenue to promote and protect the rights of indigenous peoples.[188]

i The European System of Human Rights

The second regional system to demonstrate an effective protection of indigenous peoples' rights can be found in Europe. After World War II, as part of the lessons of war, Europeans started to work to renew trust, peacekeeping, and cooperation in Europe to prevent the recurrence of war atrocities. Europeans founded three organizations: the Council of Europe (COE), the European Union, and the Organization for Security and Cooperation in Europe.[189]

Among the three, the Council is the most relevant for the promotion of human rights.[190] The Council consists of the Committee of Ministers, the Parliamentary Assembly, the Congress of Local and Regional Authorities of Europe, and the Secretary General of the Council of Europe. The Committee of Ministers is the most important institution in the council since it is the main decision-making body. The main goal of the Council is to secure democracy and prevent the recurrence of the gross violations of human rights. Therefore, according to Arthur Henry Robertson, as soon as the Council met for its first session the Consultative Assembly put on its agenda the goal of the maintenance and realization of human rights and fundamental freedoms.[191] Therefore, the Council invests much of its resources to promote human rights in Europe. Since its establishment, the Council successfully drafted several treaties and established several bodies to promote human rights. The Convention of the Human Rights is considered the leading document, while the European Court of Human Rights is considered the leading body in this regard.

ii The Convention for the Protection of Human Rights and Fundamental Freedoms

The European Convention for the Protection of Human Rights and Fundamental Freedoms is the framework document for the European system on human rights. It was adopted by the Council of Europe in 1950 and entered into force in 1953. The main provisions of the Convention were based on a draft of what is now the International Covenant on Civil and Political Rights.[192] Together with its 11 additional protocols, this Convention represents one of the most advanced and successful systems for the protection of human rights.

The European Convention on Human Rights (ECHR) was the first legal treaty the Council produced to protect human rights, as well as the first international human rights treaty with enforceable mechanisms.[193] The preamble of the Convention provides for "the maintenance and further realization of human rights and fundamental freedoms," which

> are the foundation of justice and peace in the world and are best maintained on the one hand by an effective political democracy and on the other by a common understanding and observance of the human rights upon which they depend.[194]

The European System includes many other instruments and documents that could be indirectly relevant to the protection of human rights. These include the European Social Charter of 1961; the European Committee of Social Rights; the European Convention for the Prevention of Torture and Inhuman or Degrading Treatment or Punishment; and the Framework Convention for the Protection of National Minorities (FCNM), which is the first binding international treaty to offer protection specifically for minorities; it was adopted in 1995 and entered into force in February 1998.

The Convention discusses the need to protect national minorities. The preamble of the convention states, "A pluralist and genuinely democratic society should not only respect the ethnic, cultural, linguistic and religious identity of each person belonging to a national minority, but also create appropriate conditions enabling them to express, preserve and develop this identity."[195] Among all the bodies and institutions for human rights, however, the European Court of Human Rights, which was established in 1959, is the most important.

The jurisdiction of the Court has been recognized by 47 European states. In November 1998, according to Protocol No. 11 of the Convention, the European Commission of Human Rights was abolished and the Court became to be full-time court.[196]

The Court has binding jurisdiction over COE member states that have accepted the Court's optional jurisdiction.[197] Its jurisdiction, however, does not provide the power to repeal domestic laws or administrative practices that contradict the Convention.[198]

The Court accepts applications of human rights violations from individuals as well as states.[199] Any person, nongovernmental organization, or group of individuals can submit applications against party states for violations of rights protected by the Convention. Also, any party state can bring an action against another party state in the Court for breach of the Convention.[200] Furthermore, the Court can issue advisory opinions on legal questions concerning the interpretation of the European Convention on Human Rights upon the request of the Committee of Ministers.[201]

As for the mechanism of implementation, the Committee of Ministers oversees the party states' application of the Convention and Court's decisions, and it is the body in charge of the supervision and the implementation of the Court's decisions.[202]

The Court is well respected among European member states, as most of the party states have incorporated the Convention into their own national legal orders.[203]

Although the European system of human rights was structured to protect minority rights, its structure proved to be able to also protect indigenous peoples' rights. Minority rights under the European system have successfully encompassed indigenous peoples' rights as well.

The European system is one of the regional human rights systems that have shown a special interest in the protection of human rights, and it has dealt with indigenous groups throughout Europe during the last few decades as part of its general human rights protection. As Thornberry stated, "The concern with minorities is historically embedded, even if the texts on minorities are recent products."[204] From the beginning, due to historical reasons, minority rights and human rights have been a main characteristic of the European human rights law.

In Europe, the protection of indigenous peoples is achieved through a system that protects minority rights. Although there is no specific provision for the protection of indigenous peoples' rights, the definition of minority rights according to the European system encompasses indigenous peoples' rights. Indigenous groups in Europe have employed the mechanisms of individual rights of the ECHR to advocate their rights, similar to what other indigenous groups around the world do in the UN system.[205]

Furthermore, European consciousness of the indigenous human rights issue appears to be increasing, especially as part of the increasing awareness toward human rights and minority rights in Europe.[206] During the European Conference against Racism and the Political Declaration, European states recognized the presence of indigenous peoples in Europe and the discrimination against them, especially the Roma people. In addition, several landmark Council of Europe documents included recommendations on combating racism and intolerance against indigenous groups mainly the Roma/Gypsies.[207]

Although many instruments in the European system have considerable potential to promote the human rights of indigenous groups, the abolished Commission on Human Rights and the European Court of Human Rights demonstrated that the system is able to protect indigenous peoples' rights under the rubric of the minority rights regime. The Convention on Human Rights is the basic document for human rights protection in the European system, and it includes protection for basic human rights such self-identification and ethnic identity, self-determination, nondiscrimination, dignity, and other rights especially relevant to indigenous peoples' land protection.

In several cases, the European system demonstrated its ability to protect indigenous peoples' rights under different articles of the Convention. Although sometimes the approach resulted in unfavorable decisions for the indigenous group, the approach highlights changes that indicate an increasing awareness and even support for indigenous peoples' rights, including their land and territorial rights.

Self-identification, ethnic identity, and culture

Self-identification is considered a major element of the group rights issue.[208] Issues of belonging and membership appear in the European system as they do elsewhere in the world. Europe lends this issue greater attention due to its links to WWII and its aftermath, mainly the issue of recognition of minorities and different cultures. The issue of recognition of minorities and different cultures with relation to self-identification was discussed in several cases in the European Court of Human Rights such as the case of *Ahmet Sadiq* where the court recognized the principle of minority as a right that all states must respect.[209]

In two cases involving Greece, the Court established that the existence of minorities is not a gift of the state (*Ahmet Sadiq v. Greece*) and it is a historical fact that a democratic society tolerates, protects, and supports its minorities according to the principles of international law (*Sidiropoulos et al. v Greece*). In the first case, the case of *Ahmet Sadiq v. Greece*,[210] the Court indicated that a democratic society must tolerate, protect, and support its minorities and different cultures. The case was about an applicant who was imprisoned because he published a series of communications referring to the "Turkish minority" instead of "the Greek minority of Muslim faith." The Greek court declared that "there was no Turkish minority in Western Thrace."[211] Although the European Court dismissed the case on the grounds of nonexhaustion of domestic remedies, in a dissenting decision, it considered the essence of the case to be the extent of the rights of ethnic minorities in a democratic society, suggesting that in such cases "there is no room for relying on the judgments of the national courts nor for a margin of appreciation."[212] *Ahmet Sadiq* is an opinion that led the way to recognition of the principle that minority, or indigenous, existence is not the gift of the state.[213]

In another case, *Sidiropoulos et al. v. Greece*,[214] the state of Greece refused to register a nonprofit association under the name of "Home of Macedonian Civilization." In this case, the Court, who found a violation of their freedom of association (Article 11), decided that "the existence of minorities and different cultures in a country was a historical fact that a "democratic society" had to tolerate and even protect and support according to the principles of international law."[215]

Nondiscrimination

The European Court also supports the rights of indigenous peoples under the nondiscrimination principle. Article 14 of the Convention defines the principle, and provides that "The enjoyment of the rights and freedoms set forth in this Convention shall be secured without discrimination...."

In early cases, namely *Belgian Linguistics*,[216] the Court explained, in the context of different treatment of various linguistic groups, that the principle of equality of treatment is violated if the distinction has no reasonable or objective justification.[217]

According to Thornberry, in many of the early cases the Court was reluctant to find discrimination as the relevant reason for violation of the applicants' rights.[218] Therefore, in such cases, like the Turkish cases, the Court relied on violations of other rights such as the rights to life, liberty, and property in order to avoid relying on the principle of nondiscrimination. In other occasions, the Court ignored the ethnicity of victims as a relevant factor for violation of their rights.[219] Therefore, some have been critical of the Court's reluctance to offer protection against discrimination based on national minority grounds, or protection similar to what it offers to discrimination on grounds of race and sex.[220]

Velikova v. Bulgaria[221] involves the death of an individual of Roma ethnicity where the Court developed the nondiscrimination principle in assessing the application of Article 14. It discussed the issues at hand under "ethnic origin," "ethnicity," and racial prejudice, but did not find discrimination and decided that no violation of Article 14 had been committed.[222] In *Velikova*, the Court observed that the applicant's complaint under Article 14 was based on a number of serious arguments. It also notes that the respondent State failed to provide a reasonable explanation for the circumstances of Mr. Tsonchev's death and the reasons the investigation omitted certain fundamental information, which could have shed light on the event. In the end, the Court stated that the material before it did not enable the Court to conclude beyond a reasonable doubt that Mr. Tsonchev's death and the lack of a meaningful investigation were motivated by racial prejudice; therefore, it decided that no violation of Article 14 had been established.[223]

In the case, *Chapman v. UK*, the Court refused to accept violations of Article 14 based on the nondiscrimination argument. In *Chapman*, Mrs. Chapman challenged a decision by UK national authorities that denied her family, a Roma family, permission to park a caravan on land they owned under planning reasons. The applicant claimed discrimination on the grounds of race, national or social origin, association with a national minority, and birth or other status. She claimed that discrimination was caused by popular prejudice against Gypsies and a failure by local and national governments to act despite that prejudice.[224] The Court found that the prohibition of discrimination was not violated because differences in treatment arose on the basis of legitimate aims and that any discrimination was proportionate to those aims and had a reasonable and objective justification.[225]

Second phase of decisions

Later the Court revised its decisions and, to some extent, its jurisprudence regarding the principle of discrimination and showed a development in its application of the principle in several cases. This development began with *Thlimmenos v. Greece*[226] where the Court observed that it had so far considered that the right under Article 14 "not to be discriminated against" is violated when States treat persons differently in similar situations without providing an objective and reasonable justification. In this case, the Court considered that this is not the only facet of the prohibition of discrimination. The Court found that under the Convention the prohibition is also violated when a state, without an objective and reasonable justification, fails to treat persons differently whose situations are significantly different.[227]

In 2000, the Council of Europe took additional steps to enlarge the prohibition on discrimination through Protocol No. 12. Article 1 of the Protocol states: "The enjoyment of any right set forth by law shall be secured without discrimination..." and "No one shall be discriminated against by any public authority...."[228]

Protection of indigenous peoples right to dignity

In addition, indigenous peoples advocate their rights under the right to dignity, as articulated in Article 3 of the Convention. In the case of *Kalderas Gypsies v. Federal Republic of Germany and The Netherlands*,[229] a group of Kalderas Gypsies from Germany and The Netherlands claimed that Germany and The Netherlands violated their right to dignity under Article 3 and their right not to be discriminated against under Article 14 of the Convention because Germany and The Netherlands refused to issue identification papers for the applicants. The Commission observed that refusing to grant identification documents to a nomadic group may amount to a violation of Article 3 as degrading treatment and violation of Article 14 as discrimination.

In another case in this regard, *Assenov and Others v. Bulgaria*,[230] a Roma family of Bulgarian nationality, claimed that police abused Assenov during his arrest. The family claimed that Bulgarian authorities violated Article 3 because they failed to carry out an official investigation into their allegations. The Court accepted the petition and decided that Bulgaria had violated the applicant's right to an effective remedy according to Article 13 of the Convention.[231]

The right to ways of life

The right to ways of life according to Article 8 of the Convention is one the most relevant to indigenous peoples and many cases have dealt with the characteristic ways of life of indigenous peoples.[232]

In *G. and E. v. Norway*,[233] members of the Sami community who traditionally use their lands for reindeer herding, fishing, and hunting filed an application with the Commission regarding a dam construction project and a hydroelectric plant. They claimed that the project would not only force them to lose their land, but also their identity.

Although the case was declared inadmissible by the Commission, it indicated several significant aspects of the reasoning under Article 8 of the Convention. The Commission noted that the applicants belonged to the Lapps minority group who for hundreds of years had been practicing reindeer husbandry, fishing, and hunting. It also noted that there is a great need for space to practice their way of life. Furthermore, it indicated that a minority group is entitled to the right of particular lifestyle and therefore the applicants, as a minority group, are entitled to claim a right to a particular lifestyle according to Article 8 of the Convention.[234]

In addition, the Commission stated that traditional use of land for hunting and grazing "is not a property right within the meaning of Article 1 of the First Protocol." However, the Commission did recognize their right to adequate compensation.[235] According to Thornberry, the Commission failed to protect Sami culture; instead, it assessed the effects of the project primarily in spatial and economic terms rather than in terms of cultural impact. Further, the Commission rebutted any allegation of discrimination. It noted that the European Convention does not guarantee specific rights to minorities and that the applicants had the right to vote and stand for election to the Norwegian Parliament, similar to other Norwegian citizens.[236]

In the case of *Buckley v. UK*,[237] the first Roma case to reach the European Court of Human Rights, a Roma whose family had been based in the area of South Cambridgeshire, UK claimed that UK local authorities refused to grant her permission to park her caravans on her land.[238] The Commission concluded that there had been a violation of Article 8 of the Convention and stated that "The applicant had a right to a home, an autonomous concept which did not depend on classification by domestic law."[239]

The Court, however, took a different view. It decided that there was no violation of the right to way of life and even found that the "special needs of the applicant as a Gypsy following a traditional lifestyle were taken into account."[240] Concerning the applicant's refusal to accept alternative accommodation suggested by the state, the Court stated that "Article 8 does not go so far as to allow individuals' preferences as to their place of residence to override the general interest." Moreover, the Court did not find that the applicant had at any time been deprived from her right to follow her traditional Gypsy/Roma lifestyle. On the contrary, it interpreted UK law as "aimed at enabling Gypsies to cater for their own needs."[241]

The dissenting opinion in *Buckley* is a particularly important one. In that opinion, Judge Pettiti stated that the British policy was discriminatory. He added that if the *Buckley* case were transposed to any other British family the harassment would not have occurred. J. Pettiti added that family life should not be subordinated "to the greater convenience of the local community and its greater willingness to accept others."[242] In his concluding paragraph J. Pettiti expressed his regret that the Court had lost the opportunity for a legal critique of national law transposable to the rest of Europe in partial compensation for injustices suffered by the Gypsy community.[243]

The *Buckley v. UK* case was one of the cases that introduced the inability of the European Court to recognize indigenous peoples' rights, especially the right to "way of life." Following *Buckley*, the Commission considered several applications from Gypsies under Article 8 and Article 1 of the First Protocol, and all but one was declared admissible as raising serious issues of fact and law under the Convention.[244]

The right to property

Article 1 of the First Protocol to the Convention defines property rights. It states:

> Every... person is entitled to the peaceful enjoyment of his possessions. No one shall be deprived of his possessions except in the public interest and subject to the conditions provided for by law and by the general principles of international law.[245]

The Court has taken a broad view on what constitute possessions, and it includes items having economic value such as business goodwill[246] and patents, in addition to land and chattels.[247] Such a view has benefited indigenous peoples in a way that enabled the Court to adopt some of their cultural rights as property rights protected by the Convention.

In *Konkama v. Sweden*[248] the Commission stated that herding, hunting, and fishing "are fundamental elements of the Sami culture" and recognized that specific indigenous rights excluding hunting and fishing fall within the ambit of the First Protocol of the Convention.[249] The case was initiated by Sami villagers who claimed that regulations on small game hunting and fishing violated their exclusive right to hunting and fishing, and thus violated Article 1 of the Protocol. In response, Sweden claimed that the legislation aimed "to give the general public wider access to hunting and fishing in the mountain region."[250]

The Commission observed that "reindeer herding, hunting and fishing are fundamental elements of the Sami culture. And therefore, it considered that "the exclusive hunting and fishing rights claimed by the applicant Sami villages... can be regarded as possessions" within the meaning of the First Protocol.[251] While the Commission did not resolve the question of whether the Sami villages were holders of exclusive hunting and fishing rights, since the case was declared inadmissible, the decision recognized that specific indigenous rights fall within the ambit of the Protocol.[252]

Both the Commission and the Court has dealt with indigenous peoples' rights. Although in some cases they refused to recognize basic rights for indigenous peoples, still in many cases the European system of human rights produced advanced decisions pertaining indigenous peoples. Such development recognizes the rights of indigenous peoples in regional systems and adds to the developing system of international and comparative law that interacts and informs each other.

iii Implementation of the European System of Human Rights

One of the strengths of the European system is the implementation and the execution of the Court's decisions. The Convention provides several mechanisms for implementation, namely Inter-State procedures and individual petitions, as well as a reporting mechanism that ensures the implementation of the Convention. Article 34 of the Convention establishes an individual petition system. It provides that petitions may be received from "any person, non-governmental organization or group of individuals claiming to be a victim of a violation." In 1995 the Framework Convention for the Protection of National Minorities (FCNM) adopted a provision making it a binding instrument with regard to minority rights. This is important because the ECHR does not include specific provision on minority rights, and all attempts to adopt such a provision had failed.[253] The Convention also includes a reporting mechanism according to which states must submit reports to the Secretary-General of the Council of Europe within one year of the Convention application.[254]

In sum, the protection of indigenous peoples' rights is included in the protection of minority rights in the European system. Although the Convention was designated initially to protect national minorities' rights, the definition of "minority" does not exclude indigenous groups from the protection of the Convention. Section 1 of the Convention integrates minority rights and human rights. It states that every person belonging to a national minority is to be treated without disadvantage, and it pertains to individual as well as communal exercise of rights.[255]

The Convention refers to respect of the ethnic, cultural identity of every individual. According to Article 5.1, the parties undertake to promote the conditions necessary for persons belonging to minorities "to maintain and develop their culture, and to preserve the essential elements of their identity, namely their religion, language, traditions and cultural heritage."[256]

The ECHR provides at least some protection of indigenous presence through the right to private life, property, and the principle of nondiscrimination. On the other hand, of all the global and regional instruments, the ECHR is the least developed in the field of ethnic relations and indigenous rights. Some, however, expect future development to occur.

The FCNM incorporates elements of considerable value for indigenous groups. A strong dissenting opinion in *Buckley* and narrow majorities in *Chapman* are evidence of some concern in the Court regarding the approach to the Roma indigenous people. These views could be expanded and perhaps applied to other groups. Minority protection can encompass indigenous peoples' rights. European declarations of human rights focus mainly on the "national minority," however, the term national minority is broad enough to encompass indigenous groups.[257] In some cases, the European system shows an advanced approach, recognizing that "the exclusive hunting and fishing rights claimed by the applicant Sami villages… can be regarded as possessions," as in *Konkama*.[258] Still, there is a lack of major decisions that indicate indigenous land recognition like *Mabo (No. 2)* decided in Australia and *Awas Tingni v. Nicaragua*.[259]

Notes

1 *IPP: International Instruments*, INT'L LAND COAL., http://www.landcoalition.org/global-initiatives/indigenous-peoples-and-pastoralist/ipp-international-instruments (last visited Feb. 5, 2013).
2 IPP: International Instruments | International Land Coalition, http://www.landcoalition.org/global-initiatives/indigenous-peoples-and-pastoralist/ipp-international-instruments (last visited Jan. 28, 2013).
3 RUSSELL, *supra* note 59 at 120–150 (Chapter 5).
4 IPP: International Instruments | International Land Coalition, *supra* note 504.
5 S. JAMES ANAYA, INDIGENOUS PEOPLES IN INTERNATIONAL LAW 7 (2004); Rudiger Wolfrum, *The Protection of Indigenous Peoples in International Law*, 59 HEIDELBERG J. INT'L L. 369, 370 (1999).
6 *IPP: International Instruments*, *supra* note 428.
7 Lorenzo Nesti, *The Mapuche-Pehuenche and the Ralco Dam on the Biobio River: The Challenge of Protecting Indigenous Land Rights*, 9 INT'L J. ON MINORITY & GROUP RTS. 1, 24 (2002).
8 ANAYA, *supra* note 507 at 58.
9 Nesti, Lorenzo, *Indigenous Peoples' Right to Land and Their Link to Environment Protection: The Case of Mapuche-Pehuenche.*, 11 *in* LAW & ANTHROPOLOGY: INTERNATIONAL YEAR BOOK FOR LEGAL ANTHROPOLOGY 67 (René Kuppe & Richard Potz Eds.).
10 ANAYA, *supra* note 507 at 58.
11 S. James Anaya, *Indigenous Rights Norms in Contemporary International Law*, 8 ARIZ. J. INT'L & COMP. L. 1, 7 (1991).
12 *NORMLEX: Information System on International Labour Standards*, INTERNATIONAL LABOUR ORG., http://www.ilo.org/ilolex/cgi-lex/ratifce.pl?C169 (last visited Feb. 5, 2013).

13 ANAYA, *supra* note 507 at 59.
14 Anaya, *supra* note 513 at 7.
15 ANAYA, *supra* note 507 at 60.
16 *Supervision: Conventions Regarding Indigenous and Tribal Peoples*, INTERNATIONAL LABOUR ORG., http://www.ilo.org/indigenous/Conventions/Supervision/lang--en/index.htm (last visited Feb. 5, 2013).
17 ANAYA, *supra* note 507 at 58, 226.
18 *Constitution of the International Labour Organization*, INTERNATIONAL LABOUR ORG., Apr. 1, 1919, art. 26, *available at* http://www.ilo.org/public/english/bureau/leg/download/constitution.pdf.
19 *Id.* at art. 24.
20 ANAYA, *supra* note 507 at 249.
21 *Id.* at 162.
22 Martin Scheinin, *Indigenous Peoples' Land Rights under the International Covenant on Civil and Political Rights* (Apr. 28, 2004) (Torkel Oppsahls minneseminar at Norwegian Centre for Human Rights, University of Oslo), available at http://www.galdu.org/govat/doc/ind_peoples_land_rights.pdf.
23 GILBERT, *supra* note 46 at 129.
24 *Id.*
25 It is important to notice the limitation on individual petitions in States that have refused to sign the additional protocol and therefore not bound by article 27, i.e. individuals from these States cannot use such an instrument. The Human Rights Committee may only consider individual communications relating to State parties to the First Optional Protocol to the International Covenant on Civil and Political Rights. *See Human Rights Bodies – Complaint Procedures*, OFFICE OF THE UNITED NATIONS HIGH COMM'R FOR HUMAN RIGHTS, http://www2.ohchr.org/english/bodies/petitions/index.htm (last visited Feb. 5, 2013).
26 International Covenant on Civil and Political Rights, G.A. Res. 2200A (XXI), U.N. Doc. A/6316 (1966) (Mar. 23, 1976), *available at* http://www2.ohchr.org/english/law/ccpr.htm.
27 Human Rights Comm., General Comment No. 23: The Rights of Minorities (Art. 27), 50th sess, Aug. 4, 1994 ¶ 7, U.N. Doc. CCPR/C/21/Rev.1/Add.5 (1994), *available at* http://www.unhchr.ch/tbs/doc.nsf/0/fb7fb12c2fb8bb21c12563ed004df111?Opendocument (emphasis added).
28 S. James Anaya, *Indigenous Rights Norms in Contemporary International Law*, 8 ARIZ. J. INT'L & COMP. L. 1, 17 (1991).
29 ANAYA, *supra* note 507 at 134.
30 GILBERT, *supra* note 46 at 159–160.
31 *See* Martin Scheinin, *The Right to Enjoy a Distinct Culture: Indigenous and Competing Uses of Land*, in THE JURISPRUDENCE OF HUMAN RIGHTS LAW: A COMPARATIVE INTERPRETIVE APPROACH (Theodore S. Orlin et al., eds., 2000).
32 ANAYA, *supra* note 507 at 134.
33 GILBERT, *supra* note 46 at 129.
34 Human Rights Comm., Lovelace v. Canada Communication No. R.6/24 ¶ 166 U.N. Doc. Supp. No. 40 (A/36/40) (Jul. 30, 1981).
35 *Id.*; *see also Caselaw Database: Lovelace v. Canada, Communication No. 24/1977*, INT'L NETWORK FOR ECON., SOC. & CULTURAL RTS (ESCR-NET), http://www.escr-net.org/docs/i/1307559 (last visited Feb. 5, 2013) (providing a concise case summary of Lovelace v. Canada).
36 GILBERT, *supra* note 46 at 160.
37 Martin Scheinin, *The Right to Enjoy a Distinct Culture: Indigenous and Competing Uses of Land*, in THE JURISPRUDENCE OF HUMAN RIGHTS LAW: A COMPARATIVE INTERPRETIVE APPROACH, 165 (2000).
38 GILBERT, *supra* note 46 at 128–134.

39 Athanasia Spiliopoulou Åkermark, Justifications of Minority Protection in International Law 158 (1996).
40 Human Rights Comm., Kitok v. Sweden (Communication No. 197/1985) ¶ 9.8, U.N. Doc. CCPR/C/33/D/197/1985 (Jul. 27, 1988).
41 *Id.*; *see also* Gilbert, *supra* note 46 at 129.
42 *Id.* at 129.
43 Human Rights Comm., Chief Bernard Ominayak and Lubicon Lake Band v. Canada Communication No. 167/1984, U.N. Doc. CCPR/C/38/D/167/1984 (May 10, 1990); *see also Id.* at 128–129. (discussing the cultural right to a way of life).
44 Human Rights Comm., Chief Bernard Ominayak and Lubicon Lake Band v. Canada Communication No. 167/1984, U.N. Doc. CCPR/C/38/D/167/1984 (May 10, 1990).
45 *Id.* at annex IX.A; See also S. James Anaya & Robert A. Jr Williams, *Protection of Indigenous Peoples' Rights over Lands and Natural Resources under the Inter-American Human Rights System, The*, 14 Harv. Hum. Rts. J. 33, 73 (2001).
46 Anaya and Williams, *supra* note 547.
47 Jérémie Gilbert, *Nomadic Territories: A Human Rights Approach to Nomadic Peoples' Land Rights*, 7 Hum. Rts. L. Rev. 681, 697 (2007).
48 Gilbert, *supra* note 46 at 136.
49 *Id.*
50 Benedict Kingsbury, *Claims by Non-State Groups in International Law*, 25 Cornell Int'l L. J. 481, 481 (1992).
51 Gilbert, *supra* note 46 at 130.
52 Scheinin, *supra* note 539.
53 *Id.* at 173 ("One may infer from the case that whenever a state decides to take legislation or other action in relation to earlier dispossession of indigenous lands, these measures will be subject to review despite the rationae temporis rule.").
54 Human Rights Comm., Chief Bernard Ominayak and Lubicon Lake Band v. Canada Communication No. 167/1984, U.N. Doc. CCPR/C/38/D/167/1984 (May 10, 1990); *see also* Gilbert, *supra* note 46 at 160.
55 *Id.* at 160.; Scheinin, *supra* note 539 at 173.
56 See generally Scheinin, *supra* note 539.
57 Gilbert, *supra* note 46 at 128 (discussing protection of land rights as part of the environment protection); Scheinin, *supra* note 539.
58 Human Rights Comm., Sara et al. v. Finland, Communication No. 431/1990, U.N. Doc. CCPR/C/50/D/431/1990 (Mar. 24, 1994).
59 Human Rights Comm., Lansman et al. v. Finland, Communication No. 511/1992, U.N. Doc. CCPR/C/52/D/511/1992 (Nov. 8, 1994).
60 Lorenzo Nesti, *supra* note 511.
61 Human Rights Comm., Lansman et al. v. Finland, Communication No. 511/1992 ¶9.8, U.N. Doc. CCPR/C/52/D/511/1992 (Nov. 8, 1994).
62 *Id.* at ¶ 9.3.; *see also* Scheinin, *supra* note 539.
63 Jérémie Gilbert, Indigenous Peoples' Land Rights under International Law 172 (1 ed. 2006).
64 *See* Delgamuukw v. British Columbia, [1997] 3 S.C.R. 1010 (Can.); *see also* John Borrows, *Frozen Rights in Canada: Constitutional Interpretation and the Trickster* 22 Am. Indian L. Rev. 37 (1997).
65 Human Rights Comm., Jouni E. Lansman et al. v. Finland, Communication No. 671/1995, U.N. Doc. CCPR/C/58/D/671/1995 (Oct. 30, 1996).
66 *Id.* at ¶ 10.7.
67 Gilbert, *supra* note 46 at 135.
68 Human Rights Comm., Hopu et al. v. France, Communication No. 549/1993, U.N. Doc. CCPR/C/60/D/549/1993/Rev.1 (Dec. 29, 1997).

69 GILBERT, *supra* note 46 at 135.
70 International Covenant on Civil and Political Rights, G.A. Res. 2200A (XXI), U.N. Doc. A/6316 (1966) (Mar. 23, 1976), *available at* http://www2.ohchr.org/english/law/ccpr.htm.
71 GILBERT, *supra* note 46 at 135.
72 Ostra v. Spain A303-C Eur. Ct. of H.R. xx (1994).
73 Article 8 of European Convention on Human Rights deals with the right to privacy and family life, home, and correspondence. Convention for the Protection of Human Rights and Fundamental Freedoms art. 8, Nov. 4, 1950, C.E.T.S. No. 005.
74 Lorenzo Nesti, *supra* note 511.
75 Human Rights Comm., Hopu et al. v. France, Communication No. 549/1993, U.N. Doc. CCPR/C/60/D/549/1993/Rev.1 (Dec. 29, 1997).
76 GILBERT, *supra* note 46 at 130, 134–136 (discussing land protection under the "Cultural Heritage approach").
77 *Id.*
78 Scheinin, *supra* note 539 at 162.
79 GILBERT, *supra* note 46 at 135–136.
80 *Id.* at 136.
81 *Id.*
82 Kayano et al. v. Hokkaido Expropriation Committee (Mar. 27, 1997), *translation reprinted in 38* I.L.M. 397 (1999).
83 GILBERT, *supra* note 46 at 136.
84 Kayano et al. v. Hokkaido Expropriation Committee (Mar. 27, 1997), *reprinted in 38* I.L.M. 397 (1999).
85 *Id.*
86 *See* Rep. of the Special Rapporteur on Contemporary Forms of Racism, Racial Discrimination, Xenophobia and Related Intolerance Calling for the Recognition of the Ainu as indigenous peoples, U.N. Doc. E1CN.4/2006/16/Add.2 (2006), *cited in* GILBERT, *supra* note 46 at 136.
87 *Id.* at 136.
88 *Id.* at 137.
89 *Aboriginal and Torres Strait Islander Heritage Protection Act 1984* (Cth) (Austl.); *Aboriginal Cultural Heritage Act 2003* (Qld) (Austl.).
90 *Id.*
91 *See Noonkanbah Pastoral Co Pty Ltd. v. Amax Iron Corporation* (Unreported, WA Supreme Court, June 1979) (Austl.); *see also* David Ritter, *The Fulcrum of Noonkanbah*, COUNTRY: J. OF AUSTRALIAN STUD. 2002, at 1, *available at* http://www.api-network.com/main/index.php?apply=scholars&webpage=default&flexedit=&flex_password=&menu_label=&menuID=homely&menubox=&scholar=112.
92 GILBERT, *supra* note 46 at 697.
93 *Id.*
94 Lorenzo Nesti, *supra* note 511 at 36.
95 *Id.*
96 *Id.* at 37.
97 *Procedure for Complaints by Individuals under the Human Rights Treaties*, OFFICE OF THE HIGH COMMISSIONER FOR HUMAN RIGHTS, http://www2.ohchr.org/english/bodies/petitions/individual.htm (last visited Feb. 5, 2013).
98 *See* Cynthia Price Cohen, *International Protection of the Rights of Indiginous Childern*, in THE HUMAN RIGHTS OF INDIGENOUS PEOPLES (Cynthia Price Cohen ed., 1998).
99 *Id.* at 40.
100 Nesti Lorenzo, *supra* note 511.

101 *Id.* at 41.
102 Convention against Discrimination in Education, http://portal.unesco.org/en/ev.php-URL_ID=12949&URL_DO=DO_TOPIC&URL_SECTION=201.html (last visited Jan. 6, 2012).
103 J. K. Das, Human Rights and Indigenous Peoples 72 (2001).
104 Lorenzo Nesti, *supra* note 511.
105 Robert K. Hitchcock, *International Human Rights, the Environment, and Indigenous Peoples*, 5 Colo. J. Int'l Envtl. L. & Pol'y 1, 14 (1994).
106 *Id.* at 14.
107 Ronald Paul Hill, *Blackfellas and Whitefellas: Aboriginal Land Rights, the Mabo Decision, and the Meaning of Land*, Hum. Rts. Q., May 1995 at 303, 309.
108 *Id.* at 314.
109 *History or Sustainable Development*, Vancouver Valuation Accord, http://vancouveraccord.org/the-global-context/history-of-sustainable-development (last visited Feb. 5, 2013).
110 Gilbert, *supra* note 46 at 124–128.
111 Lorenzo Nesti, *supra* note 511.
112 Gilbert, *supra* note 46 at 284.
113 Cherie Metcalf, *Indigenous Rights and the Environment: Evolving International Law*, 35 Ottawa L. Rev. 101, 101 (2003).
114 *Id.*
115 *Id.* at 104.
116 Metcalf, *supra* note 614 at 104.
117 *Id.* at 110–111.
118 The Biodiversity Convention; see also Metcalf *Id.* at 113.
119 Lorenzo Nesti, *supra* note 434 at 37; Alan E. Boyle, *The Rio Convention on Biological Diversity*, *in* International Law and the Conservation of Biological Diversity, 48 (1st ed. 1996).
120 Metcalf, *supra* note 614 at 107–109.
121 Lorenzo Nesti, *supra* note 511 at 38.
122 *Agenda 21- Chapter 26: Recognizing and Strengthening the Role of Indigenous People and Their Communities*, Information Habitat: Where Information Lives, http://habitat.igc.org/agenda21/a21-26.htm (last visited Feb. 5, 2013).
123 Draft Principles on Human Rights and the Environment, Jul. 6, 1994, UN Doc. E/CN.4/Sub.2/1994/9, Jul. 6, 1994, ¶ 74, *available* at http://www1.umn.edu/humanrts/instree/1994-dec.htm.
124 *Sustainable Development and Indigenous Peoples*, International Work Group for Indigenous Affairs, http://www.iwgia.org/environment-and-development/sustainable-development (last visited Feb. 5, 2013).
125 Metcalf, *supra* note 614 at 119–120.
126 *Id.*
127 *Id.* at 121.
128 Anaya, *supra* note 507 at 150.
129 *Id.* at 155.
130 Lorenzo Nesti, *supra* note 511.
131 *Id.*
132 *Id.*
133 World Bank, *Operational Manual Statement 2.34: Tribal People in Bank-Financed Projects*, at ¶ 6, OMS 2.34 (Feb. 1982).
134 *See Social Development: Indigenous Peoples Policy*, World Bank, http://web.worldbank.org/WBSITE/EXTERNAL/TOPICS/EXTSOCIALDEVELOPMENT/EXTINDPEOPLE/0,,contentMDK:20443667~menuPK:906528~pagePK:210058~piPK:210062~theSitePK:407802,00.html (last updated Apr. 2, 2010).

135 World Bank, *World Bank Operational Manual: Indigenous Peoples*, at ¶ 3, OD 4.20 (Sept. 1991).

136 *Id.* at ¶ 8.

137 The World Bank is comprised of four quasi-autonomous institutions supervised by a common President and personnel office. The International Bank of Reconstruction and Development (IBRD) and the International Development Association (IDA) constitute the World Bank proper, but together with the Multilateral Investment Guarantee Agency (MIGA) and the International Finance Corporation (IFC), which is legally, financially and operationally separate from the World Bank, they make up the World Bank Group. Lorenzo Nesti, *supra* note 511.

138 World Bank, *Operational Directive 4.20: Indigenous Peoples*, at ¶ 2, OD 4.20, (Sept. 1991).

139 Anaya, *supra* note 507 at 183.

140 Tom Griffiths, Indigenous Peoples and the World Bank: Experiences with Participation, Forest Peoples Programme (Jul. 2005), *available at* http://www.forestpeoples.org/sites/fpp/files/publication/2011/08/wbipsandparticipjul05eng.pdf.

141 Aharon Barak, *Human Rights in Israel*, 39 Isr. L. Rev. 12 (2006).

142 *Id.* at 25.

143 Eyal Benvenisti, *The Applicability of Human Rights Conventions to Israel and to the Occupied Territories**, 26 Israel Law Review 24–35, 24, 34 (1992).

144 HCJ 390/79 Duweikat v State of Israel LD(1) PD 1 [1979] (Isr.).

145 Guy Ophir, *Meshpat benliaomi: maamadai hameshpati shel amanoot benleaoniot baysrael [International Law: The Legal Status of International Conventions in Israel]*, Ophir Law Firm, http://www.ophirlaw.com/%D7%9E%D7%A9%D7%A4%D7%98_%D7%91%D7%99%D7%A0%D7%9C%D7%90%D7%95%D7%9E%D7%99/ (last visited Feb. 5, 2013) (discussing the status of international law in Israel); Yaffa Zilbershats, *The Adoption of International Law into Israeli Law: The Real is Ideal,* 24 Mishpatim 317 (1994); *see also* Yaffa Zilbershats, *The Role of International Law in Israeli Constitutional Law*, 4 Mishpat Umimshal 47 (1997).

146 *See* Benvenisti, *supra* note 644.; *see also* International Court of Justice, Summaries of Judgments Advisory Opinions & Orders of the International Court 53 (2003–2007).

147 G.A. Res. 2200A (XXI), U.N. GAOR, 21st Sess., Supp. No. 16, U.N. Doc. A/6316 (1966) (ratified by Israel on Jan. 3, 1992).

148 *Id.*

149 G.A. Res. 34/180, U.N. GAOR, 34th Sess., Supp. No. 46, U.N. Doc. A/34/46 (ratified by Israel on Nov. 2, 1991).

150 G.A. Res. 2106 (XX) Annex, U.N. GAOR, 20th Sess., Supp. No. 14, U.N. Doc. A/6014 (1966) (ratified by Israel on Feb. 2, 1979).

151 G.A. Res. 44/25 Annex, U.N. GAOR, 44th Sess., Supp. No. 49, U.N. Doc. A/44/49 (1989) (ratified by Israel on Nov. 2, 1991).

152 OHCHR | Session9 United Nations Fact Finding Mission on the Gaza conflict, UN Human Rights Council, https://www.ohchr.org/EN/HRBodies/HRC/SpecialSessions/Session9/Pages/FactFindingMission.aspx (last visited Mar. 26, 2020).

153 Jackson Diehl, *A Shadow on the Human Rights Movement*, The Wash. Post, Jun. 25, 2007, http://www.washingtonpost.com/wp-dyn/content/article/2007/06/24/AR2007062401373.html; *see also* Association for Civil Rights in Israel, State of Human Rights in Israel and the Occupied Territories (Dec. 2008), available at http://www.acri.org.il/pdf/state2008.pdf.

154 OHCHR | Session9 United Nations Fact Finding Mission on the Gaza conflict, *supra* note 653.

155 See generally Swirski and Hasson, *supra* note 167.
156 See Rangwala, *supra* note 391.
157 *Convention on the Elimination of All Forms of Discrimination Against Women: Why an Optional Protocol?*, Division of the Advancement of Women- Department of Economic and Social Affairs, http://www.un.org/womenwatch/daw/cedaw/protocol/why.htm (last visited Feb. 5, 2013); *see also First Optional Protocol to the International Covenant on Civil and Political Rights: Overview of Procedure*, Office of the High Commissioner for Human Rights, http://www2.ohchr.org/english/bodies/hrc/procedure.htm (last visited Feb. 5, 2013); Anaya, *supra* note 507 at 253 (discussing individual communication generally).
158 *Article 14 of the International Convention on the Elimination of All Forms of Racial Discrimination: Overview of Procedure*, Office of the High Commissioner for Human Rights, http://www2.ohchr.org/english/bodies/cerd/procedure.htm (last visited Feb. 5, 2013).
159 *Id.*
160 *See Treaties Collection Optional Protocol to the Convention on the Elimination of All Forms of Discrimination against Women*, United Nations, http://treaties.un.org/Pages/ViewDetails.aspx?src=TREATY&mtdsg_no=IV-8-b&chapter=4&lang=en (last visited Feb. 5, 2013) (listing the signatories and dates of signature, accession, ratification, and/or succession to the Optional Protocol to the Convention on the Elimination of All Forms of Discrimination against Women).
161 *Id.*; Comm. on the Elimination of Racial Discrimination, Consideration of Reports Submitted by States Parties -Concluding Observations of the Committee on the Elimination of Racial Discrimination– ISRAEL, art. 39, 70th sess, Feb. 19–Mar. 9, 2007, U.N. Doc. CERD/C/ISR/CO/13 (Jun. 14, 2007), *available at* http://unispal.un.org/UNISPAL.NSF/0/041AB84D2F05080C85257302004A9963.
162 *History or Sustainable Development*, *supra* note 534.
163 Florencia Roulet, Human Rights and Indigenous Peoples: A Handbook on the UN System 106–107 (1999); *see also* Anaya, *supra* note 507 at 226–228.
164 *Convention No. 169*, Int'l Labour Org., http://www.ilo.org/indigenous/Conventions/no169/lang--en/index.htm (last visited Feb. 5, 2013).
165 Stephen Wheatley, *The Legal Status of the UN Declaration on the Rights of Indigenous Peoples*, 7 Yale L. Pol'y Rev. Inter Alia 60, 61 (2010).
166 Ehud Ein-Gil, *Letzaarino nevtzar meetano leshkol lehitnagid [Unfortunately We Could Not Consider Objecting*], Haaretz (Oct. 1, 2007), http://www.haaretz.co.il/misc/1.1445868.
167 *Convention No. 169*, Int'l Labour Org., http://www.ilo.org/indigenous/Conventions/no169/lang--en/index.htm (last visited Feb. 5, 2013).
168 Gilbert, *supra* note 46 at 179.
169 Lorenzo Nesti, *Indigenous Peoples' Right to Land and Their Link to Environment Protection: The Case of Mapuche-Pehuenche.*, 11 Law & anthropology: Int'l y.b. for legal anthropology 67, 68 (2001).
170 *Id.* at 28.
171 *Id.*
172 *See* Aloeboetoe v. Suriname, Case 10.150, Inter-Am. Comm'n H.R., Report No. 03/90, OEA/ Ser.C./11 ¶ 96 (1991) (Suriname soldiers attacked a group of the Sarima Tribe of Maroons, killing seven).
173 *Id.*
174 Lorenzo Nesti, *supra* note 511.
175 See Jonathan L. Mannina, *Human Rights Implications of Economic Development: A Case Study of the Huaorani People of Ecuador, The* 5 Geo. Int'l Envtl. L. Rev. 117 (1992).

176 Lorenzo Nesti, *supra* note 511.

177 A. Fabra, *Indigenous Peoples, Environmental Degradation and Human Rights: A Case Study*, in HUMAN RIGHTS APPROACHES TO ENVIRONMENTAL PROTECTION 250, 260 (A. E. Boyle & M. R. Anderson eds., 1996); *see also* Francis O. Adeola, *Environmental Injustice and Human Rights Abuse: The States, MNCs, and Repression of Minority Groups in the World System*, 8 HUM. ECOLOGY REV. 1, 45 (2001).

178 ANAYA, *supra* note 507 at 137.

179 *Id.* at 134.

180 Mayagna Community of Awas Tingni v. Nicaragua, Merits, Reparations, and Costs, Judgment, Inter-Am. Ct. H.R. (ser. C) No. 79, (Aug. 31, 2001).

181 Claudio Grossman, *Awas Tingni v. Nicaragua: A Landmark Case for the Inter-American System*, 8 HUM. RTS. BRIEF 2, 8.

182 *Id.* at 2.

183 S. James Anaya & Claudio Grossman, *The Case of Awas Tingni v. Nicaragua: A New Step in the International Law of Indigenous Peoples*, 19 ARIZ. J. INT'L & COMP. L. 1, 1–2 (2002).

184 Grossman, *supra* note 682.

185 ANAYA, *supra* note 507 at 145.

186 *The European Union Strongly Criticizes Israel for Human Rights Violations – But Calls for Strengthening Economic Cooperation With It*, ADALAH, THE LEGAL CENTER FOR ARAB MINORITY RIGHTS IN ISRAEL (Jul. 29, 2012), http://www.adalah.org/heb/?mod=articles&ID=1291.

187 Eran Zedekiah & Jaob Kept-Kunz, *Yahasi yesrael vehaaihod haeropi: hakesef medaber hazak yotir mehapolitika [Israel and the European Union Relations: Money Talks Stronger Than Politics]*, CANTHINK.CO.IL (Nov. 25, 2011), http://canthink.co.il/%D7%99%D7%A9%D7%A8%D7%90%D7%9C/%D7%99%D7%97%D7%A1%D7%99-%D7%99%D7%A9%D7%A8%D7%90%D7%9C-%D7%95%D7%94%D7%90%D7%99%D7%97%D7%95%D7%93-%D7%94%D7%90%D7%99%D7%A8%D7%95%D7%A4%D7%99-%D7%94%D7%9B%D7%A1%D7%A3-%D7%9E%D7%93%D7%91%D7%A8-%D7%97%D7%96%D7%A7-%D7%99%D7%95%D7%AA%D7%A8-%D7%9E%D7%94%D7%A4%D7%95%D7%9C%D7%99%D7%98%D7%99%D7%A7%D7%94.aspx.

188 Timo Koivurova, *Jurisprudence of the European Court of Human Rights Regarding Indigenous Peoples: Retrospect and Prospects,* 18 INT'L J. ON MINORITY AND GROUP RTS. 1, 37 (2011).

189 *The European Human Rights System*, HUMAN RIGHTS ED. ASS., http://www.hrea.org/index.php?doc_id=365 (last visited Feb. 5, 2013).

190 *Id.*

191 ARTHUR HENRY ROBERTSON, HUMAN RIGHTS IN EUROPE 4 (1963).

192 William K. Coblentz & Robert S. Warshaw, *European Convention for the Protection of Human Rights and Fundamental Freedoms*, 44 CALIF. L. REV. 94, 94 (1956).

193 *Id.* at 94–95.

194 Convention for the Protection of Human Rights and Fundamental Freedoms, as amended by Protocols No. 11 and No. 14 preamble, Nov. 4, 1950, C.E.T.S. No. 194.

195 *Id.*

196 RHONA K. M. SMITH & CHRISTIEN VAN DEN ANKER, THE ESSENTIALS OF HUMAN RIGHTS 115 (2005).

197 *Id.* at 117.

198 *Id.* at 115.

199 *Id.* at 115.

200 *Id.* at 116.
201 *Id.*
202 *Id.* at 117.
203 Helen Keller & Alec Stone-Sweet, A Europe of Rights: The Impact of the ECHR on National Legal Systems (2008).
204 Patrick Thornberry, Indigenous Peoples and Human Rights 290 (2002).
205 *Id.*
206 *Id.*
207 European Commission against Racism and Intolerance, Recommendation No. 3 on Combating Racism and Intolerance against Roma/Gypsies (Mar. 6, 1998).
208 *See generally* Q. C. Boyle & Christine Lesley, *A Human Right to Group Self-Identification? Reflections on Nixon v. Vancouver Rape Relief*, 23 Can. J. of Women & L., 488 (2011).
209 Thornberry, *supra* note 705 at 291.
210 Ahmat Sadiq v. Greece, 1996-V Eur. Ct. H.R. 20.
211 *Id.*
212 *Id.*
213 Thornberry, *supra* note 705 at 291.
214 Sidiropoulos et al. v. Greece, 1998-IV Eur. Ct. H.R. 1.
215 *Id.* at ¶¶ 8, 9.
216 Belgian Linguistics Case (No. 2) 6 Eur. Ct. H.R. (ser. A) (1968).
217 Thornberry, *supra* note 628 at 293.
218 *Id.*
219 F. Hampson, *Recent Turkish Cases: Their Contribution to the Case Law of the European Court of Human Rights*, 4 Hum. Rts. L. Rev. 9 (1999).
220 Thornberry, *supra* note 628 at 294.
221 2000-VI Eur. Ct. H.R. 42.
222 Netherland Inst. of Hum. Rts. Utrecht School of L., http://sim.law.uu.nl/sim/caselaw/Hof.nsf/1d4d0dd240bfee7ec12568490035df05/59430341a8ee7a15c12568e4003919b8?OpenDocument (last updated Apr. 19, 2012).
223 Velikova v. Bulgaria, 2000-VI Eur. Ct. H.R. 42. ¶ 94.
224 *Caselaw Database: Chapman v. The United Kingdom (Application no. 27238/95)*, Int'l Network for Econ., Soc. & Cultural Rts. (ESCR-Net), http://www.escr-net.org/caselaw/caselaw_show.htm?doc_id=673056 (last visited Feb. 5, 2013); *see also* Hum. Rts. Info. Bull., Nov. 2000-Feb. 2001, at 1, 7–9, *available at* http://www.coe.int/t/dgi/publications/bulletin/hrib52_en.pdf.
225 *Id.*
226 2000-IV Eur. Ct. H.R 56.
227 *Id.* at ¶ 44.
228 Protocol No. 12 to the Convention for the Protection of Human Rights and Fundamental Freedoms, Nov. 4, 2000, C.E.T.S. No. 177.
229 No. 7823/77 and 7824/77, 11 DR (1977), 221.
230 No. 24760/94, Judgment of 28 October 1998.
231 No. 24760/94, Judgment of 28 October 1998, ¶ 118.
232 Thornberry, *supra* note 705 at 297.
233 G. and E. v Norway, Nos. 9278/81 and 9415/81, DR 35 (1983), 30–45.
234 *Id.*
235 Thornberry, *supra* note 628 at 298.
236 *Id.* at 297.
237 Application No. 20348/92. case summary: http://sim.law.uu.nl/SIM/CaseLaw/Hof.nsf/1d4d0dd240bfee7ec12568490035df05/83e28037f52484c9c1256640004c3054?OpenDocument.

238 Permission was refused because of the ugly nature of the caravans, the concentration of gypsy caravans in the area, and the availability of an official gypsy site. *Id.*
239 *Id.* at ¶ 63.
240 *Id.* at ¶ 80, *see also* THORNBERRY, *supra* note 705 at 300.
241 *Id.* at ¶ 88; *see also Id.* at 300.
242 *Id.*, *quoted in Id.* at 300.
243 *Id.* at 300.
244 *Id.* at 300.
245 Convention for the Protection of Human Rights and Fundamental Freedoms art. 1, Nov. 4, 1950, C.E.T.S. No. 005.
246 Van Marle and Others v The Netherlands (1986), Ser. A., No. 101, para. 41.
247 No. 12633/87, Smith Kline and French Laboratories v The Netherlands, DR 66 (1990), 70.
248 No. 27033/95, Konkama and 28 other Saami Villages v Sweden, DR 77/78.
249 THORNBERRY, *supra* note 705 at 305.
250 *Id.* at 305.
251 *Id.*
252 *Id.*
253 In 1995, the Committee of Ministers opened the Framework Convention for the Protection of National Minorities, Feb. 1, 1995, C.E.T.S. No. 157, which addressed the problem of lack of binding instrument in the Council of Europe, for signature. *Id.* at 307.
254 Framework Convention for the Protection of National Minorities art. 25.1, Feb. 1, 1995, C.E.T.S. No. 157.
255 *Id.*
256 *Id.* at 309.
257 *Id.* at 317.
258 *Id.* at 290.
259 GUÐMUNDUR S. ALFREÐSSON & MARIA STAVROPOULOU, JUSTICE PENDING: INDIGENOUS PEOPLES AND OTHER GOOD CAUSES : ESSAYS IN HONOUR OF ERICA-IRENE A. DAES 163 (2002).v

Bibliography

Anaya, S. J. (1991). Indigenous Rights Norms in Contemporary International Law. *Arizona Journal of International and Comparative Law*, *8*, 1.

Anaya, S. J. (2004). *Indigenous Peoples in International Law.* Oxford University Press.

Anaya, S. J., & Williams, R. A. J. (2001). Protection of Indigenous Peoples' Rights over Lands and Natural Resources under the Inter-American Human Rights System. *The Harvard Human Rights Journal*, *14*, 33.

Benvenisti, E. (1992). The Applicability of Human Rights Conventions to Israel and to the Occupied Territories*. *Israel Law Review*, *26*(1), 24–35. https://doi.org/10.1017/S0021223700010803.

Boyle, A. E. (1996). The Rio Convention on Biological Diversity. In M. Bowman & C. Redgwell (Eds.), *International Law and the Conservation of Biological Diversity* (1st ed.). Kluwer Law International, 48

Gilbert, J. (2006). *Indigenous Peoples' Land Rights under International Law* (1st ed.). BRILL.

Grossman, C. (n.d.). Awas Tingni v. Nicaragua: A Landmark Case for the Inter-American System. *Human Rights Brief*, *8*(3), 2.

Hitchcock, R. K. (1994). International Human Rights, the Environment, and Indigenous Peoples. *Colorado Journal of International Environmental Law and Policy, 5*, 1.

IPP: International Instruments | International Land Coalition. (n.d.). Retrieved January 28, 2013, from http://www.landcoalition.org/global-initiatives/indigenous-peoples-and-pastoralist/ipp-international-instruments.

Mannina, J. L. (1992). Human Rights Implications of Economic Development: A Case Study of the Huaorani People of Ecuador. *The Georgetown International Environmental Law Review, 5*, 117.

Metcalf, C. (2003). Indigenous Rights and the Environment: Evolving International Law. *Ottawa Law Review, 35*, 101.

Nesti, L. (n.d.). Indigenous peoples' Right to Land and Their Link to Environment Protection: The Case of Mapuche-Pehuenche. In R. Kuppe & R. Potz (Eds.), *Law & Anthropology: International Year Book for Legal Anthropology* (Vol. 11, p. 67). Springer.

OHCHR | Session9 United Nations Fact Finding Mission on the Gaza conflict. (n.d.). UN Human Rights Council. Retrieved March 26, 2020, from https://www.ohchr.org/EN/HRBodies/HRC/SpecialSessions/Session9/Pages/FactFindingMission.aspx.

Rangwala, T. S. (2004). Inadequate Housing, Israel, and the Bedouin of the Negev. *Osgoode Hall Law Journal, 42*, 415.

Russell, P. H. (2006). *Recognising Aboriginal title: The Mabo Case and Indigenous Resistance to English-Settler Colonialism.* UNSW Press.

Scheinin, M. (2000). The Right to Enjoy a Distinct Culture: Indigenous and Competing Uses of Land. In T. S. Orlin, M. Scheinin, & A. Rosas (Eds.), *The Jurisprudence of Human Rights Law: A Comparative Interpretive Approach.* Institute for Human Rights, Åbo Akademi University, pp. 253–286.

Smith, R. K. M., & Anker, C. van den. (2005). *The Essentials of Human Rights.* Hodder Arnold.

Swirski, S., & Hasson, Y. (2006). *Invisible Citizens: Israel Government Policy toward the Negev Bedouin.* Adva Center.

Thornberry, P. (2002). *Indigenous Peoples and Human Rights.* Juris Publishing, Inc.

Wolfrum, R. (1999). The Protection of Indigenous Peoples in International Law. *Heidelberg J. INT'L L., 59*, 369.

5 Recognition of indigenous peoples' land rights

Recognition of indigenous peoples' land rights is a long and complicated mission, but not impossible, as many cases dealing with indigenous peoples illustrate.[1] While many states continue to deny indigenous peoples' land rights, many others recognize different levels and forms of land rights for indigenous peoples. Some states recognize rights similar to ownership,[2] and others recognize different forms of rights, such as land use under different methods of rights' protection, such as rights to cultural protection, and as in the case of the indigenous Ainu in Japan, recognition of the "right to use traditional land" under the protection of their traditional lifestyle for the Sami people in Sweden.[3] Other states such as Australia and Canada offer a wider range of land recognition under the doctrine of "Native Title."[4]

This recognition resulted from a long enduring struggle and many sacrifices. Some indigenous peoples have struggled for hundreds of years and some have even engaged in war to regain rights to their traditional lands. For many native groups, this process is long and entails work on several levels, using different approaches affecting the social, political, and legal environment in the states where they are located.

The process of recognition and its results vary from one country to another. Even in countries with similar common law legal systems and similar colonial backgrounds, such as Canada and Australia, the process of the struggle and its results differ. Therefore, each movement differs in several perspectives according to historical, legal, political, and other circumstances.

Each native group's struggle for land rights and recognition provides lessons for other groups, pushing others to search for better strategies to get their rights recognized and protected. Despite the many differences between various indigenous groups, there are many common similarities in their methods, plans, and strategies that contribute to their success. These similarities constitute a roadmap for indigenous peoples' struggle for land recognition.

The choice of this research to investigate and learn from the experience of the Aboriginal peoples of Australia is not a random one. The Aboriginal case study is the most relevant to the Bedouin case, since they share many similarities. While Canada and New Zealand also recognize the land rights of indigenous peoples, Australia is the best example that can be applied to the Bedouin struggle, and provides the best methods and strategies. The indigenous struggles in Canada and New Zealand are not as well-suited because of their "treaty system," political power, and legal system.

On the other hand, the struggle of the Aboriginal peoples of Australia is comparable to the case of the Bedouins and has the potential to inform them of how to assert land rights. Despite the fact that the recognition of indigenous peoples' land rights in Australia and Canada is limited to native title (i.e., do not offer traditional land ownership),[5] native title is not an "empty" right.[6] On the contrary, native title provides many advantages and protections of their rights, culture, language, and resources, and secures the use of their traditional lands. The Australian scheme, which affords land rights to Aboriginal Australians, is considered the most successful way to recognize the land rights of indigenous people because it has the farthest-reaching level of land recognition among the Settler colonial states. In addition, judicial recognition of Aboriginal land rights could inform the struggle for the land rights of the Bedouin in Israel because of its similarities to the Bedouin legal struggle. Further, similarities in state policies against Aborigines and Bedouin, and the similarities in the two groups' life conditions, make many of the Aborigines' methods applicable to the case of the Bedouin. Further still, Aboriginal numbers among the Australian population constitute a very small percentage of the population (2.5 percent),[7] which is similar to the population of Bedouins in Israel (2.7 percent).[8] However, the most important similarity is the existence of similar legal doctrines that deny their traditional land rights – the *terra nullius* doctrine and the *Mawat* doctrine.

This section introduces the community struggle of Aborigines for land recognition in Australia and compares it with the Bedouin struggle for land recognition in order to find the basic elements and the main reasons that led to recognition of indigenous land in Australia, in order to see to what degree they are applicable to the case of the Bedouin. Then, it discusses how the Aboriginal experience can inform the Bedouin about the best plans and strategies of "struggle management."

At the end, this chapter suggests a strategy for the Bedouin struggle for land recognition and makes recommendations that could inform Bedouin leaders, nongovernmental organizations (NGOs), and activists about new and better ways of achieving land rights in Israel, as well as other places where indigenous peoples continue to fight for land rights.

Aboriginal struggle for land rights

At the beginning, it is important to introduce the environment in which the court reached its revolutionary decision in the *Mabo* case. Such introduction includes the sociopolitical background and the events that brought some kinds of land recognition prior to the *Mabo* case. It also shows that the *Mabo* decision is not the whole picture of land recognition, but only the judicial chapter of a long struggle of aboriginal land recognition.

This section describes the developments of the struggle and includes two phases: the beginning of the struggle and the effect (result) of the struggle prior to the *Mabo* decision. It also describes, in a nutshell, some of methods aborigines utilized during their struggle, such as demonstrations, campaigns, and petitions. At the end of the section it also describes some changes on the international level that affected the struggle and pushed the government to accept the demands of Aboriginal peoples.

The begininng of the struggle: the use of modern methods

The struggle of Aborigines for land rights began long before the modern land rights movement, and long before the legal struggle in the *Milirrpum* and *Mabo (No. 2)* cases.[9] During the colonization of Australia, as early as 1820, Aborigines pled for land rights and compensation for loss of their traditional land.[10] However, their modern struggle started only at the beginning of the 20th century when they started to use "the white man's political methods of struggle,"[11] especially, as Gary Foley and Tim Anderson indicate, when they found the Aboriginal political organizations,[12] and started to demonstrate, campaign, and write petitions demanding their rights.

During their longtime struggle Aborigines learned to utilize the modern technique of the political and legal struggle for their rights. From the beginning of the 20th century they learned how to demonstrate against their oppression and demand equal rights, campaign for rights, and right petitions to governmental officials. In 1939, for example, the Wiradjuri people at Cumeragunja walked off their reserve protesting the deprivation of their rights, demanding citizens' rights and controls over their own reserve.[13] Early in the 1960s, Victoria Australia decided to close Lake Tyers Reserve. In response, Aboriginal residents of Lake Tyers Reserve launched a campaign for their land rights, which was one of the first involved in the land rights movement.[14]

Aboriginal activists also employed a petition method in which petitions were submitted by Aborigines and non-Aborigines alike. These petitions were submitted frequently, especially after reports about Aboriginal status or events that highlighted blatant discrimination or deprivation of rights, such as the petitions submitted in 1957 after the publication of the Grayden Report, which introduced the hard living conditions of Aboriginal people.[15] Chiara Gamboz describes how aborigines have been submitting petitions since the 1920s and 1930, which were written by the Australian Aboriginal Progressive Association.[16] He also shows how the publication of such petitions by the media enabled their struggle to reach not only the relevant authorities but also the Australian public.[17]

During the 1960s, after they had served in two world wars,[18] Aborigines continued to live in poverty and harsh living conditions. They were discriminated against in education, health, jobs, and public spaces, and continued to be controlled by laws that forced them to live and stay in reserves. The government continued to impose a guardianship policy on Aboriginal children, which entitled the State to take Aboriginal children from their families and raise them in white Christian institutions.[19]

It is impossible not to notice the similarities between the Aborigines and the Bedouin, their living conditions and the discriminatory policies toward them. The Bedouin also continue to suffer harsh living conditions; they are the poorest, most unemployed, and most discriminated against demographic in Israel. Until 1966, the Bedouin were under an emergency regulation and military rule, and were confined to their villages and not allowed to leave without permit. They were discriminated against in education, health, jobs, and pay. In addition, they were deprived of land allocation, pastoral leases, infrastructure, and basic needs such as electricity and even drinking water. Surprisingly, both the Aboriginal peoples of Australia and the Bedouin in the unrecognized villages are still excluded from the official census.[20]

Therefore, aborigines continued to struggle in order to change their situation. They continue to protest, submit petitions, and run campaigns to bring attention to their suffering, poor living conditions, and deprivation of rights. Aboriginal struggle in this period was different; it showed the increased persistency, power, and courage Aborigines had gained by that time. Unlike in the past, Aboriginal people started to challenge acts and policies that aimed to evict them from their land.[21] In addition, the success of some "small struggles," such as the success in the struggle of Lake Tyers, which led to the recognition of Aboriginal reservation,[22] the increasing media publications of reports about poverty and blatant discrimination ignited angry reactions and added additional energy to their struggle.

In addition, during this period, Aboriginal activists continued to establish additional organizations and to initiate more campaigns for the rights of aboriginal peoples that further improved and strengthened their struggle. In 1958, Aboriginal activists established another national advocacy group called the Federal Council for Aboriginal Advancement and launched another campaign to repeal legislation discriminating against Aborigines and amend the Constitution.[23] Later in 1965, another group of students from Sydney University launched the Freedom Ride campaign, which started as a bus tour to Aboriginal towns in order to shed light on the living conditions of Aboriginal people.[24] Also during the 1960s they started several demonstrations and strikes that drove additional attention to their plight, such as the Wave Hill Walk-Off.[25]

In 1963, the Aboriginal Yolngu from the Yarrkala submitted a bark petition to the parliament to protect their land from the bauxite mine.[26] Later in 1966, the movement took shape when Aboriginal workers from the Gurindji people joined by stockmen from the Wave Hill station[27] in a protest of their working conditions.[28] A year after the Wave Hill Walk-Off, another group of the same Gurindji Aboriginal workers also walked off their pastoral station and moved to their traditional land in Wattie Creek. There they posted a sign that stated the name of their village and claimed land ownership.[29] The Wave Hill Walk-Off signaled the beginning of the land rights movement,[30] and started a new movement for land recognition in Australia.

By comparison, many Bedouin who established the Beer Hadaj, Um-Tnan, and Alalaraqib villages during the last two decades, moved back to their lands, posted signs stating the name of their villages, and claimed the land as their own, all as a part of their struggle for land rights.

The effect of the struggle: the change

As a result of the ongoing struggle, during the late 1960s, several developments and changes such as the amendment of the Constitution, political support, and legislations for land rights started to take place. The first one was the amendment of the Constitution.

The change on the constitutional level: the referendum and the amendment of the Constitution

A major development in the Aboriginal struggle took place in 1965 when the government decided to perform a referendum on the amendment of the Constitution. Prior to the referendum, the Australian Constitution included two sections that discriminated against Aboriginal peoples and prevented the government from improving their situation. Section 51 prevented the Commonwealth Parliament from enacting laws benefitting Aboriginal peoples, while Section 127 prevented counting Aborigines in the national census.[31]

In 1965, the government decided to perform a referendum vote to repeal Section 127, amend clause 26 of Section 51, and drop from the Constitution the discriminatory words "other than the aboriginal race in any State."[32] In 1967 the government performed the referendum. The results of the referendum were overwhelmingly in favor of a change that supported the rights of Aboriginal peoples. More than 90 percent of Australians voted in favor of amending the Constitution.[33] Such clear positive results led to many favorable changes for the Aboriginal people such as the amendment of the Constitution, which allowed to include Aboriginal people in the census and to legislate for them.[34]

The change on the legislative level: the first Aboriginal land legislations

The second major change took place on the legislation level. During the 1960s several states and the Commonwealth started to pass legislation that recognized some aspects of Aboriginal land rights.[35] In 1966 South Australia enacted the Aboriginal Land Trust Act,[36] which was the first land legislation for Aboriginal land rights. It provided some form of compensation and recognition for land needs rather than rights. It granted some Aboriginal people 99-year leases on their land.[37] In 1972 Western Australia also established the Aboriginal Affairs Planning Authority to administer reserve land held in trust for Aborigines.[38]

Similar changes also took place in the Commonwealth level. During the 1970s, as part of its efforts to recover land rights for Aborigines, the Commonwealth enacted several laws that supported the overall Aboriginal struggle for land.[39] The most notable law was the Aboriginal Land Fund Act of 1974, the Commonwealth enacted after the release of the Woodward Report.[40]

THE CONTINUING OPPRESSION: THE *MILIRRPUM* DECISION AND ABORIGINES' REACTION

However, despite the positive results of the referendum and some legislation in favor of Aboriginal land rights, courts refused to recognize their lan rights.[41] In 1971, the Supreme Court of the Northern Territory issued a decision in *Milirrpum v. Nabalco Pty. Ltd.*[42] (the *Gove case*) in which it rejected native title rights and confirmed the validity of the *terra nullius* doctrine.[43] The *Gove case*[44] was the first Aboriginal attempt in Australian courts to recognize their land rights, and it is considered one of the most important in the Aboriginal struggle for land rights.[45] In *Gove*, Justice Richard Blackburn approved the concept of *terra nullius*, denied Aboriginal land rights, and dismissed the case holding that the plaintiffs could not prove their right according to their traditional law.[46]

However, although the Court denied recognition of Aboriginal land rights, it did not deny the existence of their traditional legal system.[47] Justice Blackburn recognized several aspects of the Aboriginal legal system that later helped propel the Aboriginal land issue forward.[48] Blackburn accepted that "the applicants had established that under their traditional law any given part of the land could be 'attributed' to a particular clan," and acknowledged, for the first time, the existence of a system of law for Aborigines in Australia.[49] As Lewis P. Hinchman and Sandra K. Hinchman put it: "Blackburn acknowledged that 'the natives had established a subtle and elaborate system of social rules and customs' which comprised a 'recognizable... system of law.' "[50] Later, these holdings become useful for subsequent land rights cases, particularly the *Mabo (No. 2)* case. The decision indicated a beginning of several changes and relevant to land issue such as the establishment of the Woodward Commission[51] and the enactment of the first legislation for land rights such as the Aboriginal Land Act of 1976.[52]

The similarities between the *Gove* case and the first Bedouin land case, Alhawashelah (No. 1), are astonishing. For example, the reactions of both countries to both groups' land claims were similar. After the court rejected the first Bedouin land case, Israel recognized some rights and made efforts to solve the problem. Israel offered compensation and attempted to settle the Bedouin land outside the court system based on the Albeck Report.[53] It seems that countries tend to compromise by offering indigenous people compensation or limited recognition of some rights, but not land ownership, in an effort to reduce the impact of the judicial decisions that have the potential to fundamentally alter indigenous peoples' rights.

During that time, the *Gove* decision symbolized the persistent ongoing oppression and denial of Aborigines' rights, this time from the judicial system. This was especially troubling after the positive results of the 1967 referendum and the subsequent legislation enacted to recover some of the Aboriginal land. The decision symbolized that the legal system would continue to deny them basic land rights and deal with them according to the antiquated colonial policy.[54]

The *Gove* decision resulted in a reaction that generated additional support for Aboriginal rights among white Australian society. In addition, it generated a unique public sentiment toward Aboriginal equal rights that ignited an additional wave of protests for equal Aboriginal rights.

THE BEGINNING OF THE POLITICAL SUPPORT

As a result of the wide public support of the Aboriginal rights' movement, a change started to take place on the political level as well. Members of the government's counselors started to accept Aboriginal demands and consider positive responses to their demands.[55] This kind of support continued to increase, and in 1971, Prime Minister McMahon expressed his support to preserve and develop Aboriginal culture, land, traditions, and arts.[56] However, that support was limited to land use only. It did not recognize higher levels of land rights, such land ownership. This recognition could not reach the demands of Aboriginal peoples.[57]

THE TENT EMBASSY, LAND MOVEMENT, AND SUPPORT OF THE LABOR PARTY

A combination of concerns about their rights and disappointment from the McMahon land policy, mainly its limited support for Aboriginal rights, generated many different reactions amongst Aborigines that resulted in additional protests and demonstrations.[58] In one demonstration in 1972 a group of Aborigines marched to the Parliament house, camped there, and erected a tent that became be known as the "Aboriginal Tent Embassy." The Tent Embassy became a remarkable symbol for the Aboriginal struggle for their identity and land rights.[59]

The government did not condone the establishment of the Tent Embassy and demolished the tent several times until the matter reached the court. Judge Blackburn, the same judge who wrote the *Milirrpum* decision, decided that the government could not remove the tent, granting the Aboriginal peoples another victory.[60] This symbolic victory injected additional momentum into the land rights movement and the Aboriginal struggle.[61]

THE LAND MOVEMENT AND ADDITIONAL WAIVE OF STRUGGLE

The Tent Embassy movement crystallized many groups of Aborigines and non-Aborigines around the struggle for Aboriginal rights and attracted national and international attention. The Tent Embassy and the land movement started as a coalition of both Aborigines and white sympathizers who were concerned about Aboriginal land rights.[62] The movements unified Aborigines around land rights and generated additional support for the struggle among non-Aboriginal groups, and signaled the beginning of a new era of land struggle.

One of the most important achievements was the political support it succeeded to gain. As a result of that support, members of the Australian Labor Party, one of the leading political parties, joined the protest and promised to support the struggle. This event marked the beginning of successful political support for the land rights recognition movement.[63]

The change on the political level and the support for Aborigines' cause

As Peter H. Russell describes, among the many achievements, the commitment of a major political party to support the Aboriginal cause and the prevailing of that specific party in the national elections were the major achievements that put Aboriginal issues at the top of the government's agenda and led to the establishment of the foundation of their land recognition.[64]

During the 1972 election, the opposition leader Gough Whitlam visited the Tent Embassy and committed his party to a policy of self-determination for Aboriginal peoples. This commitment marked the first step in a process of successful recognition of rights. It is considered the strongest political support of a major political party that the Aborigines' cause could have. The second step occurred when the Whitlam Labor Party won the general election. The election victory gave credence to the Labor Party's commitment so that the movement had not just the support of a political party, but also had the support of the government. The third step of development in the rights movement was the establishment of the Land Rights Commission by the Whitlam government.[65]

Fourth change: the establishment of the Woodward Commission

As promised, immediately after the Labor Party won the election, the new government introduced a number of measures to reduce social inequalities regarding Aborigines, and ensured that Aborigines were equal before the law.[66] Further, and most importantly, the Whitlam government established the first land commission in Australia and appointed Justice A.E. Woodward[67] to conduct an inquiry into the appropriate means to recognize Aboriginal land rights.[68]

The Woodward Commission did not disappoint the Aboriginal peoples and issued a report that included a strong, positive mandate for the recognition of Aboriginal land rights. According to Peter Russell, the commission in Australia succeeded in issuing a brave and revolutionary report recommending that Aboriginal land rights be recognized.[69] The commission recommended recognizing land ownership of all reserves in the Northern Territory and granting them to the Aboriginal Land Trust.[70] It also recommended establishing a Land Commission to hear claims based on the traditional ownership to unalienated crown land.[71]

In contrast, in Israel, the Goldberg Commission's recommendations were very disappointing, as the Bedouin could anticipate an unfavorable decision even before the report was issued. As explained in Chapter 3, the Goldberg Commission did not recognize any historical or traditional Bedouin land rights, nor did it establish a tribunal to hear Bedouin land claims. Instead, the Commission suggested some criteria for compensation, similar to the proposals that already existed and that the Bedouin rejected for decades. In some cases, the recommendations suggested by the Goldberg Commission were actually worse than the existing policies.

It is important to recognize that while the establishment of an inquiry commission is one thing, the issuance of a brave report that recognizes their rights is totally different. While many countries may establish commissions to investigate and resolve indigenous' land issues, very few commissions dare to act against the state's traditional position of denying land rights.[72]

ACCEPTING THE WOODWARD REPORT AND THE FIRST COMMONWEALTH LAND LEGISLATION

The Whitlam government made three additional major developments leading to the enactment of the first Aboriginal Land Rights (NT) Act. First, it accepted the Woodward Report's recommendations; second, it promised to give legislative affect to the recommendation; and third, it introduced the first Aboriginal Land Rights (NT) Bill,[73] concluding another chapter of Aboriginal land rights recognition.[74]

International forces

In addition, the international atmosphere and movements against racial discrimination in the wake of the late 1960s facilitated and enabled such change. During that time South African struggle against apartheid and the African-American Civil Rights movement in the United States took place and were important issue in the international news.[75] Moreover, the United Nations was focusing on dealing with the plight of indigenous peoples around the world and released the first study on discrimination against indigenous peoples around the same time.[76]

Racial provisions in the Australian Constitution and the Australian racial immigration policy were perceived as potentially placing the country in a negative image that could harm its international reputation. At the time, Australians wished to avoid being associated with other racist states, such as South Africa.[77] This social and political climate illuminated the plight of the Aborigines amongst Australian citizens, and increased Australia's concern for its international reputation. Such concern drove the Commonwealth to change its discriminatory policies.[78]

Finally, the success of Australia's Aboriginal rights movement demonstrates the exceptional influence that a small number of people, only 2 percent of the population, can have on democratic politics.[79] The Aboriginal experience provides important lessons for the struggle for indigenous rights and has the potential to inform other indigenous groups about the major elements needed for successful assertion of rights. In addition, it encourages other groups to continue their struggle for traditional land rights, even when they make up a small portion of the population and have little or no political representation.

The Mabo (No. 2) decision and after Mabo (No. 2)

In 1992, 20 years after the *Gove* decision, the High Court in Australia delivered the landmark decision in the *Mabo (No. 2)* case.[80] According to many commentators, this decision constituted another landmark victory for indigenous peoples' land rights struggle. The decision abolished the doctrine of *terra nullius* and established native title at the judicial level.[81]

The legal process of this case began in 1982, six years after the *Gove* decision, when Eddi Mabo and other members of the Meriam Aboriginal people from the Murray Islands in the Torres Strait submitted a petition to the Australian High Court demanding recognition of their land rights.[82] They were asking for a declaration stating that they were the rightful owners by custom, the holders of traditional rights, and holders of usufructuary rights over the Murray Islands.[83]

After ten years of litigation, during which the plaintiff Eddie Mabo died, on June 3, 1992, by a majority of six to one, the High Court upheld their claims in *Eddie Mabo and Others v. The State of Queensland.*[84] In this decision, the Court recognized the existence of the Aboriginal native title, rejected the fiction of *terra nullius*, and decided that the existence of native title does not depend on positive acts of recognition by the state, but rather arises from peoples' right to use or occupy particular land.[85]

The Court stated that the Australian lands were not *terra nullius* or land belonging to no one when Europeans settled there and that the Meriam people were, "Entitled as against the whole world to possession, occupation, use and enjoyment of... the lands of the Murray Islands."[86]

In his opinion striking down the doctrine of *terra nullius*, Justice Toohey wrote, "The idea that land which is in regular occupation may be terra nullius is unacceptable, in law as well as in fact."[87] The Court also found that native title rights had survived settlement, though were subject to the sovereignty of the Crown. Further, the Court recognized the fact that Aboriginal people had lived in Australia for many years prior to colonization and enjoyed their land rights according to their customs.

Mabo (No. 2) *and the recognition of native title*

One has to notice that prior to *Mabo (No. 2)*, some states in Australia had enacted laws that recognized Aboriginal traditional land rights like the Aboriginal Land Rights Act 1976 (NT), however, such legislations were limited to a small number of states and could not recognize Aboriginal land rights on the national level. The *Mabo (No. 2)* decision, in contrast, was the first Australian judicial recognition of Aboriginal land rights on a national scale. As Gilda Rodriguez put it:

> *Mabo (No. 2)* was significant for two reasons. First, the decision rejected the common law doctrine of *terra nullius,* which had been the law for more than two hundred years. Second, the decision expanded to a national scale the return of Aboriginal land, which the Land Rights Act had begun to do in the Northern Territory.[88]

In addition, in *Mabo (No.2)*, through the recognition of native title doctrine the Court recognized Aboriginal customary law as a source of Aboriginal land rights. Up to the *Mabo (No. 2)* decision, Aboriginal land law in Australia relied on discriminatory theories, racist legal doctrines, and incorrect factual assumptions. It relied on the discriminatory idea of *terra nullius*, meaning "empty land," and the assumption that Australia was a colony acquired by settlement. It also relied on the racist doctrine that Aborigines were inhuman or an inferior and primitive civilization.[89]

Both the law and legal precedents relied on old decisions based on these antiquated premises. In a 1889 case *Cooper v. Stuart*, Lord Watson stated that the colony of New South Wales "consisted of a tract of territory practically unoccupied, without settled inhabitants or settled law, at the time when it was peacefully annexed to the British Dominion."[90] In terms of land rights, that means that by annexation there were no native inhabitants with land rights, therefore, the British Crown acquired not only political sovereignty over the territory but also absolute ownership of the land. As Russell commented, though Watson did not use the term *terra nullius de facto* he decided that Australia was a *terra nullius* when the British began to settle there.[91] That morally unjust and legally discriminatory case became the governing legal precedent. Several cases that discussed Aboriginal land rights following *Cooper* continued to establish this discriminatory legal rule making it stronger and therefore harder to refute. Even when other justices, like Justice Blackburn in *Gove,* were convinced that premises on which that law relies did not fit the facts before them, they could not change precedent and were bound to follow previous legal rules.[92]

Similarly, legal decisions regarding Bedouin land in Israel are based on the discriminatory theory that Bedouin never owned the land, never settled the land, and never cultivated the land. The *Mawat* land doctrine is based on assumptions that there was no settlement in the Negev, which means that the Negev was empty, or that Bedouin settlement should not be recognized[93] since they were not agricultural settlements. Like the Aborigines' lifestyle, the Bedouin nomadic lifestyle is not considered civilized enough to warrant recognition. According to Ronen Shamir, such assertions rely on discriminatory theories that assume that only agricultural societies are civilized.[94]

Prior to *Mabo (No. 2)* the British had considered Australia *terra nullius*. Although the British knew that Aborigines lived throughout Australia, they did not consider Aborigines to be fully human and regarded Aboriginal society as uncivilized and undeveloped. Therefore, Aborigines could not appreciate the significance of land rights and were not eligible for rights according to Western systems. Aborigines' nonagricultural lifestyle was one of the main reasons for this perception,[95] and these beliefs constituted the foundation for later decisions that denied Aboriginal rights. Judges also regarded Australia as a "colony of settlement," and believed that native people were not fully human and could not be considered bearers of rights.

During that time, Europeans did not consider indigenous people human enough (i.e., not fully human) to be considered societies with legal rights. As part of the denial of indigenous peoples' humanity and rights, English philosophers developed characteristics and theories describing the requirements of a civilized human. One of these theories was the cultivation theory, which denied the humanity of nonagriculture societies, especially the nomadic Aborigines, thus denying them of any human rights afforded civilized people.[96] Banner described:

> As a result, it quickly became conventional British opinion that the Aborigines were the most primitive people in the world. A report from 1791 characterized them as "certainly the lowest class of human beings", in part because of their lack of agriculture or houses, and in part because "they are the only people I ever heard of who did not worship some deity."[97]

By comparison, Israeli judges and officials hold similar beliefs about the Bedouin of the Negev. Judges believe that Bedouin villages are not settlements for the purpose of the land laws; their villages are not worth recognition for the purpose of official mapping or the census.[98] Moreover, some Israeli officials hold racist and discriminatory beliefs and they underlie state policy towards Bedouin. Some even express these beliefs in public. For example, in 2001 Moshe Shohat, who served as the head of Bedouin Educational Authority in the Negev, stated:

> Bedouin are bloodthirsty people who commit polygamy, have 30 children, and continue to expand their illegal settlements by taking over

> state lands. In their culture, they relieve themselves outdoors and don't even know how to use the toilet.[99]

Comparative and international laws have also informed the court in Australia. Inspired by Canadian cases and international law, the Court in *Mabo (No. 2)* first abolished old theories regarding Aborigines, including *terra nullius* and the idea that they are uncivilized people, and, second, the court adopted postimperial developments in international law and comparative law, a shift from Australia's application of colonial theories. Third, it emphasized modern norms against discrimination and recognized Aboriginal traditional law, and finally, based on the recognition of their society as a source of law, the Court recognized Aboriginal native title,[100] which is a customary land right that stems from the Aboriginal legal system and their traditional customary law.

The majority in the *Mabo (No. 2)* decision abandoned the idea that Australia was *terra nullius* when the Europeans arrived, and thus refused to apply the doctrine. They dismissed the racist evolutionary doctrine that regarded nonagricultural Aborigines as uncivilized and undeserving of rights under the European legal system.[101] In his opinion, J. Brennan stated that "the facts as we know them today do not fit the "absence of law" "or barbarian" theory underpinning the earlier decisions."[102] Justice Brennan adopted postimperial developments in international law. He cited the 1975 *Advisory Opinion on Western Sahara* case in which the International Court of Justice rejected the *terra nullius* doctrine as a legal explanation for the colonization of nomadic peoples' land.[103]

Additionally, in *Mabo (No. 2)* the court recognized Aboriginal custom as a source of law and recognized traditional rights that stem from Aboriginal laws that predated the imposition of British rule.[104] Finally, based on the recognition of rights established by traditional law, the Court recognized Aboriginal law with regard to land specifically, their connection and their relation to the land according to their traditions.[105]

The majority in *Mabo (No. 2)* denied the claim that the establishment of the British sovereignty abolished native rights, and decided that native land rights survived the establishment of British rule in Australia.[106] The majority relied on decisions of the Judicial Committee of the Privy Council,[107] which dealt with African colonies acquired by conquest of cessions rather than by settlement. In a 1919 case concerning South Rhodesia, the Privy Council ruled that in the absence of express confiscation it is presumed that the conqueror respects the rights of private property.[108] In another relevant case related to Southern Nigeria, the Council stated: "A mere change of sovereignty is not to be presumed as meant to disturb rights of private owners."[109]

In addition, the Court cited Lord Denning's decision from 1957, in which he identified a "guiding principle" of colonial constitutional law according to which preexisting property rights of inhabitants are to be "fully respected."[110] Further the majority relied on professor Kent McNeil's research about the "common law aboriginal title" in which he showed that according to the Constitution of the British Empire, the Crown's acquisition of sovereignty over a territory did not necessarily involve acquisition of Crown ownership or title to all land in the territory.[111] The majority in *Mabo (No. 2)* found that in many imperial cases "there was a presumption that native ownership continued after the annexation, so that native people did not automatically become trespassers... on their own land, immediately after the annexation."[112]

Comparative law was also a main element that the Court relied on to support its decision.[113] In particular, the Court relied on the Canadian decisions of *Calder v. British Columbia*[114] and *Guerin v. The Queen*.[115] These cases helped to put the Court's reasoning and decision in the comparative law context and allowed the majority to rely on the new norms found in comparative law that recognized Aboriginal customary land rights.[116]

In *Mabo (No. 2),* the Australian Court adopted the Canadian judicial revolution that recognizes Aboriginal land rights to support its decision.[117] The Court took into account the treatment of Privy Council precedents by the Supreme Court of Canada and how the Canadian Court treated the precedents of the Privy Council with regard to indigenous rights. J. Brennan cited Canadian Justice Emmett Hall's renunciation of Lord Watson's position in *Calder,* where Hall stated that "the proposition that after the conquest or discovery the native people have no rights at all except those subsequently granted or recognized by the conqueror or discoverer 'was wholly wrong.'"[118] Brennan also cited J. Hall's declaration that "the legal doctrines predated the empire, acknowledged the right of the Indian nations to live on their land and govern their internal affairs pre dated the imposition of European sovereignty."[119]

The Australian Court adopted the *Calder* opinion and the subsequent decision in *Guerin* in 1984. With regard to the source of indigenous rights, the Court cited Justice Hall's position in *Calder* that native title has its source in the native society that existed before European contact.[120]

The results of the **Mabo (No. 2)** *decision*

The *Mabo (No. 2)* case resulted in a huge controversy among Australians. As Harry Gibbs states, "Many decisions of the High Court have resulted in controversy, but few, if any, have given rise to such a diversity of responses, ranging from euphoria to deep anxiety as *Mabo v. Queensland*."[121]

Aborigines welcomed the decision with great satisfaction. It was a major victory and another boost to their struggle for land rights.[122] After the decision, Aborigines started to demand and push the government to legislate and recognize the land rights the High Court described in *Mabo (No. 2)* decision.[123]

On the other hand, however, many Australians were shocked and surprised by the decision.[124] The decision spread fear and worries among several sectors of non-Aboriginal Australians. There was concern among Australians in cities, such as Sydney, that some of the private and public places could be claimed by Aborigines. Such rumors developed increasing hostility to the Aboriginal land rights movement and supported demands to limit Aboriginal land rights.[125] The mining and pastoral industries, the most affected sectors, started several campaigns to limit the effect of the decision.[126] Such campaigns derogated the effect the *Mabo (No. 2)* decision could have on Aboriginal land rights.

However, despite contradictory responses the government continued to push toward a reconciliation policy. On October 1992, Prime Minister Paul Keating called on Australia to ignore the hysteria and hostility after *Mabo (No. 2)* and accept the decision "as an historic turning point, the basis for a new relationship between Aboriginal and non-Aboriginal Australians."[127] In addition, in the same year of the decision, in December 1992 Prime Minister Keating addressed a crowd in Redfern Park in New South Wales and acknowledged past wrongs.

In 1993, a year after the *Mabo (No. 2)* decision, the federal government passed the Native Title Act 1993 (NTA 1993), which enabled Aboriginal people to submit legal claims for their traditional land. Also, in 1993 Aboriginal people started to submit legal claims for their land.

Moreover, despite the "resistance" of many Australians, the Commonwealth government continued to enact laws to comply with the court decision.[128] In 1994, as part of the federal government's response to the *Mabo (No. 2)* decision, it established a Native Title Tribunal to hear Aboriginal land claims and established the Indigenous Land Fund.

Despite subsequent cases limiting some of the achievements of the *Mabo (No. 2)* decision, it opened the gates for a new judicial approach that not only recognized but also paid more attention to traditional Aboriginal land rights in Australia. Subsequent cases showed that courts, especially the High Court, did not easily accept denial of Aboriginal traditional rights.[129]

After **Mabo** *and the efforts to limit aboriginal land rights*

After the court delivered the *Mabo (No. 2)* decision many Australians, mainly those in the mining and shepherding businesses, started to express their concerns that these decisions could be detrimental to Australian rights and interests.[130] Political leaders blamed the Court for this increasing uncertainty amongst Australians. Many groups started to express worries about their interests and demanded that the results of these land cases be limited.[131] Many business groups, especially mining and pastoral groups, launched a robust campaign to lobby the government against the implications of the decision on the mining and pastoral industries. Furthermore, some politicians started to advocate for limitations of Aboriginal land rights.

In reaction, the federal government under John Howard initiated plans to limit Aboriginal land rights, and later in 1997 proposed the "Ten Point

Plan," which outlined a legislative amendment to the Native Title Act of 1993. Furthermore, the judicial system was also affected by the backlash and some of the subsequent Court decisions derogated from the achievement of the *Mabo (No. 2)* decision.[132] In the 2002 *Yarta Yarta* case, the Court refused to recognize Aboriginal land rights according to modern land rights principles. Instead, it only recognized that they hold land rights according to native title principles, which are communal and unalienable. As Graham Atkinson states, "The Court presumed that the traditional owners of that country could only be recognized as native title holders as if we had preserved our laws and customs essentially snap frozen since the assertion of British sovereignty."[133] This decision indicates some of the limitations of the "native title jurisprudence" in Australia, mainly its inability to address the cultural damage inflicted on native people by past governments.

Judicial support of Aboriginal land rights

The year 2005 witnessed another phase of judicial support of Aboriginal land rights when some decisions started to turn in favor of Aborigine's rights. In the case of the Wotjobaluk people,[134] Justice Merkel stated that the laws and customs of the indigenous peoples had not been "washed away by the tide of history,"[135] indicating that the "laws and customs" of Aborigines are still valid and continued to apply to traditional Aboriginal rights. According to Atkinson, the judgment created further public recognition of the Aboriginal traditional land ownership and laid the ground for further recognition.[136] In an additional step forward, a federal court recognized, in March 2007, the native title of the Gunditjmara people over approximately 2,000 parcels of Crown land, which constituted about 0.6 percent of the State of Victoria's Southwest territory.[137]

Finally, the recent decision of the Gunditjmara people drew attention to the worldwide trend toward the growing use of alternative dispute resolution in land conflicts.[138] Justice Tony North stated in Article 53 of his decision that:

> Some disputes are particularly appropriate for assisted dispute resolution. Many native title cases fall within this category because the issues raised often concern the very identity, beliefs, culture and history of people. It is unlikely that an enforced resolution of such issues by judicial determination will be accepted or durable. The worldwide trend is towards the development of courts with many doors. One door leads to judicial determination, but other doors lead to other forms of dispute resolution.[139]

This approach indicates the advanced stage of Aboriginal peoples' struggle for land recognition, in which courts begin to believe that the core of the disputes in many of these cases does not exist after the court recognizes

Aboriginal people's land rights. Therefore, indigenous people and the states can reach agreements without a need for litigation.

Methods of indigenous land recognition: the doctrines of native title and customary law

Inspired by Aboriginal land recognition in Australia, this section introduces the native title doctrine and customary law doctrine as methods for indigenous land recognition. Then it suggests ways to apply these methods to the Bedouin case. This section argues that the legal system in Israel includes at least two options that could recognize or facilitate recognition of Bedouin customary land rights. The first option is based on existing law as it appears in the legal codex of the State, and the second is based on general principles of the Israeli legal system, namely the principle of custom as a source of law. As an essential part of introducing these options, Bedouin customary law will also be discussed.

As introduced in the previous section, the recognition of Aboriginal land in Australia is considered one of the most inspiring cases for indigenous peoples on the community level, on the political level, and most importantly on the legal level. The Aborigines' experience continues to provide indigenous peoples and state leaders a successful example on ways and methods of land rights recognition.[140] While Chapter 5 summarized the nonlegal struggle of Aboriginal peoples in Australia, this section reintroduces the legal aspects of the Aborigines' experience and specifically the recognition of their customary land rights through the doctrine of native title.

The native title doctrine

The doctrine of native title is the major product of the *Mabo (No. 2)* decision. Through this doctrine, courts in Australia were able to recognize rights and interests in land that indigenous inhabitants enjoyed under their customs before the Crown acquired sovereignty.[141] However, *Mabo (No. 2)* does not provide a comprehensive definition of the native title doctrine. Therefore, many scholars such as Peter Sutton,[142] Janice Gray,[143] Jessica Weir, and Peter Russell have attempted to define the doctrine. According to Jessica Weir, native tile recognizes indigenous peoples' laws, customs, and connections with their lands and waters.[144] Native title transfers rights to indigenous peoples so that they may be included under state law.[145] Russell states that "native title" is not a concept of law in the common law of the dominant culture, nor is it title to land ownership. It is only a bridge, a legal connector, through which the law recognizes the traditional connection of indigenous peoples to their land.[146] J. Brennan explains: "Native title although recognized by the common law it is not an institution of the Common law."[147]

Brennan goes on to write that the rules, practices, and examples of native title are all determined by the laws and customs of indigenous peoples.[148]

The content of the rights and the identity of the beneficiaries are also determined by the traditional laws or customs of the indigenous inhabitants. According to J. Deane and J. Gaudron in *Mabo (No. 2)*, "Since the title preserves entitlement to use or enjoyment under the traditional law or custom… the content of the rights and identity of those entitled to enjoy them must be ascertained by reference to the traditional law or custom."[149] The Court explained that Aboriginal traditional laws and customs are the soul of their land rights. As long as their traditional laws exist their rights exist; if they lose those traditional laws and customs, they lose those rights as well.

Customary law as a defining feature for native title

One of innovations stemming from the *Mabo (No. 2)* decision is the recognition of Aboriginal customary law as a source for indigenous land rights. In *Mabo (No. 2)*, the Court acknowledged that Aboriginal customary law is a defining feature for native title and the basis on which the Court established native title recognition. The Court recognized that indigenous people were living on land governed by their own "system of law" at the time of the colonization and that fact constitutes a crucial defining feature of native title. As Russell put it, "For the majority, the crucial defining feature of native title was an identifiable indigenous community living on land governed by its own system of law at the time of the colonization – and maintaining that connection ever since coming under the British rule."[150]

The *Mabo (No. 2)* Court placed indigenous peoples' laws and custom in the center of the recognition of their land rights. Justice Brennan stated that indigenous peoples could lose their native title "when the tides of history have washed away any real acknowledgment of the traditional law and any real observance of traditional customs."[151]

The source of native title

While the dissenting opinion, authored by J. Dawson, claimed that imperial recognition is the source for the native rights, the majority held that native society and law are sources for indigenous rights.[152] The majority, relying on the European classical natural law writings of de Les Casas,[153] Hugo Grotius, and other founders of European international law to support their position, held that native peoples coming under British rule retain their customary land rights.[154]

John Borrows stated that "The Australian High Court has also recognized that the Common law draws on Aboriginal legal sources."[155] On the other hand, the Court found that the common law recognizes traditional interests such as native title within Aboriginal society. According to McNeil's research that was cited by the Court in *Mabo (No. 2)*, English precedent protects land rights based on customs as it protects land rights based on Crown grants·[156]

J. Toohey also approved the view of native title articulated by Canadian Judge Jadson in *Calder* where J. Jadson stated:

> The fact is when settlers came, the Indians where here, organized in society and occupying the land as their forefather had done for centuries. This is what Indian title means and it does not help one in the solution of this problem to call it a personal or usufructuary right.[157]

According to J. Toohey, Common Law recognizes the survival of traditional interests in land and even operates to protect them. In support of traditional interests, J. Toohey stated the fact that traditional ownership was different from other land rights does not mean it is less protected under the law.[158]

In *Mabo (No. 2)*, the High Court stipulated that the Aboriginal traditional legal system could coexist with the Australian legal system.[159] This coexistence led to the recognition of Aboriginal land.[160] Yvette Trahan stated that the main element of Aboriginal land recognition was "that indigenous Australians had a *sufficient system of laws* and customs and a *relationship to the land recognizable by the common law* that had survived the acquisition of sovereignty by the Crown."[161]

Most important for the following discussion regarding Bedouin land recognition is the idea that native title is a traditional interest in land that has its source in the customs of the native societies and their traditional law and also that common law recognizes traditional interests created in native society. As articulated by Trahan and Russell the *Mabo (No. 2)* decision relied mainly on three elements that are essential for indigenous peoples' land recognition: a) a customary system of law, b) connection to the land, and c) that are recognizable by the state law.

Recognition of indigenous land rights based on customary law

The recognition of land rights based on the customary law approach is not limited to Australia. Many states have adopted this approach or similar approaches to deal with indigenous peoples' land rights. Jeremie Gilbert describes several other areas, such as Quebec and South Africa, that have recognized native title or indigenous land rights based on customary law. He states "The doctrine on indigenous title is gradually becoming a global phenomenon not only limited to Canada, Australia or New Zealand."[162] T.W. Bennett and H. Powell also indicate that, while the doctrine of Aboriginal title has been developed in common law countries, several noncommon law countries have adopted the doctrine of native title. They argue that native title is *sui generis*; and at the same time, it is not part of the English common law, as declared in Canadian and Australian courts. Therefore, they claim that "Aboriginal title lies at an intersection between indigenous laws and received systems of colonial law."[163] Bennett and Powell show that the application of Aboriginal title doctrine can be found in several places.

They bring up, for example, Quebec, where, despite French rules of colonization, Canadian courts applied the doctrine. They stated, "It follows that the doctrine is applicable even in colonies, such as Quebec, which retained French law as the basic law of the land."[164]

Recognition of land based on customary law in South Africa

South Africa is another example where courts, relying on indigenous peoples' customary law, recognize customary land rights. In *The Richtersveld Community and Others v. Alexkor Limited and the Government of the Republic of South Africa,*[165] the appellants relied on the native title doctrine to recognize land rights. The court, however, decided to accept their appeal based on customary law interests. Even though the court refused to discuss whether it would recognize the native title doctrine in South Africa, the court relied on the doctrine and made reference to several cases dealing with the doctrine.[166] However, in the end, the Court held that "the Richtersveld community had a 'right in land' through a customary-law interest..."[167] and stated that "an interest in land held under a system of indigenous law is thus expressly recognized as a 'right in land,' whether or not it was recognized by civil law as a legal right."[168]

As Gilbert noticed, this approach is similar to the native title approach adopted by Canadian courts and the results are similar as well, since the courts ultimately recognized the right of land ownership based on indigenous customary law.[169] To some extent, the "customary law interest" found in the South African case of *Richtersveld* is equivalent to the notion of Aboriginal native title. As the South African Court stated, these rights are a "creature of traditional laws and customs."[170] In *Richtersveld* the Court also recognized customary law as an integral part of the state law and found that "while in the past indigenous law was seen through the common law lens, it must now be seen as an integral part of our law."[171]

Richtersveld was a dramatic development in the indigenous peoples' land recognition since it shows that other doctrines similar to the doctrine of native title can be adopted in different ways. As Gilbert stated, although land recognition in this case is the "creature of traditional laws and customs"[172] to some extent, the "customary law interest" found in this case is equivalent to the notion of Aboriginal native title.[173]

Recognition of land based on customary law in Nicaragua

Mayagna Community of Awas Tingni v. Nicaragua[174] is another instance of indigenous land rights recognition based on customary law. In *Awas Tingni* – a landmark decision that represents the ongoing development of the indigenous land rights concept based on indigenous culture, customs, and traditional legal norms – the Inter-American Court affirmed that the human right to property includes the right of all indigenous peoples to the protection of their customary land and resource tenure.[175]

While Article 21 of the American Convention on Human Rights[176] sets out the right to property only in general terms, the Court held that the right includes property held collectively by indigenous groups under customary indigenous law. In addition, the Court called upon Nicaragua to recognize indigenous land claims based on their "customary law, values, and mores."[177]

Awas Tingni is relevant to indigenous people's rights in states where, despite the existence of laws that protect and recognize their rights, the state continues to deny their rights. In Nicaragua, for example, while the Constitution includes strong protections for the rights of indigenous groups, the state continued to deny their land rights.[178] The case of the Awas Tingni shows that written provisions alone could not protect indigenous peoples' rights, especially land rights. Meaningful protection of the indigenous rights requires a genuine state desire to ensure fairness and equality for members of its society. The Nicaraguan Constitution and legal system recognized in general terms the rights of indigenous peoples to the lands they traditionally occupy and use.[179] However, in practice the state did not afford any recognition to the Awas Tingni tribe's traditional lands.[180] A similar situation exists in Israel. While the Tribal Court Regulations and other principles of law recognize Bedouin customary land rights, the State continues to deny them.

Conclusion

Ultimately, indigenous peoples' struggle for land rights is a long and hard struggle that includes a multilayered struggle on several levels, especially at the political level. Also, it must employ different methods and techniques and requires community organizations to demand and protest for rights, political organization to generate a change on the political and legislative levels, and a legal struggle to defend peoples' right in courts. In Australia, the Aboriginal struggle succeeded in changing not only discriminatory legislation, but also in changing the nation's Constitution as well.

For many years, the Aboriginal peoples of Australia struggled for their land rights. During their struggle they succeeded in navigating their struggle toward the appropriate goals, and bringing the success of their struggle through national and international dimensions, despite their limited means and small numbers.

Their struggle for land gives insight into the advancement of indigenous people and reveals several lessons. First, in terms of duration, the struggle of indigenous peoples lasts for decades. The Aboriginal struggle in Australia, for example, endured for approximately a century, during which they demanded, petitioned, demonstrated, and lobbied for their rights.

Second, in terms of organization, the Aboriginal struggle shows that organization is a key component of success for land rights. Aborigines learned to organize their struggle and their exceptional organization managed to maintain the continuity of their struggle. In fact, their struggle only began to grab attention, accumulate results, and raise public opinion after they began to establish their first institutions and organizations to fight for their rights in the beginning of the last century.

Third, in term of tools, means, and methods of their struggle, Aborigines learned how to use traditional and nontraditional methods to demand rights and grab the attention of the population. While they wrote some of their first petitions on their traditional bark, they continued to use modern methods and tools such as community organization, media, legal tools, political campaigns, and many others to generate support for their cause. At the same time, corresponding to the African American civil rights movement, they retained a pure civil and peaceful struggle that did not digress into violent armed conflict with state authorities.

Finally, the widespread impression is that the recognition of the Aboriginal land rights occurred mainly through judicial struggles as a result of the *Mabo (No. 2)* decision. Research shows, however, that Aboriginal success was made possible by their unceasing, multilayered struggle, which led to recognition of their land rights in several states, through various laws prior to the *Mabo (No. 2)* decision.

Notes

1 *See infra* Chapter 5.C; *infra* Chapter 6.A.
2 Canada and Australia have recognized native title land rights. *See infra* Chapter 5.C.
3 GILBERT, *supra* note 46 at 126.
4 RUSSELL, *supra* note 59 (discussing the recognition of Aboriginal title in Australia).
5 The recognition of native title right is not recognition of full land ownership.
6 Gary D. Meyers & John Mugambwa, *Mabo Decision: Australian Aboriginal Land Rights in Transition*, 23 ENVTL. L. 1203 (1993).
7 *Topics at a Glance – Aboriginal and Torres Strait Islander Peoples Population*, AUSTRALIAN BUREAU OF STATISTICS, http://www.abs.gov.au/websitedbs/c311215.nsf/web/Aboriginal+and+Torres+Strait+Islander+Peoples+-+Population (last updated Jan. 16, 2013).
8 See *infra* Chapter 2.
9 Ronald Paul Hill, *Blackfellas and Whitefellas: Aboriginal Land Rights, the Mabo Decision, and the Meaning of Land*, 17 HUMAN RIGHTS QUARTERLY 303–322, 305 (1995); Sandy Wood, *Aboriginal Land Rights in Australia*, 6 HUMAN RIGHTS BRIEF, 99 (1999), http://digitalcommons.wcl.american.edu/hrbrief/vol6/iss3/3.
10 Hill, *supra* note 767 at 305; Wood, *supra* note 767 at 99.
11 RUSSELL, *supra* note 59 at 130.
12 G. Foley & T. Anderson (2006). Land rights and Aboriginal Voices. Australian Journal of Human Rights, 12(1), 83. pp. 88. ??
13 *Id.*
14 *Id.*
15 JENNIFER CLARK, ABORIGINES & ACTIVISM: RACE & THE COMING OF THE SIXTIES TO AUSTRALIA 73 (2008).
16 Chiara Gamboz, "Australian Indigenous Petitions: Emergence and Negotiations of Indigenous Authorship and Writings." PhD diss., University of New South Wales, 2012. At 24. ??
17 Chiara Gamboz, "Australian Indigenous Petitions: Emergence and Negotiations of Indigenous Authorship and Writings." PhD diss., University of New South Wales, 2012. At 111.

18 Robert A. Hall, Fighters from the Fringe: Aborigines and Torres Strait Islanders Recall the Second World War, 54–55 (1995); *see also* Gina Lennox, Forged by War: Australians in Combat and Back Home, 157 (2006).
19 Russell, *supra* note 3 at 127.
20 Morad El-sana, *The Official Data on the Absent-Present Arab Bedouin, Volume 14, June 2005*, 14 Adalah's Newsletter, 1.
21 Bette Moore, *Victoria: Present Situation*, in Aboriginal Land Rights in a Handbook 150 (N. Peterson and M. Langton eds., 1981); Bain Attwood, Rights for Aborigines 245(2003).
22 Nick O'Neil & Robin Handley, Retreat from Injustice: Human Rights in Australian Law 448–449 (1994).
23 G. Foley & T. Anderson (2006). Land rights and Aboriginal Voices. Australian Journal of Human Rights, 12(1), 83. pp. 87. ??
24 *Id.*
25 Minoru Hokari, From Wattie Creek to Wattie Creek: An Oral Historical Approach to the Gurindji Walk-off. Aboriginal History 24 (2000): 98–116. At 106.
26 Russell, *supra* note 59 at 155.
27 John Chesterman, Civil Rights: How Indigenous Australians Won Formal Equality 85 (2005).
28 Russell, *supra* note 3 at 156.
29 *Id.* at 157–158; Heather Goodall, Invasion to Embassy: Land in Aboriginal Politics in New South Wales, 1770–1992 324–325 (2008).
30 Kevin Keeffe, Paddy's Road: Life Stories of Patrick Dodson 156 (2003).
31 Russell, *supra* note 3 at 157.
32 Robert French, *The Race Power: A Constitutional Chimera*, in Australian Constitutional Landmarks 180–212 (H. P. Lee & George Winterton eds., 2003).
33 Gary Foley and Tim Anderson, Land Rights and Aboriginal Voices, p. 87.
34 John Gardiner-Garden, The 1967 Referendum-History and Myths, Parliament of Australia (May 2007).
35 Russell, *supra* note 706, at 162.
36 Maureen Tehan, *Customary Title, Heritage Protection, and Property Rights in Australia: Emerging Patterns of Land Use in the Post-Mabo Era* 7 Pac. Rim L. & Pol'y J. 765, 777 (1998).
37 O'Neil & Handley, *supra* note 728, at 448–449.
38 Russell, *supra* note 3 at 162.
39 Russell, *supra* note 3 at 175.
40 *Aboriginal Land Fund Act 1974* (Cth) (Austl.).
41 Russell, *supra* note 3 at 157.
42 *Milirrpum v Nabalco Pty Ltd (Gove)* (1971) 17 FLR 141 (Austl.), known as the "Gove land rights case," was the first case to address native title in Australia. The decision authored by Justice Richard Blackburn ruled against the claimants on a number of issues of law and fact, and ultimately rejected the doctrine of aboriginal title and confirmed the doctrine of *terra nullius*.
43 Robert Van Krieken, *From Milirrpum to Mabo: The High Court, Terra Nullius and Moral Enterpreneurship*, 23 U.N.S.W.L.J. 63 (2000).
44 *Id.*
45 John Hookey, *Gove Land Rights Case: A Judicial Dispensation for the Taking of Aboriginal Lands in Australia, The*, 5 Fed. L. Rev. 85, 114 (1972).
46 Gilda C. Rodriguez, *Wik Peoples v. State of Queensland: A Restrained Expansion of Aboriginal Land Rights*, 23 N.C.J. Int'l L. & Com. Reg. 711, 718–719 (1997).
47 Hookey, *supra* note 803 at 87.
48 Marc Gumbert, *Paradigm Lost: An Analysis of Anthropological Models and Their Effect on Aboriginal Land Rights*, 52 Oceania 103–123, 107 (1981).
49 Van Krieken, *supra* note 801 at 67.
50 Lewis P. Hinchman & Sandra K. Hinchman, *Australia's Judicial Revolution: Aboriginal Land Rights and the Transformation of Liberalism*, 31 Polity 23, 35 (1998).

51 Marc Gumbert, *Paradigm Lost: An Analysis of Anthropological Models and Their Effect on Aboriginal Land Rights*, 52 Oceania 103–123, 108 (1981).
52 Larissa Behrendt, Indigenous Australia for Dummies 414 (2012).
53 Plia Albeck, *Report of the Team of Experts on the Issue of Land Settlement in the Siyag Area and the Northern Negev. Jerusalem. (In Hebrew).* 4–5 (1975); Swirski and Hasson, *supra* note 167 at 71.
54 Hill, *supra* note 767 at 304.
55 Russell, *supra* note 59 at 158.
56 Tim Rowse, Obliged to be Difficult: Nugget Coombs' Legacy in Indigenous Affairs 54 (2000).
57 Russell, *supra* note 59 at 159; Rowse, *supra* note 814 at 67.
58 Russell, *supra* note 3 at 159.
59 *Id.* at 160.
60 Due to a technical error in the ordinance, the Government tried to remove the tent, but the court rejected the Government's petition to remove the Embassy Tent.
61 Russell, *supra* note 59 at 161; Gary Foley & Tim Anderson, *Land Rights and Aboriginal Voices*, 12 Australian Journal of Human Rights 83–108, 88–91 (2006).
62 Max Charlesworth, The Aboriginal Land Rights Movement 6 (1984).
63 Rowse, *supra* note 814 at 67.
64 Russell, *supra* note 59 at 161.
65 Russell, *supra* note 3 at 161–162.
66 Cth, Parliamentary Debates, House of Representatives, Feb. 27, 1973, 14 (Austl.).
67 Woodward represented the Yolngu peoples' in *Milirrpum*.
68 A. E. Woodward & Australia Aboriginal Land Rights Commission, *Second Report of The Aboriginal Land Rights Commission* 1 (2nd ed. 1975), https://trove.nla.gov.au/version/173665448 (last visited Mar. 27, 2020).
69 Russell, *supra* note 3 at 168.
70 There were a few exceptions, including the Darwin municipality.
71 Woodward and Commission, *supra* note 826 at 129; Peter F. Rhodes, *Report of the Australian Aboriginal Land Rights Commission - A Comment, The*, 39 Sask. L. Rev. 199, 206 (1974).
72 *See infra* Chapter 3.
73 The Whitlam government could not pass its Bill due to a government crisis in 1975 when Whitlam was replaced by the opposition leader Malcolm Froster, head of the Liberal/National Country Party Coalition, who introduced and passed his own Northern Territory land legislation in 1976.
74 Bain Attwood & Andrew Markus, The Struggle for Aboriginal Rights: A Documentary History (1999); *see also* Russell, *supra* note 3 at 169.
75 *Id.* at 147.
76 *Id.* at 184.
77 John Chesterman, *Defending Australia's Reputation: How Indigenous Australians Won Civil Rights, PartII*, 32 Australian Historical Stud., 201 (2001); *see also* Russell, *supra* note 706 at 147.
78 Russell, *supra* note 59 at 147.
79 *Id.* at 161.
80 *Mabo v Queensland (No 2)* (1992) 175 CLR 1 (Austl.).
81 Meyers and Mugambwa, *supra* note 764.
82 Janice Gray, *The* Mabo *Case: A Radical Decision?*, 17 Can. J. of Native Stud. 33, 36 (1997).
83 Meyers and Mugambwa, *supra* note 764 at 1209.
84 *Mabo v Queensland (No 2)* (1992) 175 CLR 1 (Austl.).
85 Meyers and Mugambwa, *supra* note 762 at 1203.
86 *Mabo*, at 97, 110.
87 *Id.* at 20.

88 Rodriguez, *supra* note 804 at 722.
89 *Id.*
90 Russell, *supra* note 59 at 254.
91 *Id.* at 254.
92 *Id.* at 254.
93 Rangwala, *supra* note 391 at 343.
94 *See generally* Ronen Shamir, *Suspended in Space: Bedouins under the Law of Israel*, 30 L. & Soc'y Rev. 231 (1996).
95 Stuart Banner, *Why Terra Nullius? Anthropology and Property Law in Early Australia*, 23 L. & Hist. Rev. 95, 102 (2005).
96 *Id.* at 108–111.
97 *Id.* at 109.
98 El-sana, *supra* note 778.
99 Rangwala, *supra* note 314 at 437.
100 Russell, *supra* note 3 at 255.
101 *Id.* at 256; *Mabo v Queensland (No 2)* (1992) 175 CLR 1, 38 (Austl.).
102 *Mabo v Queensland (No 2)* (1992) 175 CLR 1, 38 (Austl.).
103 Russell, *supra* note 3 at 256.
104 *Id.* at 248.
105 The Australian court however did not recognize Aboriginal traditional law on all levels, but only in regard to land. *See* Garth Nettheim, *Mabo and Legal Pluralism*, in Legal Pluralism and the Colonial Legacy: Indigenous Experiences of Justice in Canada, Australia, and New Zealand (1995); *see also* Committee of Inquiry: Report on Aboriginal customary law, Northern Territory Law Reform Committee 6 (2003), *available at* http://www.nt.gov.au/justice/policycoord/documents/lawmake/ntlrc_final_report.pdf.
106 Russell, *supra* note 3 at 250.
107 The Judicial Committee of the Privy Council declared common law the constitutional law of the British Empire.
108 In re Southern Rhodesia [1919] A.C. 211, 233 (Rhodesia), *cited in* Russell, *supra* note 3 at 250. fn17.
109 Amodu Tijani v. Secratery of Southern Negeria, [1921] AC 399, 407 (Nigeria), *cited in* Russell, *supra* note 682, at 250 fn18.
110 Russell, *supra* note 59 at 252.
111 Kent McNeil, *Judicial Treatment of Indigenous Land Rights in the Common Law World* 4 (2008), http://papers.ssrn.com/abstract=1262794 (last visited Feb 3, 2013).
112 Russell, *supra* note 59 at 252.
113 *See generaly* Shirley Scott, *The Australian High Court's Use of the Western Sahara Case in* Mabo, 45 Int'l & Comp. L.Q. 923 (1996).
114 Calder v. British Columbia, [1973] S.C.R. 313 (Can.).
115 Guerin v. The Queen, [1984] 2 S.C.R. 335 (Can.).
116 Anaya, *supra* note 507 (describing new international norms that recognize indigenous peoples' rights).
117 Margaret MacMillan & Francine McKenzie, Parties Long Estranged 81 (2003).
118 Russell, *supra* note 3 at 253.
119 Russell, *supra* note 3 at 253.
120 Janice Gray, *Is Native Title a Proprietary Right*, 9 Murdoch University Electronic Journal of Law, 36 (2002), http://epress.lib.uts.edu.au/research/handle/10453/1472 (last visited Mar. 24, 2013); Russell, *supra* note 59 at 253.
121 Harry Gibbs, *Foreward,* in Mabo: A Judicial Revolution: The Aboriginal Land Rights Decision and Its Impact on Australian Law xiv (M .A. Stephenson & Suri Ratnapala eds., 1993).
122 Atkinson and Brett, *supra* note 814 at 9.

123 RUSSELL, *supra* note 59 at 286.
124 *Id.* at 279.
125 Cth, Parliamentary Debates, House of Representatives, Feb. 27, 1973, 14 (Austl.).
126 *Id.* at 284.
127 *Id.*
128 RUSSELL, *supra* note 3 at 303.
129 *See* Meyers & Mugambwa, *supra* note 684, at 1231.
130 RUSSELL, *supra* note 3 at Chapter 9.
131 *See* Rodriguez, *supra* note 748, at 712.
132 *See* RUSSELL, *supra* note 3 at Chapter 9.
133 Atkinson and Brett, *supra* note 880 at 10.
134 *Clarke v Victoria* [2005] FCA 1795 (Austl.).
135 Fergus Shiel, *Past Gives Us Strength, Aborigines Say*, THEAGE.COM.AU (Dec. 14, 2005), http://www.theage.com.au/news/national/past-gives-aborigines-strength/2005/12/13/1134236064303.html.
136 Atkinson and Brett, *supra* note 880 at 11.
137 *Id.*
138 *Id.*
139 *Lovett v Victoria* [2007] FCA 474 (Austl.).
140 Although some land rights were recognized in a few states in Australia prior to *Mabo (No. 2)*, the decision introduced for the first-time judicial recognition of Aboriginal land rights. *See* Nettheim, *supra* note 863.
141 RUSSELL, *supra* note 3 at 257.; *see also Native Title Act 1993* (Cth) pt 2 (Austl.).
142 PETER SUTTON, NATIVE TITLE IN AUSTRALIA: AN ETHNOGRAPHIC PERSPECTIVE xv, 1 (2003).
143 Gray, *supra* note 878 at 38.
144 JESSICA K. WEIR, COUNTRY, NATIVE TITLE AND ECOLOGY 6 (2012).
145 *Native Title Act 1993* (Cth) (Austl.).
146 RUSSELL, *supra* note 3 at 265.
147 *Mabo v Queensland (No. 2)* (1992) 175 CLR 1, 59 (Austl.).
148 *Id.*; *see also* RUSSELL, *supra* note 3 at 266.
149 *Id.* at 58, 74; RUSSELL, *supra* note 3 at 266.
150 RUSSELL, *supra* note 3 at 269.
151 *Mabo (No. 2)*, 175 CLR at 60.
152 *Mabo (No. 2)*, 175 CLR 1;
153

> If . . . the native peoples are . . . part of the humankind then they deserve to be respected as full, rational human being. Which means that they inhere certain fundamental rights including the right to land on which they live.

RUSSELL, *supra* note 3 at 254. (quoting Bartolome de Les Casas).
154 *Id.*
155 John Borrows, *With or Without You: First Nations Law (in Canada)*, 41 MCGILL L. J. 629, 636 (1995).
156 *See generally* Kent McNeil, *Racial Discrimination and Unilateral Extinguishment of Native Title*, 1 AUSTL. INDIGENOUS L. REP. 181 (1996); RUSSELL, *supra* note 3 at 261.
157 *Mabo (No. 2)*, 175 CLR at 195.
158 *Id.* at 187.
159 *Id.*
160 Angus Frith, *Aboriginal Law*, LAWHANDBOOK.ORG.AU, http://www.lawhandbook.org.au/handbook/ch01s01s03.php (last updated Jul. 1, 2010).
161 Trahan, *supra* note 17, at 573–574. [emphasis added].
162 GILBERT, *supra* note 46 at 66.

163 T. W. Bennett & C. H. Powell, *Aboriginal Title in South Africa Revisited*, 15 S. AFR. J. ON HUM. RTS. 449, 462 (1999).
164 *Id.* at 462.
165 *Richtersveld Community v. Alexkor Ltd.*, 2003 (2) SA 27(SCA) (S. Afr.).
166 GILBERT, *supra* note 4 at 67.
167 Yvette Trahan, *Richtersveld Community & (and) Others v. Alexkor Ltd.: Declaration of a Right in Land through a Customary Law Interst Sets Stage for Introduction of Aboriginal Title into South African Legal System*, 12 TUL. J. INT'L & COMP. L. 565, 567 (2004).
168 *Richtersveld*, at ¶ 9.
169 GILBERT, *supra* note 4 at 67.
170 *Id.*
171 *Id.* at 66.
172 *Richtersveld*, at ¶ 8.
173 GILBERT, *supra* note 46 at 66.
174 Mayagna Community of Awas Tingni v. Nicaragua, Merits, Reparations, and Costs, Judgment, Inter-Am. Ct. H.R. (ser. C) No. 79, (Aug. 31, 2001).
175 James Anaya, Divergent Discourses about International Law, Indigenous Peoples, and Rights over Lands and Natural Resources: Toward a Realist Trend, 16 Colo. J. Int'l Envtl. L. & Pol'y 237, 245 (2005).
176 Organization of American States, American Convention on Human Rights, Nov. 22, 1969, O.A.S.T.S. No. 36, 1144 U.N.T.S. 123.
177 Mayagna Community of Awas Tingni, at ¶ 164.
178 Grossman, *supra* note 682 at 2, 4, 8.
179 Grossman, *supra* note 605 at 4, 8.
180 HUMAN RIGHTS WATCH, *supra* note 125 at 105–108.

Bibliography

Albeck, P. (1975). Report of the Team of Experts on the Issue of Land Settlement in the Siyag Area and the Northern Negev. Jerusalem. (In Hebrew).

Anaya, S. J. (2004). Indigenous Peoples in International Law. Oxford University Press.

Atkinson, G., & Brett, M. (n.d.). An Historical Perspective on the Struggle for Land Justice in Victoria, Native Title Services Victoria. http://www.ntsv.com.au/document/Land-Justice-in-Vic-23Aug07-NNTT.pdf.

El-sana, M. (n.d.). The Official Data on the Absent-Present Arab Bedouin, Volume 14, June 2005. *Adalah's Newsletter*, 14.

Foley, G., & Anderson, T. (2006). Land Rights and Aboriginal Voices. *Australian Journal of Human Rights*, *12*(1), 83–108. https://doi.org/10.1080/1323238X.2006.11910814.

Gilbert, J. (2006). *Indigenous Peoples' Land Rights under International Law* (1st ed.). BRILL.

Gray, J. (2002). Is Native Title a Proprietary Right. *Murdoch University Electronic Journal of Law*, *9*(3), 1–13. http://epress.lib.uts.edu.au/research/handle/10453/1472.

Grossman, C. (n.d.). Awas Tingni v. Nicaragua: A Landmark Case for the Inter-American System. *Human Rights Brief*, *8*(3), 2.

Gumbert, M. (1981). Paradigm Lost: An Analysis of Anthropological Models and Their Effect on Aboriginal Land Rights. *Oceania*, *52*(2), 103–123.

Hill, R. P. (1995). Blackfellas and Whitefellas: Aboriginal Land Rights, the Mabo Decision, and the Meaning of Land. *Human Rights Quarterly*, *17*(2), 303–322. https://doi.org/10.2307/762519.

Hookey, J. (1972). Gove Land Rights Case: A Judicial Dispensation for the Taking of Aboriginal Lands in Australia. *The Federal Law Review*, *5*, 85.

Human Rights Watch. (n.d.). Off the Map: Land and Housing Rights Violations in Israel's Unrecognized Bedouin Villages. Retrieved September 6, 2016, from http://www.hrw.org/reports/2008/03/30/map.

MacMillan, M., & McKenzie, F. (2003). *Parties Long Estranged*. UBC Press.

McNeil, K. (2008). Judicial Treatment of Indigenous Land Rights in the Common Law World (SSRN Scholarly Paper ID 1262794). Social Science Research Network. http://papers.ssrn.com/abstract=1262794.

Meyers, G. D., & Mugambwa, J. (1993). Mabo Decision: Australian Aboriginal Land Rights in Transition. *Evironmental Law*, *23*, 1203.

Nettheim, G. (1995). Mabo and Legal Pluralism. In K. M. Hazlehurst (Ed.), *Legal Pluralism and the Colonial Legacy: Indigenous Experiences of Justice in Canada, Australia, and New Zealand*. Greenwood Publishing Group, pp. 103–130.

Rangwala, T. S. (2004). Inadequate Housing, Israel, and the Bedouin of the Negev. *Osgoode Hall Law Journal*, *42*, 415.

Rhodes, P. F. (1974). Report of the Australian Aboriginal Land Rights Commission—A Comment. *The Saskatchewan Law Review*, *39*, 199.

Rodriguez, G. C. (1997). Wik Peoples v. State of Queensland: A Restrained Expansion of Aboriginal Land Rights. *North Carolina Journal of International Law and Commercial Regulation*, *23*, 711.

Rowse, T. (2000). *Obliged to be Difficult: Nugget Coombs' Legacy in Indigenous Affairs*. Cambridge University Press.

Russell, P. H. (2006). *Recognising Aboriginal Title: The Mabo Case and Indigenous Resistance to English-Settler Colonialism*. UNSW Press.

Sutton, P. (2003). *Native Title in Australia: An Ethnographic Perspective*. Cambridge University Press.

Swirski, S., & Hasson, Y. (2006). *Invisible Citizens: Israel Government Policy toward the Negev Bedouin*. Adva Center.

Trahan, Y. (2004). Richtersveld Community & (and) Others v. Alexkor Ltd.: Declaration of a Right in Land through a Customary Law Interest Sets Stage for Introduction of Aboriginal Title into South African Legal System. *Tulane Journal of International and Comparative Law*, *12*, 565.

Van Krieken, R. (2000). From Milirrpum to Mabo: The High Court, Terra Nullius and Moral Enterpreneurship. *University of New South Wales Law Journal*, *23*, 63.

Wood, S. (1999). Aboriginal Land Rights in Australia. *Human Rights Brief*, 6(3), 5–6, 10. http://digitalcommons.wcl.american.edu/hrbrief/vol6/iss3/3.

Woodward, A. E., & Commission, A. A. L. R. (1975). *Second Report of the Aboriginal Land Rights Commission* (2nd ed.). Govt. Printer of Australia. https://trove.nla.gov.au/version/173665448.

6 Land recognition

Application of the customary land rights model in the Bedouin case

Recognition of land based on customary law: the Bedouin case

Chapters 3 and 4 showed that both domestic and international legal systems fail to recognize Bedouin land rights. On the national level, the legal system in Israel does not recognize Bedouin land and therefore does not protect such rights.[1] On the international level, international law can not offer a meaningful protection for Bedouin land rights because of the limited application of relevant international law in Israel.

Meanwhile, the increasing number of successful examples of recognition of indigenous peoples' land rights in many states around the world continues to inform the Bedouin about the potential of such methods and encourages them to continue their struggle in a similar way.

This section argues that the experience of indigenous peoples in other countries is applicable to the Bedouin land case in Israel. In order to illustrate its application, this chapter will first introduce the elements necessary for recognition and then show these elements exist in the Bedouin land case. These elements include the existence of customary law (an indigenous legal system) that recognizes indigenous/Bedouin land rights and the existence of legal recognition for such a customary system within the State's legal system.

The existence of Bedouin customary law

Bedouin customary law is Bedouin law emerged to serve the tribe's needs. It is a "system of rules" that governs tribes in different places.[2] Bedouin tribal law is only one example of tribal law systems.[3] Tribal law has existed for thousands of years in many places around the world and has organized and governed the affairs of tribal societies in activities ranging from simple transactions to major crimes. Tribal law can be found on almost every continent, including Africa, Asia, Europe, the Americas, and the Middle East. Similar to other customary law systems around the world, tribal law emerged to serve the needs of tribal societies in the absence of other law.[4] Later it continued to survive in places lacking sufficient state power to rule and enforce order, security, and law, especially in remote places like deserts.

Bedouin tribal law

Bedouin tribal law is the tribal law of Arab tribes (Bedouin) in the Middle East and North Africa. In Arabic, Bedouin tribal law is called *alu'rf wa-la'adah* meaning "that which is known and customary," or *alhaq* meaning "justice."[5] According to Clinton Bailey, in his book *Bedouin Law From Sinai and the Negev*, Bedouin law is "a system of rules that emerged in the deserts of the Middle East to serve the needs and provide a protection to individuals and nomadic society alike."[6] He goes on to say that Bedouin tribal laws can be found in Palestine, Israel, Egypt, Jordan, Saudi Arabia, Iraq, Syria, Lebanon, and many other countries.

Bedouin tribal law predates *Sharia* law (Islamic Law), which began in the sixth century,[7] as a legal system since it has existed in the desert for more than 2,000 years,[8] making it one of the oldest legal systems in the Middle East. The system originated from the Bedouin tribes in the Arab Peninsula. With the emergence of Islam in the sixth century, Bedouin law was reshaped; however, some elements remain despite Islamic influence.[9]

Bailey's book asserts that Bedouin law does exist, that it is a comprehensive system, and that it is still in practice. In addition, he argues that this system is not an isolated system but part of the Bedouin culture and legal system that has been in the desert for thousands of years and hundreds of years before Islam.[10] For generations, Bedouin lived in places that lacked governmental authority, or in places where the central government was too weak to enforce order. Therefore, there has always been a need for a legal system to fill this vacuum of central authority to regulate internal affairs and enforce order in the desert.[11]

Many scholars have recognized the existence and acknowledged the value of Bedouin tribal law.[12] The Bedouin legal system is described in many occasions as a complete and perfect legal system that includes every element for Bedouin legal needs.[13] Scholars from the Arab World,[14] such as Jordan, Syria, Iraq and Egypt, and also Western scholars like Frank Stewart and Clinton Bailey,[15] have described Bedouin law in detail.[16] In addition, many Israeli scholars such as Ben David, Abu-Rabia, and others have studied Bedouin law and described its origins and its main elements.[17] Stewart lists numerous studies that detail the Bedouin tribal justice system in the Arab world, leaving no doubt as to the existence of Bedouin law.[18]

Although some have criticized aspects of the Bedouin system, such as gender rights,[19] no researcher has claimed that Bedouin law does not exist. On the contrary, the overwhelming majority of researchers indicate the completeness of Bedouin law, and its inclusion of the basic principles of justice that arc adequate for Bedouin life.[20] In several countries in the Middle East and Africa, official law recognizes Bedouin law or at least elements of it.[21] In some states, the state's judicial system recognizes and even enforces tribal decisions.[22] In some legal systems, such as the Islamic *Sharia* law, Bedouin law is recognized as part of the *Alorf* principle, the custom principle, which constitutes a source of law in *Sharia* law.[23]

Finally, among Bedouin of the Negev, Bedouin law is still in use and continues to determine the norms of behavior of Bedouin individuals and groups in most areas of life. Many Bedouin turn to Bedouin law to resolve internal conflicts, and the system continues to answer their needs. It solves their problems and defines their rights and obligations in many areas of Bedouin life.[24]

The Bedouin legal system is well structured both procedurally and substantively. On the procedural level, it includes advanced legal procedures, such as warnings and notifications, initiation of legal actions, determination of the place of the trial, nomination of judges, determination of dates for hearings, and nomination of the courts of appeals.[25] In addition, the system distinguishes between criminal and civil legal procedures. It also includes some elements that do not exist in the modern legal systems, such as the opportunity to select judges and oppose the appointment of judges, a right that grants special advantages to the Bedouin system. In addition, the system offers courts specializing in certain matters, and even *ad hoc* courts for urgent matters. On the substantive level, the system includes well-developed law principles both in civil and criminal matters. These principles are based on Bedouin tradition, Islamic Law, and basic values of justice and natural law.[26]

Bedouin tribal law has also exercised mediation and reconciliation procedures for hundreds of years. At the beginning of each trial, the parties present their arguments, then before starting the formal trail, the judge, the representatives, and the tribal elders and other selected individuals intervene and push for a compromise. The system employs tools that include discussions of tribal and individual elements of honor; explanations of the risks and probability for success in the case; discussions of the potential gains and losses of each party, with emphasis on the social components; and other elements and techniques to reach a compromise without trial.[27]

The hard life in the desert and lack of official authority and security shaped Bedouin law and dictated some very harsh rules and principles that do not fit every society, such as collective responsibility, severe punishments, honor killings, and forced evictions. Collective responsibility is one of the main elements that distinguishes the Bedouin legal system from modern systems. The collective responsibility principle has several objectives ranging from the common interest of the parties to resolve the matter, the claimant's or victim's interest in receiving proper relief, the interests of the defendant to pay minimum damages, and the interests of the tribe as a whole. The responsibility of the tribe to its members is also a collective responsibility. These elements are a product of the hard realities of life in the desert, culture, and lack of central government that come with the Bedouin lifestyle.[28]

Implementation and enforcement of judgments in the Bedouin legal system are other elements that differ from modern legal systems.[29] Because there are no police or other official enforcement authorities, over the centuries

Bedouins have developed a unique but effective enforcement mechanism. Individuals and tribal leaders are responsible for the enforcement of judicial decisions. Judgments are usually respected and enforced, but when they are not there are several ways to enforce them. If an individual fails to respect and implement the decision, then the plaintiff and the tribe will implement the decision, first by negotiation and, only if they fail, then by force.[30]

Some people even go further to claim that, in some matters, Bedouin law is more effective than state law. In many states, such as Israel, Jordan, Egypt, and others, Bedouin law defends life and property and deters violence among the Bedouins. It also recognizes rights in areas where states do not, such as Bedouin land rights.[31] In other matters, Bedouin law protects matters where the official law provides inadequate remedies. For example, Israeli law is unable to protect Bedouin land rights because it does not recognize Bedouin law. By contrast, Bedouin law recognizes these rights and has effective and efficient tools in place that protect them.[32]

Another example from the social level is domestic violence within Bedouin families. Israel usually handles these issues under State law that is based on Western, modern ideas that do not fit the Bedouin culture. Therefore, resolution usually leads to negative results. Instead of protecting the victim, they harm the Bedouin family unit. As a result, many Bedouin women refrain from submitting complaints to the police. Another example can be found in the field of security and public order where the Bedouin law determines public order and determines the basic norms of private and collective behavior among the Bedouin population. It provides security and peace among individuals and tribes.[33]

In some places, where the state's authority is weak, or not strong enough to protect people's rights, tribal law gains tremendous strength and exceeds state power and official law. In such instances, Bedouin law could pose a threat, or could be perceived as posing a threat, to state law and authority. One recent example of this involved the Palestinian Authority. During the occupation of Palestine, Israeli authorities destroyed the Palestinian judicial system and prevented its establishment for almost 60 years.[34] As a result, Bedouin tribal law provided the only available legal system to solve disputes and serve the people's legal needs. The more people relied on the system, the more Bedouin tribal law strengthened among Palestinian society. Research completed by Birzeit University found that the status of Bedouin law among Palestinians is so strong that it poses a threat to the State official law and impedes its improvement since many Palestinians continue to resort to Bedouin law to solve their problems.[35]

Recognition of Bedouin law during the Ottoman and the British mandate rules

The status of Bedouin customary law in Israel depends on laws and legal principles from the Ottoman and British mandate periods. Therefore, in order to enable better understanding of the position of Bedouin law in Israel, this section will first introduce the recognition of Bedouin law during the Ottomans and the British Mandate periods.

Bedouin law under Ottoman rule

Both the general and the specific structures of the Ottoman Empire's system indicate that the Empire recognized Bedouin tribal law in the Negev.[36] On the general level, tribal laws were part of the Ottoman system. Since the establishment of the Ottoman state, the legal system incorporated both Islamic *Sharia* law and tribal law, and the two coexisted successfully. On the one hand, the Ottoman state practiced Islamic *Sharia* law, as it was the continuation of the Islamic State, and on the other hand, it continued to embrace tribal law as part of the tribal system that supported the first Ottoman *Sultans* that enabled them to acquire power.[37]

Furthermore, the Ottoman system recognized different models of local legal systems. Lauren Benton explains that when empires enlarge, they often streamline their legal systems.[38] This is what happened in the Ottoman Empire. During its expansion, the Ottoman Empire, at some stage, was a state with a non-Muslim majority ruled by a Muslim minority. Therefore, the Empire had to encourage integration and assimilation of other groups to hold it together. As part of this policy it offered exemptions to these assimilating groups in order to ease their integration into the Empire. These exemptions included exemptions from state legal jurisdiction,[39] and enabled the Ottomans to recognize several systems of local jurisprudence, such as the *Millet* system, which gave religious groups a certain level of autonomy to manage themselves.[40]

In addition, Ottoman power revolved around the administration of a land system called the *Timar* system, which was another factor that preserved indigenous social order. This system kept administration of the land system in the hands of the local people to collect the Ottoman taxes, and allowed them to maintain their traditional legal systems.[41]

Therefore, the general framework of the Ottoman regime revolved around diversity. It gave cultural and religious groups limited forms of autonomy to maintain their "cultural independence." Local jurisprudence and the *Millet* system "...accorded non-Muslim communities the right to manage their personal affairs according to their religion and cultural laws."[42]

Thus, the recognition of tribal law was an integral part of the system during the first years of Ottoman rule. The Ottomans also recognized local jurisprudences through the *Millet* systems and preserved the local and traditional legal systems as part of the *Timar* system.

Ottoman recognition of the Bedouin Tribal Council

On the specific Bedouin level, the Ottomans directly recognized Bedouin tribal law.[43] As mentioned above, they established the Tribal Council for

Bedouin tribes of Beer Shiva city in the Negev and nominated Bedouin *Sheikhs* (tribal chiefs) along with state officers to adjudicate disputes in the district of Beer Shiva.[44] According to a Birzeit University report, although there is no direct evidence that any Ottoman law was issued to formally legislate the practice of tribal law,[45] there is evidence showing an administrative management council comprised of Ottoman officers and Bedouin tribal *Sheikhs* that specialized in adjudicating conflicts in the district of Beer Shiva.[46] Helen Chapin Metz supports these findings. She states that although the Ottomans enforced *Sharia* law in towns and settled the countryside, in the desert they recognized customary tribal law.[47] Also, Oren Yiftachel, Alexander Kedar, and Ahmad Amara in a recent article on Bedouin land rights in Israel stated that Ottoman rule recognized Bedouin tribal law. They stated that "Until the beginning of the 20th century, the Ottomans granted broad autonomy to the Negev Bedouin… Ottoman authorities referred to the Bedouins, like many other groups, with an approach that allowed them to practice their customary law…."[48]

In conclusion, evidence shows that the Ottoman system generally recognized local legal systems, which would include Bedouin tribal law, as part of its overall policy, but also specifically recognized Bedouin tribal law through the establishment of the Bedouin Tribal Council in the Negev.

Bedouin tribal law during the British Mandate (1917–1947)

The British Mandate in Palestine that ruled from 1922 to1947 explicitly recognized Bedouin tribal law[49] by continuing to recognize the law of the Ottomans as the relevant law in Palestine.[50] Moreover, British Mandate courts continued the Ottoman practice of appointing tribal courts in Beer Shiva city and nominating Bedouin Sheikhs to serve as judges.[51] Furthermore, the British Mandate explicitly recognized Bedouin tribal law and enacted legislation that applied Bedouin tribal law among Bedouin in the Beer-Shiva district (the Negev). Section 45 of the Palestine Order in Council established tribal courts in the District of Beer-Shiva.[52] The section, titled Tribal Courts, stated: "The High Commissioner may by order establish such separate Courts for the district of Beersheba and for such other tribal areas as he may think fit."[53] The second part of Section 45 explicitly recognizes tribal law. It states: "Such courts may apply tribal custom, so far as it is not repugnant to natural justice or morality."[54] Clearly the British Mandate recognized tribal custom as applicable law in tribal courts.[55] Section 45 led to the enactment of the Tribal Court Regulation of 1937, which recognized Bedouin tribal law. The Regulation established the Tribal Courts in the Negev and authorized the Courts to adjudicate according to Bedouin law.

During the British mandate, Bedouin tribal courts were established *de facto* and authorized to adjudicate several subjects including Bedouin land rights,[56] except land ownership registered in the *Tabo* (land registry).[57] However, in cases where land rights were not registered in the *Tabo*, such as the Bedouin land rights in the Negev, the British Supreme Court gave jurisdiction to the Tribal Court.[58] This Tribal Court jurisdiction indicates that the British intended for Bedouin land rights to be adjudicated by Bedouin tribal courts according to their customary law.[59] The only reason for such jurisdiction is that Bedouin land ownership in the Negev is ownership of traditional land that has never been registered in the *Tabo*. Not one Bedouin tribe ever registered its land in the Ottoman or British *Tabo*.[60]

This point is very important for the legal status of Bedouin land rights, their tribal courts, and their customary laws. Although tribal courts had no jurisdiction over land ownership according to the Tribal Court Regulation of 1937,[61] the Supreme Court of the British Mandate interpreted the law so that it did not apply to Bedouin tribal land where lands were not registered in the *Tabo*.[62] According to this interpretation, the Supreme Court recognized Bedouin customary land rights and acknowledged their special status. The Court considered the tribal courts the "appropriate forum" and Bedouin law as the appropriate law to adjudicate any cases. According to Mansour Nasasra, the British Mandate recognized the Bedouin interterritorial tribunals as "tribal courts" and treated them as the Ottomans had handled them. The Mandate government acknowledged cultural differences and the difficulties of judging the Bedouin according to the British law and preferred to allow Bedouin to practice their tribal law.[63] Cited in Nasasra, Lord Oxford. who served as Assistant District Commissioner in Beer Shiva during the British Mandate, stated: "Sometimes, it was extremely difficult to judge cases by the British legal system and the Bedouin did not accept this. Bedouin asked us to take their laws in advance in order to accept the final decisions."[64] Nasasra explains that according to the British Report these interterritorial tribunals would be recognised by the British in order to maintain peace, order and good government for the tribes[65]:

> Under Article 17 of the Palestine Order in Council, 1922... ordinance may be made for the "peace order, and good government of Palestine," and there would not appear to be any objection in principle to an ordinance providing for the enforcement in Palestine of the judgement or orders of these inter-territorial tribunals (whether given in Palestine, Trans-Jordan or Sinai) in so far as they affect tribes in Palestine or their property there.[66]

This approach is not different from the British common law approach during colonization. British administration was based on the concept of indirect rule that allowed native chiefs to perform most executive and judicial functions.[67] According to Neville Rubin, "Indirect rule was standard practice... and it appealed to the British both because it appeared to respect native traditions and because it economized on money and manpower."[68] On the legal level, the British colonial legal system followed a two-track legal system, one for Europeans who were subject to the laws of the mother country, and the other for "natives" who were subject to local customary law.[69]

In terms of customary land rights, as mentioned earlier in the *Mabo (No. 2)* case, the British colonial system recognized customary land rights as part of the general structure of the colonial system. Relying on the decisions of the Judicial Committee of the Privy Council involving South Rhodesia in 1919[70] and Southern Nigeria -where the Council stated "A mere change of sovereignty is not to be presumed as meant to disturb rights of private owners"[71]- and citing Lord Denning's decision from 1957 in which he identified a "guiding principle" of colonial constitutional law according to which preexisting property rights of inhabitants are to be "fully respected,"[72] the court decided that the British colonial system recognized indigenous peoples' customary land rights.

Such findings show that the British Mandate in Palestine recognized Bedouin customary law as their traditional tribal law, established the Bedouin tribal courts in Beer Shiva, nominated tribal judges, and associated the tribal system with the state system.[73]

The status of Bedouin customary law in Israel and options for recognition

The status of Bedouin law in Israel is not easy to define. On the one hand, the legal system in Israel recognizes Bedouin tribal law; but on the other hand, the State does not apply that law. This bizarre, but common, contradiction between the reality of rights and the theoretical legal situation is not unique to the Bedouin in Israel but can be found in many places around the world where indigenous rights were denied *de facto* despite the recognition of their rights by the law. In the case of Australia's Aborigines, for example, the common law recognized their rights to land prior to the establishment of the colonies according to their customary law; however, for about 200 years courts refused to recognize such rights. A similar situation existed in Nicaragua prior to the *Awas Tingni* decision.

In Israel, evidence shows that the law recognizes Bedouin tribal law both directly and indirectly. Directly the law recognizes Bedouin tribal law through the Tribal Court Regulations of 1937 and Article 45 of The Palestine Council of Order of 1922; indirectly the law can recognize Bedouin tribal law through general legal principles that recognize customary laws and rights that were recognized by custom principle.

Direct recognition

The legal system in Israel, like many legal systems, includes components of a colonial period that continue to apply and shape many aspects of the modern legal system determining peoples' rights.[74] Even today there are legal institutions and legal fields that represent this heritage, and many areas of law are still rooted in that mandatory legislation.[75] The Tribal Courts Regulations of 1937 is one example of components of the colonial system that continue to exist in the State's codex of laws.[76] The Tribal Courts Regulations were adopted by the State's legal system, and they have never been abolished. Theoretically, as Eliakim Rubenstein argued, according to Section 9 of the Regulations, Tribal Courts can convene in Beer Shiva, discuss and adjudicate certain civil and criminal matters, and apply the Bedouin customary law.[77] This "preservation of traditional legal concepts, which were used in Palestine before the establishment of the state"[78] was meant to preserve the old order and people's rights and obligations under that order.

Comparatively, this situation is similar to the Aborigines in Australia and the Natives in Canada where common law doctrines recognized the rights of indigenous people before the establishment of British sovereignty,[79] even if it took the courts centuries to recognize these doctrines.[80]

Therefore, based on Tribal Courts Regulations, Bedouins should strongly demand the establishment of their tribal courts and the adjudication of their relevant matters based on their customary law. The first step for Bedouin would be to petition the Minister of Justice and demand the application of the Tribal Courts Regulations, which include the establishment of their tribal courts, the nomination of Bedouin judges, and the application of their tribal law. In the second step, they can bring their land dispute to be adjudicated in the tribal court, which will apply their tribal law and recognize customary land rights. In the third step, Bedouin would ask to bring *all* future land cases before the tribal court, which would have an exclusive jurisdiction over Bedouin tribal land issues, as mentioned by the British Land Court.

Indirect recognition: general legal principles, the custom principle

The second option for recognition of Bedouin law is based on general principles of law, namely, the principle of custom as a source of law. This option argues that, under the specific rules of customary law principle, courts in Israel can recognize some rights and obligation based on peoples' customs.

For many years, customs constituted one of the main sources for legislation.[81] In some periods, it was considered a main component of the state's binding law. However, in modern state systems where laws are codified, the status of the custom principle has been significantly decreased, and in some places, it has ceased to be a part of the state's law. In *Shatz v. Minister of Minister of Justice et al.*, Justice Cheshin stated:

> In ancient times, custom constituted an important source for creating law. In such primitive societies, countries, or quasi-countries of those days the regime was decentralized, transportation was difficult, people were illiterate, and the cumulative weight of these factors - and with other factors - led to... custom as an independent source of binding law.[82]

Although its power has been decreased, the principle of custom continues to constitute a main source for legislation in many states.[83] Some scholars continue to claim that it is not disputed that custom continues to be a good way to make law.[84] Customary international law is an excellent example of how custom can become binding law. Customary international law "consists of rules of law derived from the consistent conduct of states acting out of the belief that the law required them to act that way."[85] On the national level, consistent conduct by a group could lead to the recognition of such conduct as binding legal norms that could be enforced by law.[86]

During the Ottoman Rule, custom was a very important source for laws enacted by the Ottoman *Sultans*. The recognition of customs continued to apply during the Ottoman Empire even after the reforms of the 19th century (*Tanzimat*)[87] and that recognition was documented in the *Mejelleh* during the 19th-century reforms. Sections 36 through 45 of the *Mejelleh* recognize custom as part of the state's law.[88] Professor Ruth Gavison states that the Ottoman *Mejelleh* establishes custom as a binding legal source in the private field of law.[89] Gavison, relying on Sections 36 through 45 of the Ottoman *Mejelleh*, claims that during the Ottoman rule, custom had the same legal power as written law.[90] Section 45 of the *Mejelleh* states that "whatever is stated by custom as stated by written," meaning whatever is stated by custom is considered as stated by written law.[91]

In Israel, too, custom is a binding legal principle and courts continue to rely on it by virtue of Sections 36 through 45 of the Ottoman *Mejelleh*.[92] During the establishment of the State of Israel, it adopted Ottoman law. During its first years, Israel's legal system continued to recognize custom according to the *Mejelleh*. But in 1984, Israel abolished the Ottoman *Mejelleh*, including Sections 36 through 45, which recognized custom as a source of law. However, that abolition did not abolish the principle of custom as source of law in the Israeli system because, as noted by former Chief Justice Aharon Barak, custom has been already integrated into Israeli law and has become part of it. He stated: "Custom is a deeply rooted source of law and the dismissal of the *Mejelleh* cannot deny the power of this source."[93]

However, despite the fact that custom continues to apply in Israel and Israeli law provides that custom is binding as a legal source, the weight of the principle has been considerably decreased. Courts today give the custom principle a lesser role and weight than they used to in past days. Justice Cheshin noticed that custom is not fully defunct in the Israeli law though its power is marginal. In *Shatz*, Justice Cheshin stated:

> Custom's greatness fell down; its areas of existence are narrowed to academic research of legal jurisprudence… As experienced [Judges], we shall not say hastily that the customs of days long are already dead… But we know that its power… finds its expression in the margin.[94]

However, despite its lowered status, custom continues to have the ability to establish and produce law. J. Cheshin cites two cases to support this perspective where a State's common practice has become a binding law that determines legal rights and obligations. The first is *Kamyar*.[95] In that case, the court recognized a practice by which the government would approve international treaties without the required approval of the Knesset. The second case is *Bahmutzki* where Cheshin cited Justice Cohen's holding that the custom of making plea bargains in criminal cases is so common that it can be defined as law that binds the State.[96]

Based on these decisions, courts have the legal tools to examine Bedouin land rights based on the custom principle. The main issue a court must examine is whether the Bedouin practice falls under the category of custom that could be recognized as a binding law. According to Gavison, a binding custom has to include a combination of a factual practice, the fact that people regularly repeat a certain behavior, and a feeling of obligation to follow such practice.[97] This means that the court must determine whether there is a custom of owning or acquiring land rights based on their custom (i.e., whether there is "a combination of a factual practice and a feeling of obligation to follow such practice") with regard to Bedouin land rights.

Recognition of components of Bedouin culture and customs

In addition to the abovementioned routes for recognition, there are other secondary attitudes that recognize or acknowledge the basic components of Bedouin law, mainly the recognition of Bedouin culture. The Supreme Court, for example, recognized components of Bedouin culture on several occasions, including recognition of Bedouin customs and the unique characteristics of the Bedouin population.[98] Other courts have also recognized legal aspects of Bedouin law, such as the concept of *Sulha* reconciliation. High Court Justice Salim Jubran said:

> The customary-cultural argument, which holds that courts should take into account, in the sentence phase, the process of reconciliation (*Sulha*) between the parties, has been accepted in principle by this court... as part of recognizing the principle of restorative justice in criminal law... as well as part of the recognition of cultural considerations within the criminal justice system, due to the centrality of the institution of "*Solha*" in Arab society.[99]

Although this argument does not recognize Bedouin tribal law, it does illustrate the recognition of the Bedouin as a distinct cultural group, which is an essential element for the recognition of their different culture and different legal system.

Recognition of Bedouin as a separate cultural group

In addition, several decisions by the Israeli Supreme Court support the recognition of Bedouin as a separate cultural group, similar to the way the

Ottomans and the British dealt with the Bedouin.[100] In practice, courts in the Negev indirectly recognize the *Sulha* concept in several matters, especially in intertribe conflicts and disputes. In the Islamist *Sharia* courts in particular Bedouin customs get better acknowledgment.[101] This practice is more prominent in the attitude of governmental institutions toward Bedouins. Almost all the governmental institutions in Beer Shiva, especially those that deal with Bedouin matters involving land, security, and public order, are aware of Bedouin customs, culture, and law. When they deal with Bedouin matters, they take their culture into consideration, especially their tribal law. As part of the State recognition of Bedouin cultural distinctions it established separate institutions and governmental offices to deal with Bedouin matters, such as the Bedouin Educational Authority and the Bedouin Land Development Authority. Moreover, governmental offices interact with Bedouins as a separate cultural group. Often government officials, such as police commanders, work with tribal leaders (*Sheikhs*) to reach a truce and to make peace between tribes while relying on tribal law. One prominent example is demonstrated by police reliance on the Bedouin law to reach a truce in case of fights between tribes and to make peace between Bedouin tribes. In many incidents, authority figures like policemen, officers from The Ministry of Interior use tribal customs to settle conflicts. They ask tribal leaders to accompany them to help reach *Atwah,* a truce, according to the Bedouin customs.[102]

Summary and conclusions

In summary, based on the Australian experience, this chapter introduces the idea of recognizing Bedouin land rights based on the recognition of their customary law. To illustrate this idea, this chapter introduced the recognition of Aboriginal land in Australia and then applied the Australian model in the Bedouin case in Israeli.

The recognition of Aboriginal land rights in Australia relies mainly on the existence of three elements. The first is the existence of a system of law, such as Aboriginal customary law; the second is the existence of a connection to land, which means the existence of traditional land rights system; and the third element is the existence a legal recognition option for these elements in the state legal system, such as the native title doctrine in Australia. This last element constitutes a bridge that connects the indigenous peoples' customary law with the state law and enables the state to recognize indigenous peoples' customary law and their rights under their customary system.

The second part of this chapter addressed Bedouin land recognition. This part applied the Australian model of land recognition to the Bedouin case. It mainly showed the existence of the three elements for recognition in the Bedouin land case in Israel. First, it demonstrated the existence of Bedouin traditional system of law; second the existence of Bedouin connection to the land[103]; and then it introduced the third element, two "bridges" that could work as a connection between Israeli and Bedouin customary law. The first bridge option is through Tribal Courts Regulations and the second is the principle of custom as a source of law.

In conclusion, similar to Australia's and other countries' legal systems that have recognized indigenous land rights, the legal system in Israel includes sufficient elements that can lead to the recognition of Bedouin traditional law that would inevitably bring recognition of their traditional land rights.

Notes

1 Shlomo Swirski & Yael Hasson, Invisible Citizens: Israel Government Policy toward the Negev Bedouin 5 (2006).
2 Clinton Bailey, Bedouin Law from Sinai and the Negev: Justice without Government 1 (2009).
3 *Id.*
4 *Id.*
5 *Id.*
6 *Id.*
7 Mohammad Sadiq Al Sadr, Fiqh al-'Asha'ir [Tribal Jurisprudence] (2008) (dealing with the reconciliation of tribal and religious law, and many Iraqi Shi'a have surely been influenced by his teachings to view the two as compatible).
8 Bailey, *supra* note 55.
9 *Id.*
10 Bailey, *supra* note 2 at 60–67.
11 *Id.*
12 Ahmad Uwaidi Alabadi, Alaqadaa End Alashaer Alurdonea [Law among the Jordanian Tribes] 1–32 (2007).
13 *Id.*; Bailey, *supra* note 2 at 1.
14 Muhammad Abu Hassan, Alaqadaa End Alashaer Alurdonea [The Bedouin Legal Heritage] (1974); Ahmad Uwaidi Alabadi, Alaqadaa End Alashaer Alurdonea [Law among the Jordanian Tribes] 1–32 (2007); Arif Alarif, Law among the Bedouin (1933).
15 *See generally* Bailey, *supra* note 2 at 1.
16 *See* Frank H. Stewart, *Tribal Law in the Arab World: A Review of the Literature*, 19 Int'l J. Middle E. Stud. 473 (1987).
17 Bailey, *supra* note 2.
18 Stewart, *supra* note 904.
19 Jenna Browning, Book Annotation, *Bedouin Law from Sinai and the Negev, Justice without Government*, 42 N.Y.U. J. Int'l L. & Pol. 1428 (2009).
20 Bailey, *supra* note 55; Alabadi, *supra* note 12 at 1–32.
21 *See id.*
22 *See generally* Ahmad Alabadi, Alaqadaa End Alashaer Alurdonea wadmjehe attakamoli fe nezam addawlah [Law among Bedouins: Customary Tribal System and Its Incorporation in the State and Its Policy from 1921 until 1982] (1988); *Article title in Arabic/Roman Letters [Title in English]*, Name of Website (date of posting), http://www.lob.gov.jo/ui/laws/search_no.jsp?no=107&year=1936.
23 Azizah al-Hibri, *Islam, Law and Custom: Redefining Muslim Women's Rights*, 12 Am. U. J. Int'l L. & Pol'y 1, 6 (1997); Mustafa Abdul Rahim Abu Agila, Alorf wathrahu fe attashrea [Custom and its Impact on Islamic Law] (1975).
24 Bailey, *supra* note 2 at 1–3.
25 See generally *id.*; Abu Hassan, *supra* note 902; Alabadi, *supra* note 12 at 1–32.
26 *See generally* Bailey, *supra* note 55, at Chapter 1.
27 Joseph Ginat, Blood Revenge: Family Honor, Mediation and Outcasting (2 Sub ed. 1997) (discussing mediation and reconciliation among Bedouin).

28 BAILEY, *supra* note 55 at Chapter 3.
29 *See generally id.*, at Chapters 2–4.
30 GINAT, *supra* note 27 (discussing mediation and reconciliation among Bedouin).
31 AHMAD UWAIDI ALABADI, ALAQADAA END ALASHAER ALURDONEA [LAW AMONG THE JORDANIAN TRIBES] 1–32 (2007); Bailey, *supra* note 2.
32 *See infra* Chapter 3 (It argues that the state recognizes some of Bedouin land rights such as possession and rights of use but does not protect these rights either).
33 BAILEY, *supra* note 2.
34 BIRZEIT UNIVERSITY, INFORMAL JUSTICE: RULE OF LAW AND DISPUTE RESOLUTION IN PALESTINE (2016).
35 The Palestinian Authority complains that people tend to rely on tribal law and trust it over the state official courts. *Id.*
36 Oren Yiftachel, Alexander (Sandy) Kedar & Ahmad Amara, *Re-Examining the 'Dead Negev Doctrine': Property Rights in the Bedouin-Arab Space*, 14 MISHPAT UMIMSHAL, 101 (2012).
37 *Islamic Monarchy*, SCIENCE ENCYCLOPEDIA, http://science.jrank.org/pages/10291/Islamic-Monarchy-Post-Mongol-Period.html#ixzz1FrArYpjb (last visited Feb. 5, 2013).
38 LAUREN BENTON, LAW AND COLONIAL CULTURES: LEGAL REGIMES IN WORLD HISTORY, 1400–1900 109 (Text is Free of Markings ed. 2001).
39 *Id.*
40 *Id.* at 109–110.
41 *Id.* at 109.
42 FEDERAL RESEARCH DIVISION, JORDAN: A COUNTRY STUDY p.16 (Helen Chapin Metz ed., 1989).
43 Oren Yiftachel et al., Tokhnit av lehakarah bakfarim haarvim habedouim ban-gev [Master Plan for recognizing Arab Bedouin villages in the Negev] 7, *available at* http://www.wisdom.weizmann.ac.il/~oded/X/bedouim.pdf).
44 BIRZEIT UNIVERSITY, INFORMAL JUSTICE: RULE OF LAW AND DISPUTE RESOLUTION IN PALESTINE (2016).
45 *Id.* at 31.
46 ARIF ALARIF, LAW AMONG THE BEDOUIN 12 (1933).
47 FEDERAL RESEARCH DIVISION, JORDAN: A COUNTRY STUDY Chapter 1 (Helen Chapin Metz ed., 1989).
48 Oren Yiftachel, Alexander (Sandy) Kedar & Ahmad Amara, *Re-Examining the 'Dead Negev Doctrine': Property Rights in the Bedouin-Arab Space*, 14 MISHPAT UMIMSHAL, 101 (2012).
49 LAUREN BENTON, LAW AND COLONIAL CULTURES: LEGAL REGIMES IN WORLD HISTORY, 1400–1900 10 (Text is Free of Markings ed. 2001).
50 *See generally* Assaf Likhovski, *between Two Worlds: The Legacy of tile Mandatory Judicial System in the Early Years of the State of Israel*, in JERUSALEM AND THE BRITISH MANDATE 253 (Yehoshua Ben-Arieh ed., 2003).
51 Arif Alarif, Law among the Bedouin (1933).
52 Ruth Gavison, *Abolition of the Mejelle: Custom and the Fiqe Principles*, 14 MISHPATIM 325, 339 (1985).
53 Palestine Order in Council, 1922, 13 Geo. 5, art. 46 (Eng.), *available at* http://unispal.un.org/UNISPAL.NSF/0/C7AAE196F41AA055052565F50054E656.
54 *Id.*
55 Section 45 of the Palestine Order in Council is still valid in Israel; the law has never been abolished, although it is not applied in courts.
56 The court authority was limited to land use only. *Cf.* Tribal Court Regulation of 5715, 1937, KT 483, 123 (Isr.) (tribal courts refrained from discussing matters of land ownership).
57 During a dispute in a land possession case between the Tribal Court and Land Court in Jerusalem, the Supreme Court decided that the Tribal Court has the

appropriate jurisdiction over that matter. Further, regarding land matters, the court stated that

> given the fact that there is no land documentation in the Beer Shiva region, and according to the obligation to produce title deed according to article 24 of the Magistrate Act, in this kind of lawsuits tribal law should be applied according to article 45 of the Palestine Constitution.

AL-ARIF, *supra* note 902, at 72 (author's translation).

58 *Id.*

59 See *id.*; *see also* YIFTACHEL, *supra* note 91 at 7–10.

60 HUMAN RIGHTS WATCH, *Off the Map: Land and Housing Rights Violations in Israel's Unrecognized Bedouin Villages* 15, http://www.hrw.org/reports/2008/03/30/map (last visited Sept. 6, 2016).

61 Tribal Court Regulation of 5715, 1937, KT 483, 123 (Isr.).

62 BIRZEIT UNIVERSITY, *supra* note 972 at 32.

63 Mansour Nasasra, *The Ongoing Judaisation of the Naqab and the Struggle for Recognising the Indigenous Rights of the Arab Bedouin People*, 2 SETTLER COLONIAL STUDIES 81, 95–96 (2012).

64 *Id.* at 85.

65 *Id.*

66 According to this report found in the Public Record Office at Kew, the Mandate government was willing to understand how the Bedouin tribunal system worked in order to avoid clashes between the British and the Bedouin. *Id.*

67 Alexander Lee & Kenneth A. Schultz, *Comparing British and French Colonial Legacies: A Discontinuity Analysis of Cameroon*, 7 Q. J. OF POL. SCI., 12 (2012).

68 NEVILLE N. RUBIN, CAMEROUN: AN AFRICAN FEDERATION 74 (1971).

69 Alexander Lee & Kenneth A. Schultz, *Comparing British and French Colonial Legacies: A Discontinuity Analysis of Cameroon*, 7 Q. J. OF POL. SCI., 11–13 (2012).

70 In re Southern Rhodesia [1919] A.C. 211, 233 (Rhodesia).

71 Amodu Tijani v. Secretary of Southern Nigeria, [1921] AC 399, 407 (Nigeria).

72 *Id.*

73 BIRZEIT UNIVERSITY, *supra* note 1 at 32, 39–44.

74 Eliakim Rubinstein, *From the Ancient East to the Middle East: legal dimensions of belonging and distinction between Israel and the neighboring countries*, http://www.lifshiz.macam.ac.il/m/pages/m0581/m0581194a.html (last visited Oct. 16, 2012).

75 *Id.*

76 *See* Tribal Court Regulation of 5715, 1937, KT 483, 123 (Isr.).

77 In practice Israel has never applied the law, has never established any Bedouin tribal courts, and has never applied or recognized Bedouin tribal law. However, this law continues to be valid since Israel has never revoked it.

78 Rubinstein, *supra* note 73.

79 KENT MCNEIL, *Judicial Treatment of Indigenous Land Rights in the Common Law World* 5 (2008), http://papers.ssrn.com/abstract=1262794 (last visited Feb. 3, 2013).

80 PETER H. RUSSELL, RECOGNISING ABORIGINAL TITLE: THE MABO CASE AND INDIGENOUS RESISTANCE TO ENGLISH-SETTLER COLONIALISM (2006).

81 DAVID J. BEDERMAN, CUSTOM AS A SOURCE OF LAW ix (2010).

82 HJC 849/00 Shatz v. Minster of Justice 56(V) P.D. 571[2000] (Isr.).

83 See generally BEDERMAN, *supra* note 80; Gavison, *supra* note 51 (outlining custom principles in the Israeli legal system).

84 Gavison, *supra* note 51.

85 SHABTAI ROSENNE, PRACTICE AND METHODS OF INTERNATIONAL LAW 55 (1984).

86 *See generally* G. S. NARWANI, TRIBAL LAW IN INDIA (2003); Bederman, *supra* note 967.

87 Mejelleh is the civil code of the Ottoman Empire during the late 19th and early 20th century and can be written as Majallah or Mecelle.
88 Gavison, *supra* note 940.
89 *Id.* at 347.
90 *Id.*
91 *Id.*
92 Aharon Barak, *Heheser (lacuna) bameshpat vehok yesudut hamespat [The Lacuna in the Law and the Foundations of Law Act]*, 20 MISHPATIM 233, 325 (1991).
93 Barak, *supra* note 91; See also Gavison, *supra* note 51; Gad Tedeschi, *Hamenhag bamishpatino hanahug wehaatidi [Custom in our Law, Practice, and the Future]*, 5 MISHPATIM 233 (1972).
94 HCJ 849/00 Shatz v. Minster of Justice 56(V) PD 571[2000] (Isr.).
95 CA 131/67 Kamyaar v. State of Israel 12(2) PD 85 [1967] (Isr.).
96 CA 537/71 Bahmutzki v. State of Israel 26(1) PD 543 [1971] (Isr.).
97 Gavison, *supra* note 51 at 333–334.
98 Ronen Shamir, *Suspended in Space: Bedouins under the Law of Israel*, 30 L. & Soc'y Rev. 231, 249 (1996).
99 *See* CA 9896/09 Fares Mashehreh v. State of Israel (unpublished) (2009) (Isr.) (discussing "Solha"). *See generally* Nurit Tsafrir, *Arab Customary Law in Israel: Solha Agreements and Israeli Courts*, 13 ISLAMIC L. & SOC'Y 76 (2006).
100 Nasasra, *supra* note 62 at 30–34.
101 *See generally* Edo Shahar, *Trelemah bdeyuni bet hadin hasharai bbeer sheva kenekudat mifgash [Trilemma in Court: The Shari'a Court in Beer-Sheva as a Convergence Point of Three Law Systems]* JAMA'A, MONTH 1997, at 11.
102 *See* Artzi Halfon, *Harog ve 11 ptzoeem baekvot krav yeriot ben bedouim [One Killed and 11 Wounded after Shootout between Bedouin]*, YNET.CO.IL (NOV. 14, 2002), http://www.ynet.co.il/articles/0,7340,L-2247833,00.html (police turn to Bedouin Shieks to calm things down).
103 *See infra* Chapters 2 & 3.

Bibliography

Alabadi, A. U. (2007). *Alaqadaa End Alashaer Alurdonea [Law among the Jordanian Tribes]*. Dar Jarir.

Arif Alarif. (1933). *Law among the Bedouin*.

Bailey, C. (2009). *Bedouin Law from Sinai and the Negev: Justice without Government*. Yale University Press.

Barak, A. (1991). Heheser (lacuna) bameshpat vehok yesudut hamespat [The Lacuna in the Law and the Foundations of Law Act]. *Mishpatim*, *20*, 233.

Bederman, D. J. (2010). *Custom as a Source of Law*. Cambridge University Press.

Benton, L. (2001). *Law and Colonial Cultures: Legal Regimes in World History, 1400–1900* (Text is Free of Markings). Cambridge University Press.

Birzeit University. (2016). *Informal Justice: Rule of Law and Dispute Resolution in Palestine*. CreateSpace Independent Publishing Platform.

Gavison, R. (1985). Abolition of the Mejelle: Custom and the Fiqe Principles. *Mishpatim*, *14*, 325.

Ginat, J. (1997). *Blood Revenge: Family Honor, Mediation and Outcasting* (2 Sub). Sussex Academic Press.

Human Rights Watch. (n.d.). *Off the Map: Land and Housing Rights Violations in Israel's Unrecognized Bedouin Villages*. Retrieved September 6, 2016, from http://www.hrw.org/reports/2008/03/30/map.

McNeil, K. (2008). *Judicial Treatment of Indigenous Land Rights in the Common Law World* (SSRN Scholarly Paper ID 1262794). Social Science Research Network. http://papers.ssrn.com/abstract=1262794.

Nasasra, M. (2012). The Ongoing Judaisation of the Naqab and the Struggle for Recognising the Indigenous Rights of the Arab Bedouin People. *Settler Colonial Studies*, *2*(1), 81–107. https://doi.org/10.7790/scs.v2i1.305.

Rubinstein, E. (n.d.). *From the Ancient East to the Middle East: Legal Dimensions of belonging and Distinction between Israel and the Neighboring Countries.* Retrieved October 16, 2012, from http://www.lifshiz.macam.ac.il/m/pages/m0581/m0581194a.html.

Russell, P. H. (2006). *Recognising Aboriginal Title: The Mabo Case and Indigenous Resistance to English-Settler Colonialism.* UNSW Press.

Swirski, S., & Hasson, Y. (2006). *Invisible Citizens: Israel Government Policy toward the Negev Bedouin.* Adva Center.

Tedeschi, G. (1972). Hamenhag bamishpatino hanahug wehaatidi [Custom in Our Law, Practice, and the Future]. *Mishpatim*, *5*, 233.

Yiftachel, O. (2012). *Re-Examining the 'Dead Negev Doctrine': Property Rights in the Bedouin-Arab Space, 14 Mishpat Umimshal, 7.*

Yiftachel, O., Kedar, A. (Sandy), & Amara, A. (2012). Re-Examining the 'Dead Negev Doctrine': Property Rights in the Bedouin-Arab Space. *Mishpat Umimshal, 14.*

Index

Note: Page numbers followed by "n" denote endnotes.